Motivation in Education

EDUCATIONAL PSYCHOLOGY

Allen J. Edwards, Series Editor
Department of Psychology
Southwest Missouri State University
Springfield, Missouri

Phillip S. Strain, Thomas P. Cooke, and Tony Apolloni. Teaching Exceptional Children: Assessing and Modifying Social Behavior

Donald E. P. Smith and others. A Technology of Reading and Writing (in four volumes).

> Vol. 1. *Learning to Read and Write: A Task Analysis (by Donald E. P. Smith)*
> Vol. 2. *Criterion-Referenced Tests for Reading and Writing (by Judith M. Smith, Donald E. P. Smith, and James R. Brink)*

Joel R. Levin and Vernon L. Allen (eds.). Cognitive Learning in Children: Theories and Strategies

Vernon L. Allen (ed.). Children as Teachers: Theory and Research on Tutoring

Gilbert R. Austin. Early Childhood Education: An International Perspective

António Simões (ed.). The Bilingual Child: Research and Analysis of Existing Educational Themes

Erness Bright Brody and Nathan Brody. Intelligence: Nature, Determinants, and Consequences

Samuel Ball (ed.). Motivation in Education

J. Nina Lieberman. Playfulness: Its Relationship to Imagination and Creativity

In preparation:

Donald E. P. Smith and others. A Technology of Reading and Writing (in four volumes).

> Vol. 3. *The Adaptive Classroom (by Donald E. P. Smith)*
> Vol. 4. *Preparing Instructional Tasks (by Judith M. Smith)*

Harry Hom, Jr. (ed.). Psychological Processes in Early Education

Harvey Lesser. Television and the Preschool Child: A Psychological Theory of Instruction and Curriculum Development

Donald J. Treffinger, J. Kent Davis, and Richard E. Ripple (eds.). Handbook on Teaching Educational Psychology

Motivation in Education

Edited by

SAMUEL BALL

Educational Testing Service
Princeton, New Jersey

ACADEMIC PRESS   New York   San Francisco   London   1977

A Subsidiary of Harcourt Brace Jovanovich, Publishers

ACADEMIC PRESS, INC.
111 Fifth Avenue, New York, New York 10003

United Kingdom Edition published by
ACADEMIC PRESS, INC. (LONDON) LTD.
24/28 Oval Road, London NW1

Library of Congress Cataloging in Publication Data

Main entry under title:

Motivation in education.

    (Educational psychology series)
    Includes bibliographies.
    1.   Motivation in education.   I.   Ball, Samuel.
LB1065.M67   370.15'4   76-27432
ISBN 0−12−077450−X

Contents

4 ACHIEVEMENT MOTIVATION   67
DEREK C. VIDLER

5 ANXIETY   91
RICHARD A. HANSEN

6 ATTITUDES   111
DEREK H. GREEN

List of Contributors

Numbers in parentheses indicate the pages on which the authors' contributions begin.

Samuel Ball (1, 189), Educational Testing Service, Princeton, New Jersey

Gerard C. Fanelli (45),* Educational Psychology Department, Newark State College, Union, New Jersey

Derek H. Green (111), The Psychological Corporation, 757 Third Avenue, New York, New York

Richard A. Hansen (91), Educational Psychology Department, CUNY, City College, New York, New York

Langbourne W. Rust (131), Langbourne Rust Research, 96 Round Hill Road, Briarcliff, New York

Derek C. Vidler (17, 67), Educational Foundations Department, CUNY, Hunter College, New York, New York

Margaret Nancy White (147, 173), Department of Sociology, Northeastern University, Boston, Massachusetts

*Present address: Kean College of New Jersey, Union, New Jersey.

Preface

There are many textbooks in the area of educational psychology (well over 50 at the last count). Almost all of these have at least one chapter on the topic of motivation. Unfortunately, the overlap in content covered from motivation chapter to motivation chapter is not extensive. Some concentrate on reinforcement theory and practice; and they counsel educators to spend much of their time rewarding appropriate student behavior. Others concentrate on the student's inner need to know; and they counsel the teacher to build on the intrinsic motives of the student. There are more integrated statements to be found in the literature, but the relationship among them is by no means clear; and, in many cases, their relationship to education is not clear either.

The unhappy fact is that there is no previous book that relates the psychology of motivation to the needs of the educator. We have, therefore, taken the approach of relating to the educator (preservice or in-service teacher, educational administrator, educational or school psychology student) a number of the most important motivational constructs with which we think an educated educator ought to be familiar. We asked the question: What factors influence the arousing, directing, and sustaining of student behavior in the educational process? In answering this question, we arrived at our chapters on curiosity, locus of control, achievement motivation, anxiety, attitudes, and interests. These, of course, were not our comprehensive list of candidates—rather, they were our final short list of factors we considered most important both for substantive reasons and in order to provide coverage of important areas in the psychology of motivation.

A common format has been attempted within these chapters, detailing important motivational constructs. Each has sections on definition and conceptualization, measurement considerations, educationally relevant correlates, the growth and development of the motive, and educational implications.

A chapter is also included on motives that are socially mediated in a classroom. Education is a social process: While each student brings a distinct motivational style to the classroom, there also exists a network of social relationships that affect each member's motivational state.

We also included an initial chapter that provides a setting, rationale, and background understanding of how to encourage and develop well-motivated students, and a chapter relating health and nutritional considerations to motivation in the classroom (a grossly neglected problem). Motivation is a psychological process that is at least partly dependent on the nutritional status of the individual. Failure to satisfy vital nutritional needs leads to the death of the individual. Less observably, insufficient nutrition leads to a student with learning and motivational handicaps which should be recognized, not only in so-called underdeveloped countries but also in the most industrially developed countries. The final chapter looks forward to the time when a more integrated approach to motivation in education is available and suggests a way of bringing about this needed development.

We think this book will help the educator clarify his/her values concerning motivation. And it provides some practical ideas and useful implications about how to structure the educational process in order to operationalize those values. What varieties of motivational style in the student does the educator value?—a high level of internal locus of control and of curiosity? Then the chapters of these topics will provide ideas on what to do to promote high levels in these motivational areas.

In addition, this volume provides insights to enable a better understanding of what is is happening in the school and the classroom. But we hope that the educator will not expect to find recipes that will say exactly what to do in the detailed day-to-day running of the school or classroom. In our view, there is no simple, single recipe.

This book does not pretend to be a complete and comprehensive compendium of all that is known about motivation in education. However, it presents a body of empirically researched knowledge and wise speculation that educators (both teachers and administrators) will find useful and usable.

Acknowledgments

The work that culminated in this book was initially inspired by a request by the United Nations Scientific and Cultural Organization (UNESCO) for a short monograph of about 30 pages on the topic of motivation in education. This request was made to the International Evaluation Association (IEA) in Stockholm, Sweden, which had already convened a committee of three* to consider the topic (with a view to generating a research proposal). As a member of that committee, I agreed to develop such a monograph on condition that the product be expanded. To write something useful in 30 pages on such a vast topic was, I felt, too difficult. This was the roundabout beginning to a complex task.

In collaboration with a group of colleagues who all† obtained their doctorates at Teachers College, Columbia University, the present book was produced. I wish to thank my erstwhile students and research assistant who collaborated with me. Rarely can it be said that the production of a book was an enjoyable process. Too often the labor pains predominate. However, in this instance, from conception to delivery it has been a pleasure and I want to thank my colleagues for so motivating me.

*Heinz Heckhausen, Psychologisches Institut, Ruhr-Universitat Bochum, 436 Bochum-Querenburg, Ruf 399, Postfach 2148, Germany; John Raven, 30 Great King Street, Edinburgh EH3 6QH, Scotland; Samuel Ball, Division of Educational Studies, Educational Testing Service, Princeton, New Jersey.

†The exception was Ms. Margaret Nancy White who was then a research assistant at Educational Testing Service and who is now a doctoral student in sociology at Northeastern University.

Motivation in Education

1

Introduction*

SAMUEL BALL

Educational Testing Service

DEFINITIONS

A teacher sees a student as motivated if the student wants to do, and does, those things the teacher thinks the student should do. By the same token, a student is seen by the teacher as unmotivated if the student will not do, or has to be made to do, those things that a teacher thinks the student should do.

We begin with these rather simple, functional definitions of *motivated* and *unmotivated* because they carry with them two important messages. The first message tells us that, at least in the educational process, motivation or lack of it is a subjective matter. For example, consider a child who is willing to sit long hours at her desk working steadily at a task given her by her teacher. One teacher might say, "What a well-motivated child." Another teacher might demur and say, "It is good that she is persistent; but she asks no questions, and she seems to be working only because a teacher has set her a task to do. This child is not well-motivated in my view. I think a well-motivated student is less passive than this one."

The other message we wish to emphasize is that motivation is a central concept in any theory of education. When a failure occurs in an education

*Prepared for UNESCO under contract with IEA, ref. 206612, and published by its permission. © UNESCO 1977.

system, motivation is often blamed. If aboriginal children in central Australia or if economically disadvantaged black children in urban America fail to do well in school, many of their teachers will point to the children's poor motivation, which they will blame on the home background. The parents will deny this blame and say that the failure is the result of bad teaching—that there is nothing wrong with the home background and that a good teacher would be able to motivate the children.

Responsibility is not a question we wish to pursue at this stage. The point to be made is simply that motivation is a central topic in education. At the end of this book, in a postscript, we shall return to motivation in education as a subjective but central topic. We shall turn now to the psychology of motivation, because it is in the discipline of psychology that motivation theory has been treated most systematically and tested empirically.

The term *motivation* is usually defined by psychologists as the processes involved in arousing, directing, and sustaining behavior. It is used to indicate, for example, why an organism is awake and active rather than asleep, why it works at one task rather than others that it could work at, and why it persists at that task rather than moving on to other activities.

Five major problems must be emphasized at this point. First, when we define motivation in this way we must recognize that motivation is a hypothetical construct. That is, we cannot directly observe a person's motivation—all we can observe is a person's behavior and the environment in which a person is active. Motivation for the person's behavior is something we *infer*.[1] It is something within the individual, interacting with the environment, that we suppose arouses, directs, and sustains behavior. This something is not directly measurable, given our current knowledge. Furthermore, motivation has conceptual implications, because it reminds us that in discussing motivation we are talking about a conceptual scheme that helps us understand behavior. If that scheme is useful, if it helps us predict and control behavior, we think our inferences and concepts are correct. However, they remain inferences and concepts, they are fallible, and we must remain open to revising them.

A second problem associated with our definition of motivation is that we tend to overuse motivation as an explanatory concept. We want to be able

---

[1] By the same token, we cannot directly measure a person's intelligence or creativity. All we can measure is his or her behavior, be it intelligent behavior or unintelligent behavior, be it creative behavior or routine behavior. How much intelligence or creativity a person has remains an inference.

to explain *why* people[2] behave in certain ways. Strictly speaking, we can, at this point, only *describe* people and their behavior as they interact with their environment. It is presumptuous to claim we are *explaining* the behavior. After all, what we have to work with are descriptions of a person's behavior (for example, scores on tests, reactions to certain stimuli), plus some inferences based on that behavior. To say the inferences explain the behavior is to make an unjustifiably long logical leap. From a practical point of view this limitation need not be a problem; but it often becomes one. For example, take a situation where a child is failing to learn much in school, even though he or she has ability to learn. Perhaps the child seems to lack interest in school subjects and regards education as being of little value. A teacher, wishing to explain the child's poor school performance might say, "That child is doing poor work *because* he is uninterested." Note, however, that the inference that the child is uninterested in school work is based on observing the poor behavior of the child in school, and that this behavior is what we are trying to explain. Thus, to say the child is uninterested in school is quite circular and, worse still, tends to keep the teacher from looking for concrete reasons for the child's behavior. The teacher should look to see *why* the child seems uninterested and should not be content with naming the condition.

The third problem to be pointed out concerning our definition of motivation is that motivation is but one set of elements in the web of factors determining behavior. Whether or not a child does well in school is, to be sure, partly a function of motivational forces. It is also partly a function of innate and learned abilities. Thus, while we hope this monograph will shed some light on motivational processes in education and thereby enable educators to educate their students better, no spectacular results should be expected. A teacher who understands motivational processes, consciously *or* intuitively, will be better able to ensure that students are more active, better directed, and more persistent. But motivation is after all a matter of degree, and, as we shall see, a teacher does not by any means have total control over the motivational processes in the classroom. Students with low entry-level skills and with little help from their home and community might be helped to do better than might otherwise be predicted, if helped by a teacher with good understanding of and control over motivational processes. However, these students are unlikely to surpass others with much higher entry-level skills,

---

[2]We have tried throughout this book to avoid sexist language. We have used plurals where possible, and tried otherwise to assign female and male identities without prejudice.

who have supportive home and community backgrounds, but who have a teacher with a somewhat less well-developed ability to motivate.

A fourth problem is that motivation, as here defined, involves many processes. No current theory can provide a full picture of motivation in education. No theorist has a monopoly of knowledge or understanding of the topic (although some theorists write as if they did). If we want to understand the processes underlying why children are roused to learn in a classroom, why they direct their attention at certain tasks over others, and why they are persistent despite distractions, we must range across a great panorama of research and theory. In this book we will attempt to weave together some of these theories and the related research into a fabric that we hope will at least partly cover the educators' major concerns. We do not pretend that this fabric will be suitable for those who wish to apply the psychology of motivation to applied areas other than education.

Finally, we wish to emphasize from our definition of motivation that a quite important matter of values is involved. In manipulating and controlling a child's motivations in a classroom, a teacher is helping to mold that child's personality. As long as the teacher is carrying out that task intuitively and in the traditional ways of a society, there is usually no problem. But as soon as teachers try to change children so that the children will grow up to help change the society, controversy is almost bound to occur. We must realize that certain ways of teacher and of organizing classrooms and schools lead to changes in student motivations that may, in turn, have marked effects eventually on society. We educators must ask whether we want, for example, a society that presses to achieve economic growth (perhaps at the risk of environmental disaster), a society where citizens are taught to respect and obey authority (perhaps at the risk of totalitarian takeover), or a society where citizens are taught to question authority and to be autonomous (perhaps at the risk of a breakdown in the established law and order). Probably the decision is not in our hands. An educator is rarely able to make important changes without the agreement of the political zeitgeist. As Socrates discovered some 2500 years ago, to attempt to defy the politicians in power is not a healthy activity for an educator.

In this first section of the introduction, we have pointed out that an educator's definition is likely to be subjective and to depend on the values he or she brings to the teaching–learning process. Psychologists, on the other hand, are likely to be more descriptive in their approach and, perhaps, more tentative. They see motivation as an important element in behavior; but they point out that it is an inference, that it can be misused, that it is not the sole element determining behavior, and that it is not a unitary process.

Finally, in discussing the definition of motivation we pointed out that motivation in the classroom, from any viewpoint, inevitably leads to contact with values. For, as we motivate children or develop their motivations, we affect the kinds of people they become and the society they live in.

HOW MOTIVES ARE LEARNED

In the following chapters, we will be considering a number of motives that are important for learning in school. In each instance, we shall also be considering some evidence on how each of those motives is developed in the child. We realize that such motives as anxiety, curiosity, and the need to achieve, are part of our human inheritance. But, by school age, it is clear that how these motives are expressed, and whether they are expressed at all in the classroom setting, depend heavily on the experiences (learnings) of the child. If we want to be able to help the child be more curious about science, want to achieve better in mathematics, and be less or more anxious in learning to read, then we need to know more about how motives are learned.

There is no *one* learning process—there are many. Teachers should realize, therefore, that there are many ways whereby a child's motives can be modified through learning. In the following pages we shall present three of the most important learning processes that might be useful in modifying the motives of children in the classroom.[3]

Classical Conditioning

This model of learning was first described in the late nineteenth century by Ivan P. Pavlov (1849–1936), a Russian physiologist. Figure 1.1 indicates the processes in this conditioning. The model was extended to educationaly meaningful applications by John Watson, the founder of behaviorism, in an experiment with an 11-month-old child called Albert. Before the experiment had begun, it was observed that a loud sound caused fear in Albert. It was also observed that Albert reached for a white rat whenever it came into his view. In the experiment, the white rat (CS) was presented and then a loud noise (UCS) was made just behind Albert's head. After only a few of these experiences, Albert showed great fear (CR) of the white rat though he previously had enjoyed patting it (Watson & Rayner, 1920). The new associa-

---

[3]A more comprehensive description is provided by Ball (1970) and some of the sections in this discussion are based on that source.

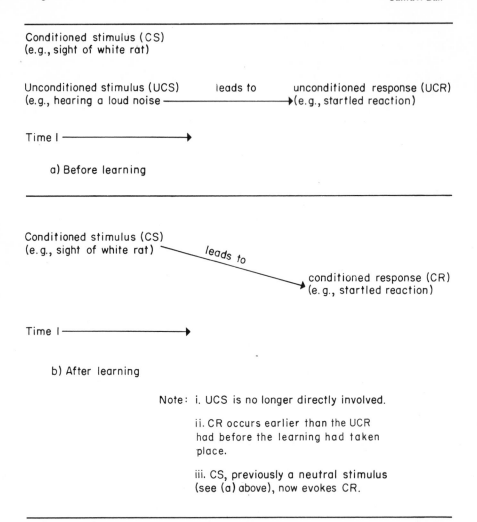

Figure 1.1 A graphical representation of the classical conditioning model of learning (a) before learning takes place and (b) after learning takes place. [From S. Ball, "Learning and teaching," in J. R. Davitz and S. Ball, *Psychology of the Educational Process* (New York: McGraw–Hill, 1970).]

tion of an emotional state with a previously neutral stimulus remains one area in which classical conditioning theory does seem to be an appropriate model.

The importance of this experiment to education is clear. Although we often teach as though a major goal is the delivery of some particular knowledge or skill, we should realize that it is at least as important that the student associate positive emotions with the subject matter we teach. The teacher's words or the printed words of the textbook can be thought of as conditioned stimuli either for positive emotions—or for negative ones. Teachers and books that become associated with negative emotions will cause the learner to remove himself from the learning situation as soon as he reasonably can. School dropouts typically have negative feelings about teachers and the curriculum. In a study by Frankel (1960), bright underachievers, in comparison to overachievers who were matched for IQ, disliked school and most school subjects. We suggest that the dislike had been built up, at least in part, by experiences arranged in terms of the classical conditioning model.

Reinforcement (Instrumental Conditioning)[4]

Edward Thorndike (1874–1949) was one of the first to express the thought that learning (the association of responses with stimuli) depended on what happened *after* the response (whether a reinforcement is presented). His ideas on reinforcement are seen in his law of effect, which states, in part: When a modifiable connection between a stimulus and response is made, and this connection is followed by a satisfying state of affairs, the connection is strengthened (Thorndike, 1913). Another reinforcement theorist, B. F. Skinner (1904–   ), defined reinforcement in operational terms. That is, any stimulus following a response is a reinforcer, in the Skinnerian system, if it increases the probability of the preceding response's recurring in the future (Skinner, 1953). Whatever the particular definition favored, the point is that if a response that once had a low probability of occurrence now has a higher probability of occurrence, then a change in behavior (learning) has come about. Reinforcement at least facilitates learning, whether or not it is essential for learning.

Almost every book on educational psychology or human learning makes this point explicit. Authors of such books cite, for example, Elizabeth Hurlock's (1925) classic research on the effects of praise and blame on performance in arithmetic. The praised group did best over a 5-day period when compared with a reproved group, and control groups. More recently, Anderson, White, and Wash (1966) have further shown that the effects of praise are generalized, positively affecting not only performance on the subject matter concerned but also performance on other subjects. Perhaps

---

[4] The term *instrumental conditioning* is used to label this learning model because the responses or behavior that the learner emits are "instrumental" in modifying the environment. A synonymous term *operant conditioning* is also used. Instrumental (operant) conditioning is subsumed in the term *reinforcement theory.*

one of the best pieces of research on the facilitating effects of reinforcement, from a methodological standpoint as well as from the standpoint of usefulness to the teacher, was conducted by Page (1958). He conducted his experiment using more than 2000 children in 74 high school classrooms. All teachers gave an objective test to their students, who were subsequently assigned to one of three conditions. One-third of the students received no comment on their tests, one-third received specified comments of a rather stereotyped nature such as "Excellent! Keep it up," and the final one-third received a personal comment freely written by the teacher and designed to encourage that student. On a later test the free-comment group did best and the no-comment group did worst. The greatest improvement was shown by the poorest students in the personalized-comment group. Apart from the fact that these students had great room for improvement, the reasonable assumption might also be made that for them an encouraging comment might be even more potent as a reinforcement than for a student who was already doing quite well. Note that in experiments such as these, the particular response being reinforced is not clearly shown. Probably it varies from student to student and probably all we are observing is an average, overall result.

An analysis of reinforcement techniques indicates two major areas of effectiveness. The first technique involves taking a piece of behavior already in a person's repertoire and increasing the likelihood of its occurrence. This technique is illustrated, for example, in the work of Verplanck (1955), who found that selectively reinforcing a speaker's conversations by showing interest and agreement with the speaker's statements of opinion subsequently increased the probability of the speaker's expressing opinions.

In education, however, increasing response rates of students is only one aspect of a teacher's role. A high school English teacher may not merely want to increase the number of books independently read by students each month; she may also want to change the type of book the student chooses to read, or, in certain regrettable cases, she may even be forced to aim at getting the student to read a book independently for the first time. When change of behavior is wanted, as distinct from increasing the rate of behavior already exhibited, reinforcement theory suggests the technique of shaping. This technique constitutes a second major effective application of reinforcement theory to learning.

A simple example of the shaping of behavior is provided by Harris, Johnston, Kelley, and Wolf (1964) in their presentation of a case study of a nursery school child called Dee. Little Dee had regressed to the extent that she crawled and would not walk. Before the experiment, the less she walked, the more attention she got from her teachers. The experimenters decided to reverse this procedure. Using adult social attention as the reinforcement, her teachers attended to her only when she moved from the crawling position and withdrew attention when she reverted to crawling. They were able, by using shaping techniques, to restore her walking within a few days. Then, to show that social reinforcement was the causative factor in this changed behavior, the teachers attempted to reinstate off-feet behavior. "In addition to personal reluctance to institute the process, the staff at this point seriously questioned their ability to succeed in getting Dee again into off-feet behavior" (Harris *et al.*, 1964, p. 37). The staff nonetheless quickly succeeded, by using a reversal of previous reinforcement procedures. Finally, the teachers reinstated Dee's walking. At the time of publication of this research (a year after the experience), Dee was walking and crawling at appropriate times.

Granted, then, that reinforcement is useful both in more firmly establishing existing behavior patterns and in developing new behavior patterns, a major problem remains for educators. When applying reinforcement to students, how can we know beforehand what is a productive reinforcement and whether it works well for all the students?

Age and background of the student seem clearly to affect the applicability and strength of a particular reinforcement. Consider, for example, adult social commendation or attention as a reinforcement for desired student behavior in class. A teacher saying, "I like to see children with straight backs" might cause a roomful of middle-class first-graders to sit with ramrod erectness, a roomful of lower-class first-graders to stare back with some puzzlement, and a roomful of eighth-graders from any social class to wonder about the sanity of the teacher. The fact that the same action on the teacher's part can have different degrees of reinforcement is further illustrated in research conducted by Mischel (1961a, b). He found that delinquent and lower-class children preferred a small, immediate reward to a larger, delayed reward. For older and middle-class children, the position was reversed. In short, the teacher at best can make a shrewd guess about reinforcements based on earlier experiences. For example, the teacher can ask, "Will the anticipation of success on a final test serve as an effective reinforcement of student effort early in a course?"

A possible clue for the teacher in deciding which reinforcements are appropriate for a given child is provided by the work of Premack (1959, 1965). He notes that the activities in which a person engages can be ordered in terms of that person's preferences. For example, a student reading this book might prefer, first, to watch the news on television; second, to wash her car; and, third, to study her schoolwork. A teacher might simply find out the preferences by asking the student directly, or with younger children, by observing what the child does when he is free to do any of the activities (discovering the free-operant level of the behaviors). Premack further argues that a more preferred activity can be used as a reinforcement for a less preferred one by making the former contingent on the completion of the latter. Thus, with the example above, a person will study if she is allowed to wash the car when she is finished studying, or she will wash the car if she is allowed to watch television when the car is clean. However, she is not likely to be encouraged to watch television merely on the condition that when the game is over she will be allowed to study her/his schoolwork. This argument has some research verification in a study charmingly noteworthy for its irreverence of tradition (Homme, deBaca, Devine, Steinhorst, & Rickert, 1963).

Note, in passing, that the Premack principle takes into account not only the fact that a given event is a reinforcement for one person but not for another person, but also the fact that a given event may be reinforcing to a person at one time and highly aversive to the same person at another time (Helson, 1964). The change would be explained in terms of changes in the person's preferences and changes in the availability of alternatives.

Another practical problem is that, even if the teacher knows what reinforcements are effective, it would be rare indeed for her or him to be able to control, in the classroom, all the sources of reinforcement for a particular student. Therefore, even if teachers were to select and use intelligently the potent reinforcement in their control, the changes in behavior they had hoped to see occur in their students might not occur. For example, perhaps the students may find that the laughter of fellow students at their wisecracks is more satisfying than the teacher's smiles or commendations for their more serious efforts. Thus, Goldiamond (1965) notes that, when attempting to use negative reinforcement[5] techniques to cure stuttering, a therapist sometimes finds the patient will simply "go elsewhere, where the consequences will be favorable" (Goldiamond, 1965, p. 155). It has been argued, in response to this point, that the reinforcement model of learning is espoused by a number of eminent learning theorists and has considerable usefulness in both the acquisition of new behaviors and in the strengthening of old behaviors.

It should also be remembered that reinforcement techniques can be

---

[5]Negative reinforcement is the removal of aversive (punishing) stimulation. To use this technique in learning, aversive stimulation first must be applied in order to allow its removal to occur. For example, "I'll stop giving you Fs when you start doing some work."

used to develop motives in children. We can show pleasure (social reinforcement) when a child asks questions (displays curiosity). Or we can provide a payoff to develop the child's need for achievement when a child takes moderate risks to achieve some goal. Thus, while reinforcement can be used as a motivating force in its own right, its most potent value is probably in the development of self-sustaining motivational habits in the learner.

Imitation

The learning model of imitation has been one of the most recent to achieve systematic attention from psychologists. Pioneers in the area were Miller and Dollard (1941), who attempted to show that imitation was itself, at least in part, a learned type of behavior. They showed that, with appropriate reinforcements, frequency of imitative behavior could be raised. A different argument, that imitation might be an essentially innate tendency, has also been put forward, particularly by ethologists. They have based their arguments on inferences made from studies showing, for example, that birds of certain species learn to chirp by imitating the sounds from the adult birds in their nests, even when these adults are not of their species. That is, the chirping pattern itself is not innate, but the tendency to imitate chirping patterns is innate. For teaching, however, it is not particularly profitable to examine this argument further. The children who enter our classrooms are all imitative at least to some degree. This fact seems to be the sensible starting point for discussion.

That the teacher in the classroom may serve effectively as a model for imitative learning has been shown. Anderson and Brewer (1946) found that more aggressive teachers tended to have more aggressive students. Similarly, Kounin and Gump (1961, p. 49) concluded that when compared with children who have nonpunitive teachers, children who have punitive teachers "manifest more aggression in their misconducts." Imitation as a model for classroom learning is clearly seen in action in physical and cognitive as well as emotional areas.

Bandura has been a prolific researcher on the topic of imitation. Basically, his argument is that imitation can be considered as "no-trial learning." As he sees it, through the process of observing a model, and without recourse to practice or the need of reinforcement, three different sorts of behavior change may occur. New responses that did not occur before may be acquired, inhibitory responses may be weakened or strengthened, and responses that were already acquired may be facilitated. Each of these three aspects of learning through imitation is illustrated in an experiment by

Bandura, Ross, and Ross (1963). In this experiment, some children observed various types of aggressive models, others observed nonaggressive models, while still others served as a control group, observing no model at all. Observing an aggressive model led to the acquisition of certain aggressive verbal and physical responses not previously observed in the children's repertoire (e.g., "Pow, sock him in the eye"). Observing aggression also led to the disinhibition of aggressive responses the children had earlier learned to control. For example, those children who observed the aggressive model exhibited about twice as many aggressive acts as did the control group. On the other hand, the children who observed the nonaggressive model exhibited significantly less aggression than the control group and thereby also testified to the potential inhibitory effects of observing certain types of behavior in a model. The response facilitation effect was observed when children, who had observed toy hammers being used aggressively on dolls, subsequently used these hammers themselves significantly more often than the other children in the socially approved manner of hitting pegs through boards.

Children learn a great number of roles through observation of others playing those roles. For example, any child functioning in our society is aware of and potentially could carry through roles such as murderer and thief, but fortunately most decide not to play these roles, presumably because they fail to see sufficient reinforcements emanating from the performance of them. One might also speculate that many underachieving children know what it takes to become a better achiever, but that the necessary performance does not occur because they, too, fail to see that there are intrinsic or extrinsic reinforcements that compensate them for the extra effort they would have to expend.

The importance for educators of taking into account the interaction between learner and the model being imitated will be indicated here by reference to a particular experiment. Using the autokinetic effect,[6] Fisher (1966) has demonstrated that imitation, in the sense of conforming to an authority's judgments, partly depends on the person's perceptions of himself. Freshman college students were given a test of dogmatism, and those scoring in the middle range were then randomly divided into two groups. One group was told that the test indicated they would be successful in life because they were cooperative and got along well with others; the second group was told

---

[6]When a person is placed in a room that is completely darkened and when a ray of light shines on the opposite wall, it seems to him as though the light actually moves on the wall. Each person has his own impression of how far and in what direction the light has moved. This apparent movement is known as the *autokinetic effect*.

they would be successful because they stood up for themselves and were independent thinkers. These verbal manipulations apparently were effective, because the members in the first group subsequently showed considerable tendency to conform to an authority figure's judgments (imitated) whereas the members in the second group tended to reject these judgments (failed to imitate).

In the second phase of this experiment, the authority figure's credentials and credibility were subtly devalued in the eyes of the subjects. The effect of this devaluation was to cause the rejectors to change and to become conforming by following the authority figure's judgments. Presumably, without much status, the authority figure was not worth rejecting. The conforming group members tended to change too. They became less conforming; however, the significant feature of their behavior was the distortion with which they viewed their relationship with the model. There was considerable underrecall of their disagreements with the model. In short, whether behavior of an imitative type will occur seems to depend on the perceived personality of the model, the personality of the learner, and the interaction between these two factors.

The gap between learning in the schools and learning experiments in the psychological laboratory is wide enough to suggest that adequate empirical bridges should be built between the two before crossings are attempted. Therefore, the best that can be culled for education from Fisher's research is a series of questions concerning educational practices. For example, what are the effects on conforming, imitative, middle-class children when they begin to realize that their teachers and other authority figures are not omniscient? Is one result a cultural alienation, a rejecting of the middle-class values portrayed by their middle-class models? What are the effects, on rejecting, nonimitating, lower-class adolescents, of placing them in an educational setting where the authority does not play its role in a traditional manner? Will they then tend to conform to the values of the models they have to that stage rejected?

Imitation is a useful model for learning motives. Teachers should be curious and enquiring if they want their students to be curious and enquiring. A teacher who conforms quietly to the school system might be expected to have students who themselves conform to authority. Consider a science teacher who models the role of the enquiring scientist seeking to solve puzzling phenomena; contrast this teacher with one who teaches from a textbook and has the students memorize formulas, and learn by rote, with proper reinforcements, a series of scientific principles. What kinds of students would you expect these two prototypic teachers to have?

Of course, classical conditioning, reinforcement, and imitation are not the only ways children learn the motives that affect their performance in the classroom. In each of the following chapters a section is devoted to how the motive under discussion is developed. The three learning processes we have presented here are important and basic—but, as the child grows and becomes increasingly autonomous, the likelihood is reduced that the teacher can successfully manipulate the learner's motives using these learning processes. When dramatic changes occur in the adult or adolescent learner's motivations they are usually associated with that person's reassessment of preferred values and life-style. Although such a reassessment may be associated with conditioning, reinforcement, and imitation, it is also associated with problem solving and with the person's creative manipulation of his or her environment to achieve valued goals. In older children and in adults, cognitively based values arouse, direct, and sustain behavior and tend to override the more ephemeral reinforcements that occur in a given situation. To say more here about the development and learning of motives would perhaps undermine the integrity of the succeeding chapters.

REFERENCES

Anderson, H. E., Jr., White, W. F., & Wash, J. A. Generalized effects of praise and reproof. *Journal of Educational Psychology,* 1966, *57,* 169–173.

Anderson, H. H., & Brewer, J. T. Studies of teachers' classroom personalities: Effects of teachers' dominative and integrative contacts on children's classroom behavior. *Applied Psychology Monographs,* 1946, *8.*

Ball, S. Learning and teaching. In J. R. Davitz & S. Ball (Eds.), *Psychology of the educational process.* New York: McGraw-Hill, 1970. Pp. 5–59.

Bandura, A., Ross, D., & Ross, S. A. Imitation of film-mediated aggressive models. *Journal of Abnormal and Social Psychology,* 1963, *66,* 3–11.

Fisher, H. Conformity, negativism, and dissonance in the devaluation of authority. Unpublished doctoral dissertation, Columbia University, Teachers College, 1966.

Frankel, E. A comparative study of achieving and underachieving of high school boys of high intellectual ability. *Journal of Educational Research,* 1960, *53,* 172–180.

Goldiamond, I. Stuttering and fluency as manipulatable operant response classes. In L. Krasner & L. P. Ullman (Eds.), *Research in behavior modification.* New York: Holt, 1965. Pp. 106–156.

Harris, F. R., Johnston, M. K., Kelley, C. S., & Wolf, M. M. Effects of positive social reinforcement on regressed crawling of a nursery school child. *Journal of Educational Psychology,* 1964, *55,* 35–41.

Helson, H. *Adaptation-level theory.* New York: Harper & Row, 1964.

Homme, L. E., deBaca, P. C., Devine, J. V., Steinhorst, R., & Rickert, E. J. Use of the Premack principle in controlling the behavior of nursery school children. *Journal of the Experimental Analysis of Behavior,* 1963, *6,* 544.

Hurlock, E. B. An evaluation of certain incentives used in school work. *Journal of Educational Psychology*, 1925, *16*, 145–159.

Kounin, J. S., & Gump, P. U. The comparative influence of punitive and nonpunitive teachers upon children's concepts of school misconduct. *Journal of Educational Psychology*, 1961, *52*, 44–49.

Miller, N. E., & Dollard, J. *Social learning and imitation.* New Haven: Yale University Press, 1941.

Mischel, W. Delay of gratification, need for achievement and acquiescence in another culture. *Journal of Abnormal and Social Psychology*, 1961, *62*, 543–552. (a)

Mischel, W. Preference for delayed reinforcement and social responsibility. *Journal of Abnormal and Social Psychology*, 1961, *62*, 1–7. (b)

Page, E. D. Teacher comments and students' performance. *Journal of Educational Psychology*, 1958, *49*, 173–181.

Premack, D. Toward empirical laws: Positive reinforcement. *Psychological Review*, 1959, *66*, 219–233.

Premack, D. Reinforcement theory. In M. R. Jones (Ed.), *Nebraska symposium on motivation.* Lincoln: University of Nebraska Press, 1965.

Skinner, B. F. *Science and human behavior.* New York: Macmillan, 1953.

Thorndike, E. L. *An introduction to the theory of mental and social measurements.* New York: Teachers College, Columbia University, 1913.

Verplanck, W. C. The control of the content of conversation: Reinforcement of statements of opinion. *Journal of Abnormal and Social Psychology*, 1955, *51*, 668–676.

Watson, J. B., & Rayner, R. Conditioned emotional reactions. *Journal of Experimental Psychology*, 1920, *3*, 1–14.

2

Curiosity

DEREK C. VIDLER
Hunter College of CUNY

DEFINITIONS OF CURIOSITY

The term *curiosity* has a lengthy and respectable lineage. In recent years, like antique furniture, it has again come into vogue. Yet, the term, though familiar, is deceptively simple, defying easy analysis. One of the more noticeable features in the literature on curiosity has been the relative scarcity of descriptive statements offered by researchers, and the absence of adequate definitions. Few writers seemingly have felt troubled to explain just what they conceive curiosity to consist of, and yet the term, undefined, is bandied about with fair regularity.

Equally as noteworthy as the absence of definitions is the lack of reference to their absence. Most writers assume, it seems, that what constitutes curiosity can be recognized and generally agreed on, but that an attempt to define it is still both premature and unprofitable. At all events, one must agree with Maw and Maw (1964) that "nowhere in the literature is there a precise statement as to the nature of curiosity" (p. 6). Furthermore, as Bindra (1959) comments, many of the attempts to discuss the nature of curiosity have had recourse to hypothetical constructs that provide "redundant descriptions, not systematic explanations" (p. 288).

Fowler (1965) deals directly with the central problem of definition.

The task of defining curiosity and exploration seems difficult if not impossible, fe₁ there appears to be no goal object or condition to and for which the organism responds. We might consider that the organism explores in order to acquire new forms of stimulation and, thus, as a first attempt at definition, view curiosity and exploration as behaviors that have the sole function of altering the stimuli that impinge on the organism. [p. 23]

Fowler goes on to point out that this definition is unsatisfactory, because changing the organism's stimulus field appears characteristic of all behaviors, whether food seeking, pain escaping, or otherwise. Note, too, that Fowler sees exploratory behavior as the overt manifestation of curiosity.

Fowler cites Berlyne, perhaps the major theorist in the area of curiosity. Berlyne (1963) makes the point that exploratory and nonexploratory behaviors differ in that the latter are accompanied by biologically important effects on tissues other than the sense organs and the nervous systems. Curiosity and the resulting exploratory behavior may refer thus to a great variety of events that possess little in common other than "our failure to recognize a specific biological function that can be associated with them" (p. 288). Curiosity is thus curiously defined not in terms of conditions under which it takes place, but in terms of the *absence* of certain conditions.

Berlyne draws a useful distinction, between intrinsic and extrinsic kinds of exploration, which has aided clarification of curiosity and at the same time has guided research. Aspects of behavior that have clearly definable consequences are classed as *extrinsic* (for example, food seeking and goal reaching), the presumed motivational indices being conditions of deprivation or excessive stimulation. The term *intrinsic* as applied to types of exploration refers to those behaviors that seem unrelated to any goal attainment or reinforcement activities—activities "for their own sake."

Berlyne also makes a further distinction between epistemic curiosity and perceptual curiosity. Epistemic curiosity concerns enquiry about knowledge and is shown, for example, when a child puzzles over some science problem he has come across. Perceptual curiosity concerns increased attention given to objects in the child's immediate environment as, for example, when a child stares longer at an asymmetrical rather than a symmetrical figure on a screen. Curiosity related to work in school settings seems to belong more to epistemic than perceptual curiosity.

Various approaches and views are presented by writers as to the nature and characteristics of curiosity. Curiosity is often closely linked to a number of other variables and at times considered virtually synonymous with them. The extent of these relationships and the stress placed on them not unnaturally vary with the individual author's perspective and preferential bias. Taking collectively views put forward by a variety of researchers, curiosity is frequently connected with "exploration," "manipulation," "activity," "interest," and "attention." Thus, Bindra (1959) refers to a primary drive, which "has been variously designated as exploratory drive, curiosity, or manipulatory drive, and exploratory activity is assumed to reduce this drive" (p. 15).

Fundamentally, there have been two major theoretical positions as to the motivational origin or source of curiosity, or exploratory behavior. Initially, these positions were mostly grounded on research with subhumans, though more recently humans have been accorded their due share of investigation. These two positions are outlined by Fowler (1965).

One view has been that mild and novel external forms of stimulation motivate the organism to explore and investigate them. The organism becomes curious about the novel or unfamiliar stimuli and hence responds to them. The novel stimulus not only directs, but also activates or energizes behavior. Thus Montgomery (1953) supposed that a novel stimulus situation would evoke in an organism an "exploratory drive," which would decrease with continued exposure to novel stimuli. Harlow (1953) referred to a "manipulation drive," and a "visual exploration drive" that motivated the organism to explore and manipulate. Berlyne (1950) prefers to talk of an "exploratory drive." For him, curiosity is a drive state induced by experienced novelty or uncertainty, or, more generally, by lack of sufficient information in a given environmental situation.

> When a novel stimulus affects an organism's receptors, there will occur a drive-stimulus-producing response which we shall call "curiosity." . . . as a curiosity arousing stimulus continues to affect the organism's receptors, curiosity will diminish. [p. 79]

The other position has been derived from the assumption that familiar and unchanging stimuli of the organism's present or recent environment motivate exploration or the response to change, the novel or unfamiliar stimuli being simply cues that direct this behavior. In this view, the externally elicited drive of exploration is treated in a fashion analogous to hunger and thirst. Stimuli that are homogeneous, unchanging, and therefore monotonous evoke a "boredom" drive that can be reduced by sensory variety (Myers & Miller, 1954; Glanzer, 1953).

As might be expected, out of the two main theoretical approaches grew others that considered both views as necessary to a more complete understanding. Thus, theories that have taken account of the fact that both rises and falls in the level of curiosity depend on the state of the organism and the conditions of the external environment have been more favored. These theories of "optimal stimulation" are exemplified in theoretical frameworks proposed by Berlyne (1963) and Fiske and Maddi (1961).

A number of studies of curiosity have provided descriptive evidence of curiosity, especially in young children. Perhaps the most important of studies on the human level is that by Maw and Maw (1964). These researchers have explored a large number of techniques for assessing curiosity and laid the groundwork for others to follow. Subsequent researchers have depended heavily on their methods and procedures, as well as on their definition. According to Maw and Maw (p. 2), curiosity is demonstrated by an elementary schoolchild, when he:

1. reacts positively to new, strange, incongruous or mysterious elements in his environment by moving toward them, or by manipulating them;
2. exhibits a need or a desire to know more about himself and/or his environment;
3. scans his surroundings seeking new experiences;
4. persists in examining and exploring stimuli in order to know more about them.

With only slight modifications, these criteria have been used by a number of researchers (Penney & McCann, 1964; Minuchin, 1968; King, 1968).

Other writers have offered their views of what constitutes curiosity. Beswick (1965) conceived it more loosely, defining it in terms of openness to unusual experience, the desire to understand novel experience and to incorporate it into one's map of the world. And, most recently, Livson (1967) suggests: "Curiosity is a tendency, or motive to acquire or transform information under circumstances that offer no immediate adaptive value for such activity" (p. 76). But one searches in vain through the literature for anything more precise. Curiosity is almost always defined as a personality trait or motive that has generality over time, tasks, and circumstances. The evidence for this "big-C" approach to curiosity (general curiosity) as opposed to the "many little-c's" approach (specific curiosities) is not at all clear. Although we have all come across people who seem generally curious and others who seem generally incurious, it is also true that we commonly find ourselves to be curious about some things and not at all curious about others.

Possibly the truth lies somewhere in between. As noted in the chapter on anxiety, there is strong evidence, from factor analysis, of an anxiety trait (long-term general anxiety) *and* anxiety states (specific to tasks or situations). Perhaps the same might be true for curiosity—but there is a lack of experimental evidence on the question. As we shall see in the next section of this chapter, the measures available usually assume a general curiosity valid across many tasks and conditions.

Thus, despite the increasing interest in curiosity, progress toward its identification and definition has been slow and unsteady. Nonetheless, the various views presented have a good deal in common, and the sometimes small differences among them may be exaggerated because of differences in approach.

MEASURES OF CURIOSITY

Assessments of curiosity have included as wide a variety of measuring instruments as is to be found for any motivational construct. This variety undoubtedly has in part been caused by the relative difficulty in studying curiosity. This difficulty has, in turn, encouraged the trend toward exploring new avenues of approach and stimulated investigations of an exploratory nature. The measures employed have commonly been dictated by the nature of the population sampled, the need to tailor the measures to the level of functioning of the individual (or organism), and the need to take into account the practical restrictions of the situation.

Studies on the subhuman level have normally focused on variables such as "exploration," "activity," and "manipulation" as measures of curiosity. Typically, animals are observed in various laboratory situations, mazes, unfamiliar settings, and so on, and their exploratory activity recorded. The common assumption is that the level of activity or exploration of animals in these situations represents the degree of their curiosity.

Studies on the human level have allowed for a greater variety of measuring instruments and researchers have been given more scope to follow their own inclinations. With preschool and elementary school children, who have formed the populations for most of the studies at the human level, measures mostly have been observations of the children's behavior in the classroom setting and ratings of the children, both by themselves and by others—usually their teachers or peers.

On the high school level and beyond, an area not as extensively explored to date, more frequent have been true–false scales, on which the subject rates himself against a list of statements. Perceptual measures involving judgments of a subject's curiosity on the basis of his looking at stimulus figures have also been used.

A major researcher in this latter area has been Berlyne. He has attempted to discover the conditions that arouse curiosity, mostly using perceptual measures. The basic paradigm usually employed is to present subjects with a series of pictures that vary as to their supposed curiosity-arousing properties. Berlyne feels that a number of "collative" variables, such as novelty, incongruity, and complexity, in stimulus figures are important aspects in the arousal of curiosity. The pictures typically are flashed on a screen and the subject's viewing time for each figure is recorded, the length of viewing time being a presumed measure of the subject's curiosity in regard to that stimulus figure. Berlyne has mostly been interested in the properties of objects and the conditions that stimulate curiosity rather than in individual differences in level of curiosity. For his purpose, subjects for the study have been less important than the materials and the conditions of the study.

A study by Pielstick and Woodruff (1964) employed similar perceptual measures. With 30 children from the second and sixth grades, they used both observational data on the exploratory behavior of the children and perceptual measures of pictures of different stimulus variables, the length of viewing time of each subject being recorded. They, like Berlyne, assumed that a preference for the novel or unfamiliar indicated curiosity, and that those children who viewed the figures high in novelty and unfamiliarity for longer periods of time were the more curious.

Starkweather (1966) developed a perceptual task suitable for even younger children, 3 to 6 years old, which was designed to measure the child's preference for the novel. In the curiosity task, each child was exposed to and given the chance to become familiar with several designs by looking at them and talking about them with the experimenter. The child was then offered a choice in a series of paired designs, one of which was familiar to him and the other novel, his curiosity level being determined by his selection. Hess, Shipman, Brophy, and Bear (1967) used a perceptual curiosity task with 163 6–7-year-old black children. They presented 16 pictures divided into 8 complex–simple pairs of similar stimulus types. The children were asked to look at them and were rated as to curiosity by the length of viewing time of the complex as opposed to the simple design.

Perhaps the simplest procedure has been the adjective checklist. Despite its ease of administration, however, it does not seem to be highly regarded enough to have justified extensive usage. Hogan and Greenberger (1969) developed a brief adjective checklist for use with elementary school children. On the basis of total agreement among a selected group of 12 judges, the curious child was considered to be "active, adventurous, curious, energetic, enthusiastic, imaginative, and with wide interests." Of the 12 judges, 11 also agreed that the curious child was "alert, assertive, clever, enterprising, intelligent, restless." Each child was accordingly judged curious to the extent that he conformed to these descriptions.

Somewhat similar in approach to the adjective checklist was Maw and Maw's (1964) attempt to find dimensions of the curious person. They had 146 college sophomores rate a list of words on a 0–4-point scale as indicating curiosity. Most related words were *explorer, discoverer, adventurous,* and *questioning;* and the next most, *venturesome, scouting, thinking,* and *prodding.*

Projective techniques have not been commonly employed to measure curiosity. Beswick (1965), following McClelland's need-for-achievement measures, outlined a method for the content analysis of written story productions evoked by a standard set of pictures. The assumption as with other projective techniques was that the presentation of vague, ambiguous stimulus situations as a basis for story productions would evoke imagery that reflected degree of curiosity. A person was judged curious to the extent that curious images or ideas were present in his stories. Greenberger, O'Connor, and Sorenson (1968) revised and modified Beswick's scoring system for their own use and provided further statistical data on the technique. They set out examples of the scoring procedure using various protocols and the rationale for scoring, through their basic assumptions and procedure were not essentially different from that of Beswick.

Greenberger and Entwistle (1968) also used similar pictures to elicit stories from subjects. The pictures contained elements similar to the Thematic Apperception Test (TAT) pictures and presented a series of vague, ambiguous scenes. One picture, for example, showed an inventor in his laboratory with a large light bulb in front of him; another showed two boys on a beach, one bending to pick up a bottle. As before, subjects' stories were analyzed and scored for curiosity imagery present in them.

More common, especially with preschool and elementary school children, have been ratings of curiosity by teachers or, occasionally, other significant adults, as well as by peers. The reasonable assumption has been that those who come into contact with the children most often, their teachers and their peers, are in the best position to judge their curiosity.

In one study (Hess, 1967), these ratings were made by the mothers of the children. The mothers were read the items from the Plutchik Exploratory-Interest Questionnaire, which described activities classified as *exploratory* and *nonexploratory,* and asked if the children liked or disliked the activity. Exploratory items included "meeting new people," "reading about distant lands," and "listening to stories"; nonexploratory items included "seeing sporting events," "socializing," "writing letters," and "shopping for clothes." The more exploratory activities liked, the more curious the child was considered to be. One cannot help but wonder why listening to stories is considered exploratory but shopping for clothes is not.

Minuchin (1968) explored various techniques to describe expressed curiosity and "constructive exploration" among disadvantaged preschool children, with a sample of 18 4-year-old black children. Among other measures, teachers were asked to rank the children in curiosity level on the basis of their experience with the children. Each child thus received a ranking relative to the other children in the classroom.

Maw and Maw (1964) obtained teachers' judgments of curiosity in students. They gave their own definition of the word *curiosity* and asked the teacher to describe their curious students on this basis. In the same study, judgments of curiosity by peers were assessed, somewhat indirectly, through the "Who should play the part" test. This test was a play situation in which children were asked to assign roles to the other children in the class, the roles characterizing the curious and noncurious children. Self-judgments were also assessed in "About Myself," in which each subject rated himself on items such as "When I see a neighbor digging in my yard, I wonder what he's doing!" and "If a grown-up says something, I believe it." An affirmative answer to the first of these statements and a negative answer to the second were assumed to indicate curiosity.

Other self-report measures have been developed both for use with children and adults, though clearly their use with children below certain ages is impractical. Penney and McCann (1964) constructed a scale of "reactive curiosity" for use with children in Grades 4–6. They labeled it *reactive curiosity* since it was felt a child may be curious but not display it. The scale contained 90 items on which the subject rated the statements as they were true or false in describing himself, and contained items such as: "I like everyone I know," "I like to look at magazines," "I don't like to eat in restaurants."

More recently, Day (1969), following closely the theoretical position of Berlyne, constructed a test of curiosity suitable for a population of "unselected" adults. On the basis of a theoretical description of selected characteristics and expected behaviors, specific curiosity was conceptualized as a three-faced cube: Face 1 is the nature of the stimulation (complexity, novelty, ambiguity); Face 2 is the nature of the response (observation, questioning, thinking); and Face 3 is interests (outdoors, scientific, mechanical).

Distinguishing between *specific* and *diversive* curiosity, Day felt the former characterized the individual who

> reacts with positive affect towards situations high in novelty and complexity and
> who tends to approach them with the purpose of exploring the stimulation,
> reducing uncertainty, and gaining information. [p. 4]

The diversively curious person, on the other hand, tends to be "restless, easily bored, continuously seeking change, but possibly fails to concentrate on these situations until full understanding is reached" (p. 4). Day developed a 36-item self-report scale measuring extent of interest and willingness to approach a wide range of stimuli with high collative properties. The test has to date been used with college subjects and a simplified version with sixth-, seventh-, and eighth-graders.

Day has also developed a more comprehensive questionnaire (110 items) for adults—the Ontario Test of Intrinsic Motivation (OTIM). It is designed to measure both specific and diversive curiosity. The subscales of the specific curiosity part identify the individual who is stimulated largely by novelty, complexity, and/or ambiguity, and who reacts generally by observation, consultation, and/or thinking. This part also divides specific curiosity into ten areas of interest. The scale includes items such as: "I try to think of answers to the problems of international social relationships" and "I enjoy trying to identify old themes in new songs." This approach comes close to the argument that curiosity should not be considered solely as a general, single-dimension trait.

A more recent scale, suited to high school and college students, is the outcome of a factor-analytic study of academic motivation by Chiu (1967). (This study and its implications are discussed in more detail in the final chapters of this book.) Chiu selected items from a variety of tests and questionnaires considered to be related to motivation in the classroom, administered the items to a large sample, and factor analyzed the results. On the basis of his analysis, one of five factors identified was labeled "curiosity."

Not infrequently, investigators have included a number of measures in their studies, hoping thus to more closely identify the nature of curiosity. The most comprehensive of these studies has been the milestone study by Maw and Maw (1964), who explored the possibility of developing a large number of paper-and-pencil test instruments and techniques to yield reliable measures of curiosity among elementary school children. After several preliminary phases of experimentation, they selected 11 tests for final use. These tests included: *(1)* "Picture and Story Satisfaction," in which the subject was presented with a picture of, for example, a Chinese musical instrument or a scientist, and was asked what else he would like to know about the picture, his curiosity being rated on the basis of the questions he wanted to know; *(2)* "Preferred Behavior," in which the child was given a number of situations and alternative responses, some being judged more curious than others (one item in the test was: "If you were walking across an open field and you found an old golf ball that had been knocked out of shape, would you give it a kick, throw it away, cut it up to see how it was made, or play golf with it?"); *(3)* "Preference for the Unbalanced," in which the subjects were presented with a number of varied figures two at a time, the choice of the more unbalanced indicating curiosity; and *(4)* "Which Saying Do You Believe," in which the subject was given two proverbs and asked to state which one was most nearly true most of the time, such as: "Look before you leap," and "Who stands still in the mud sticks in it."

As one might expect, the extensive range of measuring instruments employed in the studies of curiosity has meant that they have frequently had little in common with each other and hence at best have shown only modest intercorrelations. However, certain relationships have been noted. McReynolds, Acker, and Pietila (1961) found significant correlations between object curiosity scores, in which an observer rated a subject on his manipulations of objects, and teachers' ratings of curiosity (.37). Maw and Maw (1964) found peer and teachers' judgments to be positively related (.54). Minuchin (1968) showed that measures of curiosity and exploration tended to confirm each other and to suggest a generaly consistent pattern of reaction on the part of the children. Poore and Lang (1963), however, found little relationship between parent rating, teacher rating, and children's self-rating of curiosity, and other studies have occasionally found similar results. Thus, although there is some evidence that the various measures of curiosity share a common base, and are measuring the same variable, this comparability is not as great as might be desirable and tends to suggest that curiosity might indeed be a multidimensional construct.

CORRELATES OF CURIOSITY

Since adequate definitions of curiosity are hard to come by, and since different measures of curiosity have not always shown strong interrelationships with each other, it is hardly surprising that curiosity itself has not proved to be strongly related to other variables. There is abundant testimony of opinion and speculation to the effect that curiosity is connected with a number of other factors, but experimental evidence to support such notions is less clear-cut. The majority of studies have investigated areas where a relationship is at least plausible, although the results have usually shown either an absence of any significant relationship or a moderate relationship in the direction expected. Yet, though relationships are rarely strong, there has been some consistency in findings of the different studies.

To back up the numerous suggestions in the literature that associate curiosity with IQ, research has provided some moderate evidence. At one extreme, some authors have been unable to establish any significant relationship. King (1968) found with 4- and 5-year-olds that intelligence was not related to any of seven different measures of curiosity. Day (1968a) argued that test scores of children on curiosity and IQ tend to be uncorrelated and suggested the two dimensions are independent. Penney and McCann (1964) found no relationship between IQ and their Reactive Curiosity Scale for children.

Others have found more positive results. Hogan and Greenberger (1969) present evidence for a positive relationship between curiosity and standardized measures of intelligence. Kagan, Sontag, Baker, and Nelson (1958), analyzing a number of personality variables in children and comparing them with changes in IQ, found that children with maximum increases in IQ showed greater curiosity about nature. Hoats, Miller, and Spitz (1963) showed that high-grade mentally retarded males showed less perceptual curiosity than did combined groups of equal mental and chronological age normal males. Maw (1967), arguing that level and functioning of intelligence seems to play an important role in determining curiosity level, showed a positive correlation of .36 with the Lorge–Thorndike IQ Test, with fifth-graders. With 225 eleventh-graders, Demel and Hansen (1969) found that a standardized measure of IQ correlated .24 with Chiu's self-report scale of curiosity.

More significantly, perhaps, Maw and Maw have felt IQ to be strongly enough related to curiosity that they have controlled for IQ when investigating other variables. Thus, they have frequently matched subjects for IQ (Maw & Maw, 1963, 1970). Note, however, that no study has found more than a low to moderate relationship between curiosity and IQ.

One might expect a relationship between curiosity and achievement. It seems reasonable to suppose the academically curious child would perform better on achievement tests though the relationship would probably depend on how rigid the school and classroom are, how much emphasis is placed on rote learning and how much credit is given to students who show initiative rather than passive acceptance in learning. The available research supports such a relationship, even though the measures of achievement vary greatly. With fifth-graders, Maw and Maw (1961) showed that highly curious children performed better on a test of general information. In another study, highly curious children also tended to sense the meaning of sentences more accurately than less curious children on a reading comprehension task (Maw & Maw, 1962). Maw and Maw (1961) showed also that highly curious children remembered more material on a story retention task than less curious children, in that they either learn more from a given period of exposure, or they remember longer what they learn. Hogan and Greenberger (1969) present evidence for positive relationships between standardized measures of academic achievement and curiosity. Demel and Hansen (1969) found a small positive correlation of .15 between Chiu's scale of curiosity and a test of arithmetic concepts.

The positive relationship of curiosity to creativity has received virtually unanimous support. No one seems to dispute the presumed connection between these two variables, such a relationship in fact being commonly taken for granted (Leuba, 1958; Torrance, 1967). Studies for the most part have borne out the evidence of opinion. Day (1968a) found, with a group of 75 nursing students, a significant relationship between curiosity and creativity, using two self-report measures of curiosity and the Remote Associates Test, and also between a measure of perceptual specific curiosity and Barron Welsh Art Scale scores. The latter finding partly results from the fact that both tests use visual stimulus materials, which vary in the same dimensions of complexity and symmetry. Penney and McCann (1964) found scores on their curiosity scale correlated with Guilford's Unusual Uses Test. Joesting and Joesting (1969) modified Penney and McCann's scale for use with undergraduates and found that it correlated substantially (.58) with a checklist of characteristics of highly creative people developed by Torrance. Maw (1967) found small positive correlations between the Word Association Test and several indices of curiosity.

One of the clearest indications of a relationship between curiosity and creativity is found in a statement by Torrance (1967), who appears to consider curiosity as virtually synonymous with creativity. To identify creative talent in sixth-graders, he made use of Maw and Maw's (1964) definition of curiosity, and obtained "excellent differentiations on all the measures of creativity between the two groups of children nominated as most and least curious. Almost all of those nominated among the more curious made higher scores on each of several tests of creative thinking than their equally intelligent but less curious classmates" (p. 243).

Many theorists have suggested an inverse relationship between curiosity and anxiety. Hebb (1955), in discussing the curve of arousal in motivation, labeled one end of the continuum "increasing alertness, interest, positive emotion," and the other "increasing emotional disturbance, anxiety." Levitt (1967) states simply and directly, "It follows that anxious people will be less motivated by curiosity: will not evince as much interest in exploring new arenas, and in having new experiences" (p. 162).

Maw (1967) notes that the results of research tend to be ambiguous. Vidler (1972), using 212 college students, found no significant relationship between Chiu's scale of academic curiosity and Sarason's test-anxiety scale. On the other hand, Penney (1965) found that children's reactive curiosity was negatively related to manifest anxiety. Children who are reactively curious exhibit less anxiety than children who are not as reactively curious. Negative relationships between curiosity and anxiety are also reported in two studies at the adult level. Zuckerman, Kolin, Price, and Zoob (1964) showed their Sensation-Seeking Scale (SSS) containing items that deal with preference for the new, unfamiliar and irregular, and a measure of anxiety on the Multiple Affect Adjective checklist were negatively correlated. McReynolds (1958) found some evidence for a negative relation between anxiety and curiosity in a group of psychiatric patients.

There is, further, a large body of research dealing with variables related to anxiety, which has consistently shown interrelationships between these personality variables and measures of curiosity. These variables include "psychological adjustment" (McReynolds *et al.*, 1961); "mental health" (Day, 1969); "security" (Maw & Maw, 1968); and "positive self-image" (Minuchin, 1968).

McReynolds *et al.* (1961) reported findings that suggest that "those aspects of classroom learning which depend on curiosity are hindered by the anxieties of students" (p. 397), and found, with 30 sixth-graders, a negative correlation of .42 of curiosity with "nervous behavior," and −.27 with "worry over achievement." Maw and Maw (1970) showed that highly curious fifth-grade boys are more secure and more free from nervous symptoms than less curious boys. Maw and Maw (1970) also found that "the less curious boy does not feel he is well regarded by others; he believes his ability is less than average; he feels he is not attractive," whereas the highly curious boy is greater in "self-reliance, sense of personal freedom, feeling of belonging, and strong self-sentiment" (p. 127).

The implicit argument behind much of this research is set out at greater length by Maw and Maw (1965a):

Tolerance toward an ambiguous stimulus might be considered an indicator of mental health, since the individual seems to be more realistic in his evaluation of the world around him, more aware of his own limitations, and more willing to admit that he does not know the answer to the problem. Intolerance of ambiguity indicates a need to structure the world, even at the expense of neglecting reality. [p. 21]

Lesser (1971) provides the link between tolerance and curiosity.

Tolerant, open-minded or complex individuals tend to prefer stimulation high in uncertainty or other collative properties, or at least are willing to expose themselves to such stimulation. Work with specific curiosity tests suggests that not only do individuals high in this characteristic tolerate such stimulation, they are also interested in actively exposing themselves to, and exploring, these environments. [p. 324]

In contrast to studies that have related curiosity to anxiety and related variables, other studies have focused on the nature of the curious person in an attempt to identify the particular attributes he possesses. These studies have, generally speaking, come to many of the same conclusions. Thus, King (1968) found that well-adjusted children were slightly more curious than poorly adjusted children; children who did well in school were more curious than children who did not do well; curious children tended to talk more; children who got along well with others tended to be more curious than others.

On the basis of their large-scale research, Maw and Maw (1964) arrived at a number of specific characteristics that were true of the curious person. For example, children with high curiosity ask more and better questions; select more outgoing, adventurous activities; have more general information about the world in which they live; can recall more specific facts; relate more frequently to the unbalanced and the unfamiliar; persist longer at problem solving; and are more alert to verbal absurdities.

Furthermore, Maw (1967), on the basis of a factor-analytic study of curiosity, concluded that personal and social factors differentiate highly curious from less curious children. Highly curious boys are, according to Maw:

self-actualized, creative—look in terms of finding unique immediate solutions and in seeking long-range, well-considered answers to problems, emotionally mature, capable of abstract thinking and considerable leadership, while being persistent and desirous of having ideal or moral qualities. [p. 64]

Other variables have been studied, but not in any depth, perhaps partly because of the preoccupation with the more fundamental problems that has kept researchers from more specific investigations. It is reasonable to add that, where plausible potential relationships have so far eluded the grasp of researchers, this difficulty has been caused in part by the inadequacy of the instruments to measure curiosity, by the lack of substantial correlations so far demonstrated between them, and by the sometimes considerable differences between the kinds of instruments used in one study and those in another. If greater concern were given to these issues, stronger relationships would probably emerge.

GROWTH AND DEVELOPMENT OF CURIOSITY

Discussions of methods of developing curiosity presuppose that curiosity is a desirable quality to promote. Curiosity has not always been seen in a favorable light, nor always been considered an attribute deserving of encouragement. The proverb "curiosity killed the cat" contains in a nutshell what some have presumably felt to be the negative effect of this attribute. In more modern times, such couplets as Tennyson's "Theirs not to reason why, / Theirs but to do and die" suggest that at a national level, there is some pressure not to develop overly enquiring minds in the citizenry. However, the great majority of writers on curiosity, both past and present, have accorded it a favorable status, and considered it a quality to be worthy of encouragement; and at the present time it would seem to be enjoying as high a status as it has ever achieved in educational thought.

As to the typical course of the development of human curiosity, most writers are in basic agreement. Ashbaugh (1929) feels that it is during the preschool years that curiosity is given full scope. After all, it is during the early years of life and the early years of school that the greatest amount of novelty occurs. Hammond (1958) argues that, by the sixth grade, curiosity normally declines. Hasbrouch (1935) considers children's curiosity at its height between the ages of 4 and 10. Averill (1949) lists the kinds of things children are curious about, and feels that curiosity is greatest in the elementary school. A more comprehensive statement is offered by Vernon (1969):

> This motivation towards achieving an understanding of the nature and causes of events appears, as we have shown, particularly strongly in the curiosity and exploration of children. It tends to die down at adolescence, and to remain only at a moderate level in the lives of most adults. But with a relatively small number of people, it remains high throughout life, appearing as a strong and persistent interest in invention, discovery, scientific research and the pursuit of truth. [p. 92]

As to how to promote curiosity, asking questions has for some considerable time been considered one of the principal ways to do so. Lombard (1940) urges teachers and parents to encourage children to ask questions in order to develop inquiring minds in their children. Evans (1956) felt that sustaining and increasing curiosity required supplying children with accurate information, while promoting critical thinking and dissent fostered self-reliance and originality in behavior. Sherwood (1933) claimed that parents and teachers limit the child's opportunity to clarify his surroundings when they give evasive and impatient answers to the child's questions. Courtis (1940) felt the answers should be self-obtained as far as possible, without adults giving friendly, helpful guidance. By helping a child find his own answer, the adult will help him develop his own intellectual curiosity. Thus, the kind of question asked is very important. Some questions are merely meant to generate conformity. For example, "We all like to read, don't we?" is meant to arouse a resounding "yes"; it is not likely to arouse curiosity. On the other hand, the teacher who raises open-ended questions such as "I wonder why this is happening?" (in a science lesson) or "Why is it that every time I double a number it comes out as an even number?" is likely to stimulate a good deal of interest.

Somewhere between these two extremes is the most commonly asked type of question in the classroom—questions seeking to find out what a student is supposed to know already. These questions, designed to elicit facts ("What is the square root of 49?" "What is the capital city of Egypt?") do *not* generate curiosity.

Sometimes a child will ask a question apparently spontaneously. Maybe an insect flies into view, or a new word is heard and the child asks, "What is it?" or "What does it mean?" Whether a reinforcement now occurs will help determine whether the child will continue to show curiosity. Consider such answers as "It's dirty. Don't touch" in contrast to "It's an insect. Look at its six legs." Or consider the answer, "Don't you know anything!" or "Don't you ever stop asking questions!" in contrast to "Oh! That word means to run and jump. Do you know other words that mean that?" The way parents and teachers ask questions and answer questions is a potent means of stimulating curiosity.

A number of other ways to stimulate curiosity have been suggested. Oswald (1932) listed several conditions that he felt might encourage curiosity. These conditions included notions others have frequently taken for granted: teachers' recognition of the importance of curiosity; attempts to "inspire" pupils; a society that does not demand conformity; high IQ; small classes in schools; avoidance of standardized exams; in-depth study of subject matter; abolition of grading systems; and reducing the completeness of textbooks.

What children will be curious about depends in large part on the nature of the world about them and their previous experiences in it. Clearly the external environment is a strong determinant of the form curiosity will take. Davis (1932), who analyzed 3000 questions posed by 73 children, found that children are not curious about things that have not been encountered in some form in their own experiences. Almost all of their questions resulted from the immediate situation. Evidence from research shows, further, that the presence of a manipulable object in the environment tends to stimulate exploratory behavior (Miles, 1958). Other determinants of the situation are outlined by Vinacke (1952). The consequences of exploring and manipulation depend on what there is to explore and manipulate, on the codes that govern the child's activities, and on the rewards that accrue from them. In some classrooms, the rules of conduct include having the child remain seated at his desk, not touching anything unless told to, and not speaking unless spoken to by the teacher. Inquiring attitudes will soon be stifled in these kinds of classrooms. At the same time, the child's own tissue system determines to a large degree how active he is in exploring, how rapidly he develops, and how strongly he reacts emotionally.

Berlyne (1957) also acknowledges the effect of experience on curiosity. Curiosity can also be increased with a number of "collative" variables that, he argues, are significant in arousing curiosity. In an interesting experiment (Berlyne, 1954a), he also showed how material could be presented in such a way as to increase curiosity in students. He gave subjects a pretest about invertebrate animals, some statements that included answers to the questions, and then a posttest similar to the pretest. He found that prequestioning increases curiosity; statements recognized as answers to questions from the prequestionnaire are more likely to be recalled in the postquestionnaire; questions about more familiar animals and questions whose concepts seem incompatible increase curiosity; and statements containing an element of surprise are recalled more frequently than other statements.

On the other hand, when the same material is presented repeatedly, exploratory behavior declines. Berlyne (1960) noted that, as a curiosity-arousing stimulus continues to affect an organism's receptors, curiosity will diminish. Similarly, Welker (1956) presented chimpanzees with manipulable objects over several sessions and showed that handling of these objects declined from session to session. When new objects were introduced, a revival of exploratory behavior occurred.

One of the most consistent findings of research has been that extremes

of stimulation are antithetical to the arousal of curiosity, whereas intermediate degrees of arousal are likely to elicit curiosity. Neither too much nor too
little stimulation is desirable, but, somewhere between, there is the optimal
level for curiosity arousal. Too much arousal and novelty leads to fear and
anxiety; too little leads to boredom. Aestheticians have often asserted that an
intermediate degree of complexity makes for a maximum appeal. Berlyne
(1958) showed that subjects preferred to look at stimuli possessing novelty
and incongruity. He assumed that such factors elicited curiosity in individuals. Yet, at the same time, it was clear that stimuli that were too complex or
novel might have caused subjects to prefer looking at the less novel and less
complex stimuli.

Maddi (cited in Murray, 1964) demonstrated children's preference for a
moderate degree of novelty. Nursery school children were allowed to play
with a group of small toys on a table. They were then allowed to choose one
of five other tables of toys, some of which contained more "novel" toys than
others. As a group, the children selected tables with toys of 25–75% novelty,
avoiding the extremes of complete familiarity or novelty.

Curiosity in monkeys was studied by Butler (1953). Monkeys were
placed in a dimly lit, opaque box with two small, covered windows. One
window was always locked, the other always unlocked. If the monkey pushed
the unlocked window, it would swing open and allow a view of the laboratory
for a brief period. The monkeys learned this response, and showed very little
satiation in the process, with a fairly constant rate of visual exploration over
several days. The strength of the motive to open the window depended on the
stimulus. Thus the sight of another monkey or a train constituted a "reward."
But the window was not opened, as Murray (1964) points out, to see a large
dog or another monkey in pain.

Analysis of children's humor illustrates the same point. Thus, Zigler,
Levine, and Gould (1967) showed, on a third-grade level, that, with regard to
jokes, complete and easy comprehension does not result in the greatest
amount of laughter. Children obtained the highest mirth response in the
intermediate range of difficulty. They explain their findings thus:

> This is in keeping with a variety of theoretical views and everyday observations
> that have emphasized that children enjoy most that which lies at the growing
> edge of their capacities. While here variables of enjoyment and preference were
> under study, it seems reasonable to assume these are related to curiosity arousal.
> [p. 335]

More recently, a study most relevant to education by Evans (1969) has
shown that students rate as most interesting textbook material that is some-

what more complex and beyond their usual level of comprehension. In explanation, it seems that, far from being something to be avoided, complexity up to the point that it can be comprehended with a degree of effort is perceived as challenging and therefore desirable. Thus it seems, teachers need not worry so much about presenting complexity to pupils, but must control the degree of complexity. In regard to the arousal of curiosity, then, the golden mean prevails. The teacher's problem is to find out (or help the students find out) where the right amount of complexity is for each student. It is doubtful whether the same level of complexity will generate curiosity for all students in the one class.

EDUCATIONAL IMPLICATIONS

It should be reemphasized at this point that curiosity or exploration is better conceived not just as a desirable attribute, but rather as a need that the organism or individual has for its normal functioning. Over and above normal physiological needs, the exercise of the cognitive capacities through curiosity is necessary to proper healthy development, just as, conversely, deprivation can lead to stunted psychological growth.

Thus Nissen (1951) states: "Exploratory behavior may also be thought of as reflecting a primary tendency of all tissues, including the sense organs and their central nervous connections towards functional expression" (p. 357). The principal function of curiosity seems to be to gain an understanding of the environment, and to make use of it more effectively. These themes are common not only in the literature of curiosity but also in related theoretical viewpoints. Thus, in Woodworth's "behavior primacy theory" the most fundamental type of motivated behavior takes the form of attempts to deal effectively with the environment, and these attempts are not random, but selective, directed, and persistent. White's concept of competence stresses that directed and persistent behavior takes place in order to master the environment through interaction with it.

As was noted earlier, findings of research generally supported the view that curiosity was positively related to IQ and creativity, and inversely related to anxiety. Correlational studies indicate the extent of relationships and say nothing about cause and effect. Nevertheless, it would appear reasonable to suggest that the same conditions that favor curiosity would also tend to facilitate intellectual and creative performance. A classroom with a relaxed atmosphere, which allows each child a degree of freedom to explore the world around him, and which displays a tolerant approach toward deviations from the norm, is likely both to encourage curiosity, and at the same time foster intellectual and creative processes. Conversely, a classroom setting where exams are emphasized, rigid and conformist behavior required, and excessive stress laid on high marks, would be likely to promote anxiety. These same pressure-creating situations are detrimental to the arousal of curiosity. Since further curiosity does not appear when activity is predominantly goal directed, what is needed in schools for its appearance is free time during which no specific result necessarily has to be produced (Arnstine, 1966).

For this reason, the optimal time for the development of curiosity would appear to be the preschool and elementary school years. As one progresses through school, there is decreasingly less time to devote to exploring interests outside a somewhat restricted educational program, and larger educational goals become subordinated to more narrow perspectives that necessarily force more limited, goal-directed activities. During the earlier years, one has the opportunity to explore and investigate the world in a setting and at a time relatively unencumbered by pressures to succeed in formal academic courses, and achieve in accordance with standardized tests and curricula.

There are also other reasons to suggest that preschool and elementary school offer the most opportune time. As mentioned earlier, not only is it true that at this time curiosity is most clearly seen in the child, but there is a well-established psychological view that those values and attitudes developed early in life have a profound and lasting effect on subsequent development. Curiosity developed early in a child's career is likely to be maintained throughout life. These ideas are as familiar to the psychoanalysts as to Montessori and Piaget, both of whose theoretical positions implicitly assume curiosity as a primary motivational force for the growth of the child's understanding about the world.

Research evidence was also discussed earlier that showed that an intermediate degree of stimulation was most likely to arouse curiosity. This central concept is discussed in terms of satisfaction of expectation by Arnstine (1966):

> If, for example, the events that follow the arousal of an expectation are perceived just as they were expected to be, interest wanes in seeking to maintain or reinstate the original cue. In human contexts this state of affairs is called boredom, and it can occur whether the cue for an expectation is a school lesson, a work of art, or a personal acquaintance.... The series of events has become too familiar to remain attractive and maintain interest or curiosity....
>
> On the other hand, attention is not likely to be maintained when we don't know what to expect. Under these conditions, when the cues are remote from our experience and we have only the vaguest of expectations, we are likely to

experience discomfort. Thus when a situation is either too familiar or too remote, curiosity is inhibited and attention wanes. We may feel discomfort, boredom, restlessness, or aversion, and the situation is made worse if we cannot escape it. [p. 598]

The fundamental problem for educators would, therefore, seem to be to determine this intermediate degree in any given situation so as to be able to regulate or modify methods and materials to be presented both on an individual and group level. Unfortunately, this determination is not so simple in practice. For one thing, the term *right* or *appropriate* has frequently been applied after the fact—what happens to be curiosity arousing is then by definition labeled "appropriate." In many situations, further, this "optimum" level cannot be known beforehand and has to be discovered through a process analogous to trial and error or to intuition.

A more specific educational application is illustrated in a study by Berlyne (1954a), referred to earlier. From Berlyne's findings, it would seem that a period of prequestioning prior to the presentation of material increases students' curiosity about the material, and improves retention of the material both immediately following the presentation and afterward. Furthermore, questions whose concepts appear incompatible are also more likely to create conflict and hence to increase subject's curiosity; and statements that are surprising are more likely to be recalled.

In another most relevant article, Berlyne (1965) expands on some of these implications, and discusses ways in which curiosity can be used in educational situations. As elsewhere, he distinguishes between perceptual curiosity, a state of conflict that additional information will relieve, and epistemic curiosity, the result of conceptual conflict, or conflict caused by discrepant thoughts, beliefs, or attitudes. Concentrating on the latter, he shows specifically how epistemic curiosity can be induced through conceptual conflict and subsequently relieved to provide reinforcement for school learning. Thus,

> in several subject matters, but especially in the natural sciences, it is possible to present the student with a phenomenon that violates expectations derived from existing beliefs, a phenomenon that his prior training and experience have led him to regard as improbable or impossible. The motivational potentialities of surprise are commonly utilized in lessons using demonstrations of physical, chemical or biological phenomena. The skills of the experimenter and the stage magician have, in fact, been fruitfully combined on many such occasions. [p. 78]

Berlyne cites as an example, the familiar physical experiment in which a brass bell that is just small enough to pass through a ring, will not pass through the same ring when it is heated. The student is invited to find an explanation by putting questions to the teacher, and as the reality of the surprising phenomenon is established and explained, the conflict caused by surprise is eventually eliminated.

Conceptual conflict can be induced in other ways as well as by "surprise." Thus, "bafflement" occurs when a student is confronted with a situation in which a number of apparently irreconcilable demands are made on him. Until he finds a course of action that satisfies all of these demands, he tends to inhibit his responses and remain unsatisfied. A student is asked, for example, to consider how he would find out where he is—what the longitude and latitude of his location are—in the middle of the desert. His conceptual conflict is relieved only when he finally discovers a method of solving the problem. Likewise, "perplexity," "doubt," and "contradiction" are types of conceptual conflict that arouse epistemic curiosity, and can provide reward for learning. Response patterns that relieve the motivating conflict, and solve the motivating problem, thus further understanding and integration, and are reinforced by the reduction of the conceptual conflict.

What Berlyne calls *contradiction* contains within it the idea of paradox—when an apparently simple and familiar event defies a simple and familiar explanation. A specific example of paradox is given with reference to social studies, by Arnstine (1966):

> The presentation of paradox is equally helpful in arousing curiosity in the social studies. Much of what we might want to teach, for example, about wages and prices, production and distribution, may appear formal and rather forbidding to students. But to present the paradox of a nation whose productivity is so high that surplus foods must be destroyed or buried, while at the same time some of its citizens go hungry, is to make a strong appeal to curiosity and interest. The presentation of a paradox arouses curiosity by altering the nature of what was expected. When one hears that food is overproduced, he does not expect to hear that people are hungry. [p. 601]

These ideas, centering on conceptual conflict, can easily be put into practice by teachers. They relate to virtually any subject matter, and involve largely the manner of presentation of the material.

One should note, finally, that educational implications based on the study of curiosity are necessarily limited in the absence of answers even to some of the most basic questions about curiosity. Thus, for example, it is not at all clear, as we have pointed out, whether curiosity can be considered as unidimensional. The most reasonable position to take would be to conceive of it as multidimensional, the different dimensions not necessarily possessing a great deal in common. It is unlikely that being curious about trying new kinds of food, taking a clock apart to see how it works, and looking up complicated words in a dictionary represent the same dimension. Yet such items are commonly included together on self-report scales of curiosity, measuring supposedly a unitary dimension. Researchers have not often enough taken account of this multidimensionality.

As Berlyne (1965) points out, the experimental analysis of attention, curiosity, and interest is just beginning. With further research, we may eventually reach the position whereby "the zest for action, including intellectual action, of the normal child that so often obstructs the teacher's efforts can be pressed into service as a potent ally" (p. 87).

ANNOTATED BIBLIOGRAPHY

Berlyne, D. E. *Conflict, arousal and curiosity.* New York: McGraw-Hill, 1960.
> Eleven chapters deal with attention, exploratory behavior, arousal, epistemic behavior, art and humor, conceptual conflict, and epistemic curiosity. Berlyne presents his own theoretical position, a highly modified drive-reduction theory, incorporating evidence from neurophysiology; shows interrelationships between curiosity and other variables, and synthesizes a large and extensive body of knowledge from different sources, summarizing a great deal of research. The most extensively developed theoretical formulation and integration of ideas. 350 pages in all, with a substantial bibliography of more than 30 pages.

Fowler, H. *Curiosity and exploratory behavior.* New York: Macmillan, 1965.
> The book is divided into two parts. The first part deals with problems in the study of curiosity, the nature of exploration, applications of contemporary theory, and recent developments—a well-written, concise summary of theoretical and research evidence. The second part consists of 14 major experimental studies relating to curiosity, reprinted in full. 13-page bibliography.

Maw, W. H., & Maw, E. W. An exploratory investigation into the measurement of curiosity in elementary school children (Cooperative Research Project No. 801). University of Delaware, Newark, 1964.
> A large-scale empirical exploration of curiosity in fifth-grade children in Delaware public schools with a large sample of subjects, comprehensive in scope. The authors devised, tested, and modified a wide variety of measurement techniques, mostly paper-and-pencil tasks, over several stages of experimentation. A definition of curiosity offered, and an extensive review of research, including correlates of curiosity. Lengthy bibliography.

REFERENCES

Arnstine, D. Curiosity. *Teachers College Record*, May 1966, *67*, 595–502.
Ashbaugh, E. J. Curiosity. *School and Society*, 1929, *30*, 590–593.

Averill, L. A. *The psychology of the elementary school child.* New York: Longmans Green, 1949.

Berlyne, D. E. Novelty and curiosity as determinants of exploratory behavior. *British Journal of Psychology,* 1950, *41,* 79.

Berlyne, D. E. An experimental study of human curiosity. *British Journal of Psychology,* 1954, *45,* 256–265. (a)

Berlyne, D. E. A theory of human curiosity. *British Journal of Psychology,* 1954, *45,* 180–191. (b)

Berlyne, D. E. Conflict and information—Theory variables as determinants of human perceptual curiosity. *Journal of Experimental Psychology,* 1957, *53,* 399–404.

Berlyne, D. E. The influence of complexity and novelty in visual figures on orienting responses. *Journal of Experimental Psychology,* 1958, *55,* 289–296.

Berlyne, D. E. *Conflict, arousal and curiosity.* New York: McGraw-Hill, 1960.

Berlyne, D. E. Motivational problems raised by exploratory and epistemic behavior. In S. Koch (Ed.), *Psychology: A study of a science.* Vol. 5. New York: McGraw-Hill, 1963. Pp. 284–364.

Berlyne, D. E. Curiosity and education. In J. D. Krumboltz (Ed.), *Learning and the educational process.* Chicago: Rand McNally, 1965. Chap. 3.

Beswick, D. Theory and measurement of human curiosity. Unpublished doctoral dissertation, Harvard University, Cambridge, Mass., 1965.

Bindra, D. *Motivation: A systematic reinterpretation.* New York: Ronald Press, 1959.

Butler, R. A. Discrimination learning by Rhesus monkeys to visual-exploration motivation. *Journal of Comparative Physiological Psychology,* 1953, *46,* 95–98.

Chiu, L. H. A factorial study of academic motivation. Unpublished doctoral dissertation, Teachers College, Columbia University, 1967.

Courtis, S. A. Developing an inquiring mind. *Childhood Education,* 1940, *16,* 197–200.

Davis, E. A. The form and function of children's questions. *Child Development,* 1921, *3,* 57–74.

Day, H. I. A curious approach to creativity. *Canadian Psychologist,* 1968, *9,* 485–497. (a)

Day, H. I. The role of specific curiosity in school achievement. *Journal of Educational Psychology,* 1968, *59,* 37–43. (b)

Day, H. I. A progress report on the development of a test of curiosity. Paper presented at the National Seminar on Adult Education, Toronto, Ontario, Can., February, 1969.

Demel, A., & Hansen, R. Reliability and validity data on a multi-dimensional scale for measuring classroom motivation. Paper presented at the National Council on Measurement in Education, Los Angeles, California, 1969.

Evans, B. Our responsibility to the intelligent. *National Parent Teachers,* 1956, *51,* 8–10.

Evans, D. R. Conceptual complexity, arousal and epistemic behavior. Unpublished doctoral dissertation, University of Toronto, 1969.

Fiske, D. W., & Maddi, S. R. A conceptual framework. In D. W. Fiske & S. R. Maddi, *Functions of varied experience.* Homewood, Ill.: Dorsey Press, 1961. Pp. 11–56.

Fowler, H. *Curiosity and exploratory behavior.* New York: Macmillan, 1965.

Glanzer, M. Stimulus satiation: An explanation of spontaneous alternation and related phenomena. *Psychological Review,* 1953, *60,* 257–268.

Greenberger, E., O'Connor, J., & Sorenson, A. *Content analysis of stories for curiosity imagery: A manual.* Baltimore: The Center for the Study of Social Organization of Schools, The Johns Hopkins University, 1968. (Report No. 35.)

Greenberger, E., & Entwistle, D. R. *Need for achievement, curiosity and sense of control.* Baltimore: Johns Hopkins University, Report No. 35, 1968.

Hammond, S. B. Curiosity and creativity. *Journal of Engineering Education,* 1958, *42,* 392–393.

Harlow, H. F. Motivation as a factor in the acquisition of new responses. In *Current theory and research in motivation.* Lincoln: University of Nebraska Press, 1953. Pp. 24–49

Hasbrouch, P. D. Enquiring eddies. *Progressive Education,* 1935, *12,* 267–269.

Hebb, D. Drives and the C.N.S. *Psychological Review,* 1955, *62,* 243–254.

Hess, R. D. *The cognitive environments of urban preschool children. Manual of instructions for administering and scoring the Plutchik Exploratory-Interest Questionnaire.* Chicago: University of Chicago, 1967.

Hess, R. D., Shipman, U. C., Brophy, J., & Bear, R. M. *The cognitive environments of urban preschool children. Manual of instructions for administering and scoring the curiosity task.* Chicago: University of Chicago, Urban Child Center, 1967.

Hoats, D. L., Miller, M., & Spitz, H. Experiments on perceptual curiosity in mental retardates and normals. *American Journal of Mental Deficiency,* 1963, *68,* 386–395.

Hogan, R., & Greenberger, E. The development of a curiosity scale (Report No. 32). Baltimore: Johns Hopkins University, Center for the Study of Social Organization of Schools, 1969.

Joesting, J., & Joesting, R. Torrance's Creative Motivation Inventory and its relation to several personality variables. *Psychological Reports,* 1969, *24,* 30.

Kagan, J., Sontag, L., Baker, C., & Nelson, V. Personality and IQ change. *Journal of Abnormal and Social Psychology,* 1958, *56,* 261–266.

King, J. B. Curiosity in young children. Unpublished doctoral dissertation, University of Colorado, 1968.

Lesser, G. S. (Ed.). *Psychology and educational practice.* Glenview, Ill.: Scott, Foresman, 1971.

Leuba, C. A new look at curiosity and creative activity. *Journal of Higher Education,* 1958, *29,* 132–140.

Levitt, E. E. *The psychology of anxiety.* New York: Bobbs-Merrill, 1967.

Livson, N. Towards a differentiated construct of curiosity. *Journal of Genetic Psychology,* 1967, *111,* 73–84.

Lombard, E. C. Our adventures with children: Developing an inquiring mind. *School Life,* 1940, *26,* 71–72.

Maw, W. H. A definition of curiosity: A factor analysis study (Cooperative Research Project S-109). University of Delaware, 1967.

Maw, W. H., & Maw, E. W. Information recognition by children with high and low curiosity. *Educational Research Bulletin,* 1961, *40*(8), 197–201; 223–224.

Maw, W. H., & Maw, E. W. Children's curiosity as an aspect of reading comprehension. *Reading Teacher,* 1962, *15,* 236–240.

Maw, W. H., & Maw, E. W. The differences between the scores of children with high curiosity and children with low curiosity on a test of general information. *Journal of Educational Research,* 1963, *57*(2), 76–79.

Maw, W. H., & Maw, E. W. An exploratory investigation into the measurement of curiosity in elementary school children (Cooperative Research Project No. 801). University of Delaware, 1964.

Maw, W. H., & Maw, E. W. Differences in preference for investigating activities by school children who differ in curiosity level. *Psychology in the Schools*, 1965, *2*, 263–266. (a)

Maw, W. H., & Maw, E. W. Personal and social variables differentiating children with high and low curiosity (Cooperative Research Project No. 1511). University of Delaware, 1965. (b)

Maw, W. H., & Maw, E. W. Self-appraisal of curiosity. *Journal of Educational Research*, 1968, *61*(10), 462–465.

Maw, W. H., & Maw, E. W. Self-concepts of high and low curiosity boys. *Child Development*, 1970, *41*, 123–129.

McReynolds, P. Exploratory behavior as related to anxiety in psychiatric patients. *Psychological Reports*, 1958, *4*, 321–322.

McReynolds, P., Acker, M., & Pietila, C. Relation of object curiosity to psychological adjustment in children. *Child Development*, 1961, *32*, 393–400.

Miles, R. C. Learning in kittens with manipulatory, exploratory, and food incentives. *Journal of Comparative and Physiological Psychology*, 1958, *51*, 39–42.

Minuchin, P. Processes of curiosity and exploration in preschool disadvantaged children. Bank State College of Education, New York, 1968. [Eric no. ED023470.]

Montgomery, K. C. Exploratory behavior as a function of "similarity" of stimulus situations. *Journal of Comparative and Physiological Psychology*, 1953, *46*, 129–133.

Murray, E. J. *Motivation and emotion.* New York: Prentice-Hall, 1964.

Myers, A. K., & Miller, N. E. Evidence for learning motivated by "exploration." *Journal of Comparative and Physiological Psychology*, 1954, *47*, 428–436.

Nissen, H. W. Phylogenetic comparisons. In S. S. Stevens (Ed.), *Handbook of experimental psychology.* New York: Wiley, 1951.

Oswald, F. W. Obstacles to the development of intellectual curiosity. *Clearing House*, 1932, *6*, 349–351.

Penney, R. K. Reactive curiosity and manifest anxiety in children. *Child Development*, 1965, *36*(3), 697–702.

Penney, R. K., & McCann, B. The children's reactive curiosity scale. *Psychological Report*, 1964, *15*, 323–334.

Pielstick, N. L., & Woodruff, A. B. Curiosity arousal and its effects on learning (Cooperative Research Project No. 1962). Northern Illinois University, 1964.

Poore, P. J., & Lang, G. Curiosity in elementary school children: A comparison of parent, teacher, and self-ratings. Paper presented at American Psychological Association, Philadelphia, August, 1963.

Sherwood, G. H. How, when and why? *Child Study*, 1933, *11*, 65.

Starkweather, E. K. *Potential creative ability and the preschool child.* Stillwater: Oklahoma State University, 1966. [ERIC no. ED018900.]

Torrance, E. P. Non-test ways of identifying the creatively gifted. In J. C. Gowan, G. D. Demos, & E. P. Torrance (Eds.), *Creativity: Its educational implications.* New York: Wiley, 1967.

Vernon, M. D. *Human motivation.* London: Cambridge University Press, 1969.

Vidler, D. C. The relationship between convergent and divergent thinking, anxiety and curiosity. Unpublished doctoral dissertation, Teachers College, Columbia University, 1972.

Vinacke, W. E. *The psychology of thinking.* New York: McGraw-Hill, 1952.

Welker, W. I. Some determinants of play and exploration in chimpanzees. *Journal of Comparative and Physiological Psychology*, 1956, *49*, 84–89.

Zigler, E., Levine, J., & Gould, L. Cognitive challenge as a factor in children's humor appreciation. *Journal of Personality and Social Psychology*, 1967, *6*, 332–336.

Zuckerman, M., Kolin, E. A., Price, L., & Zoob, I. Development of a sensation-seeking scale. *Journal of Counsulting Psychology*, 1964, *28*, 477–482.

3

Locus of Control

GERARD C. FANELLI

Kean College of New Jersey

INTRODUCTION

The term *locus of control* refers to the perceived causality of behavioral outcomes. At one extreme (internal), the individual thinks of himself as being responsible for his own behavior. At the other extreme (external), the individual sees others or luck or circumstances beyond his control as responsible for his behavior. The internal person blames himself for his failures and accepts praise as deserved for his triumphs. The external person will not blame himself for his errors and will not think his successes are caused by his own efforts.

The concept of locus of control has appeared in many forms throughout the history of mankind. The ancient Greek tragedies abound with notions of man's helplessness before gods and fate. Shakespeare's plays illustrate both tragic predestination (Romeo and Juliet, the "star-crossed" lovers) and free will ("The fault, dear Brutus, lies not in our stars, but in ourselves," *Julius Caesar*). Philosophers have wrestled with the concept of locus of control as determinism versus free will; sociologists, as autonomy versus alienation (powerlessness); and psychologists, as behaviorism versus mentalism. Nietzsche has called power the most important psychological phenomena and Adler, in his system of individual psychology, suggests that feelings of inferiority are overcome through the exercise of personal power.

45

As a formal psychological construct, however, the concept of locus of control had its origin about two decades ago. A closely related concept—attribution of responsibility—has also undergone considerable investigation in recent years. This chapter attends to both concepts, although the primary emphasis is on locus of control.

THE CONCEPT OF LOCUS OF CONTROL

First introduced by Rotter (1954), the locus of control concept has become increasingly of more importance in theoretical and practical considerations of motivation. Rotter's social learning theory, from which the concept of locus of control comes, suggests that a person enters a situation with expectancies concerning the probable outcomes of his possible behaviors. These expectancies are presumed to be based on the person's past experiences. These experiences might be divided into two categories: general and specific. The latter includes those experiences that are similar to the current situation; the former, the sum total of all other experiences. According to Rotter, the probability of a certain behavior will vary lawfully with the person's expectancy regarding the outcome of that behavior. (This rule can be formulated $pB = f(E) + r.v.$, where pB is probability of behavior, $f(E)$ is function of expectancy, and $r.v.$ is reinforcement value.) This formulation predicts that the frequency of a certain behavior will increase if past and current experiences suggest that a rewarding outcome will result from that behavior; and the frequency will decrease if the anticipated outcome is nonrewarding. The implication for education is: If a teacher makes it consistently clear (1) that a particular student behavior will result in a rewarding outcome for the student, then the likelihood of that behavior's recurrence will be increased; (2) that another student behavior will result in a nonrewarding outcome for the student, then the likelihood of that behavior's recurrence will be decreased.

The impetus for the incorporation of the locus of control construct as a modification of this formula came from two kinds of discrepancies that resulted from related research. The first discrepancy is that the predicted changes in the probability of a behavior occur only when the outcome is perceived by the person to have been contingent on (the result of) his behavior. If an outcome is perceived to be the result of luck, chance, or the influence of others, then it is reasonable for the person to discount that particular outcome with regard to the "lawful" alteration of the probabilities of his behaviors. Phares (1957), for example, found that changes in expectancies after success and failure were greater if skill determined the outcome than if chance determined the outcome. Classroom implication: A student will not "lawfully" alter the probabilities of his behaviors on the basis of rewarding and nonrewarding outcomes unless he is convinced that the outcomes were directly attributable to his behaviors. If the student believes that the teacher's reward and punishments are given at random (without regard for his behaviors), then the likelihood of his repeating the behaviors might be unaffected (or be affected in a "nonlawful" manner).

The second discrepancy is reported in an extensive review by Rotter (1966). In ambiguous tasks, where causality for outcomes was in doubt, the behavior of some people followed the expectancy formula, whereas the behavior of others did not. The latter group more often attributed causality to luck, fate, chance, or other people, while the former group more often attributed causality to themselves. Apparently, in those tasks where either skill or chance might be at work, some people believe that skill is the major factor and other people believe that chance is the major factor. Classroom implication: Some students might characteristically view the occurrence or nonoccurrence of reinforcements as being beyond their control. Then, even if the teacher exercised care in reinforcing certain behaviors, these students might still refuse to acknowledge the relation between their behaviors and the outcomes. Then the anticipated "lawful" changes would not occur.

MEASURES AND CORRELATES
OF LOCUS OF CONTROL

Before the notion of a characteristic tendency to attribute causality to one's self or to chance could be incorporated into the social learning theory formula, it had to be determined if one could measure this tendency, and, if indeed, it were a generalizable trait. Rotter (1966) devised a questionnaire that attempts to determine the degree to which a person generally attributes responsibility to himself rather than to other factors. The questionnaire consists of 29 pairs of statements that require the respondent to select the one statement of each pair with which he more strongly agrees. One statement places responsibility within the person's power ("The grades I get depend on how hard I study"); the alternative statement places responsibility outside the person's power ("Sometimes I can't understand how teachers arrive at the grades they give"). One point is given for each "external" statement selected. Six of the items are fillers (items designed to introduce other ideas to the questionnaire so that the questionnaire is not too transparent). Filler items are not scored. Thus, the possible range of scores is from 0 to 23. A considerable number of studies, using a wide variety of subjects, obtained reliabilities of about .70 both for internal consistency and for test—retest reliability. Franklin (in Rotter, 1966) factor analyzed the scores of 1000 high school students and found that all the items correlated significantly with one general factor and that this one factor accounted for 53% of the total scale variance. Rotter labeled the tendency to attribute responsibility for outcomes to oneself as a generalized expectancy for internal locus of control and the tendency to attribute responsibility for outcomes to luck, fate, chance, or powerful others as a generalized expectancy for external locus of control. Subjects who demonstrate the former tendency are often referred to as *internals*, while those who demonstrate the latter tendency are referred to as *externals.*

Many studies have related scores for internals and externals (I—E) on Rotter's questionnaire to other variables and have reported significant differences between the two types. Hersch and Scheibe (1967) found that internals were higher than externals on the Dominance, Sociability, Intellectual Efficiency, Tolerance, Good Impression, and Well-Being scales of the California Psychological Inventory. They also found that internals were more likely than externals to describe themselves on the Adjective Checklist as achieving, assertive, independent, effective, powerful, and industrious. Strickland (1970) found that internals attend better to outcomes, retain more of the relevant information given, are more aware of cues, and tend to resist subtle suggestion more than externals do. In relation to self-esteem, Epstein and Komorita (1971) found that both low-esteem and moderate-esteem subjects were significantly more external than high-esteem subjects. This finding supports the hypothesis held by several researchers that greater internality is found among high-esteem subjects.

Internals perform better under skill rather than chance instructions, whereas externals perform better under presumed chance conditions (Rotter, 1966). A typical "skill" instruction is to tell students that their scores on a test or at a game depends on how good they are and how hard they try. A typical "chance" instruction is to tell students that their scores depend on how lucky they are. The preference that internals have for skill-oriented situations and that externals have for chance situations has been explained by Schneider (1972) as self-fulfilling prophecy. That is, a person will anticipate (or predict) an event and this anticipation will regulate his behavior such that the likelihood of the occurrence of the predicted event is increased. So a person whose locus of control is internal will anticipate that he has control and will, therefore, choose those situations that allow him to exercise this control. A person whose locus of control is external, on the other hand, would choose those situations that support his expectation that he is, in fact, unable to control what happens to him.

Internals tended to prefer moderate risks in terms of the probabilities of success in various tasks. Externals preferred choices with low probabilities of success in a dart-throwing game (Julian, Lichtman, & Ryckman, 1968). Such choice patterns might be explained as follows: Since the selection of a behavior whose probability of success is low all but guarantees failure, the chooser is freed from the pride–shame reaction to success–failure. He suffers no shame from frequent failure because this outcome is expected. On the other hand, the choice of intermediate-risk behaviors (those whose probability of resulting in a successful outcome is about 50%) makes the outcome least certain of all the probability levels and thus places greatest responsibility for the outcome on the performer's ability and effort. Additionally, the actual results of these intermediate-risk level tasks give more information about the performer than do the outcomes of lower or higher levels of risk. Since externals tend to avoid these intermediate-risk tasks, they might be demonstrating a fear of self-disclosure or of self-discovery. This thought suggests that externality might be akin to a psychoanalytic defense mechanism, the purpose of which is to permit the person to reject new information about himself and to maintain a posture of helplessness. Adler viewed neurotic symptoms (of which the patient complains) as the patient's means for exerting control (power) over others, without feeling responsible for doing so. This position suggests that a "normal" person feels autonomous and accepts responsibility for his behaviors, whereas a "neurotic" person feels powerless and does not accept responsibility for his behaviors.

Several studies have explored the relationship between psychological adjustment and locus of control. Shybut (1968) found that psychotic subjects had higher externality scores than did neurotic and normal subjects. Feather (1967) reported that external subjects of both sexes scored significantly higher than internal subjects on a measure of "debilitating" anxiety. Fanelli (1972) found that females who were external reported more anxiety on the Achievement Anxiety Test (Alpert & Haber, 1960) than those females who were internal. With the same subjects, Fanelli also found that females who accepted more responsibility for the outcomes of various tasks reported significantly less anxiety than females who accepted less responsibility. Nowicki, Bonner, and Feather (1972) found that patient's views of the therapeutic relationship in counseling experiences were a function both of locus of control and of the procedures employed. The resistance to influence that is characteristic of internals suggests a need to maintain the belief in personal control. This finding suggests that extreme internality might be as defensive as extreme externality.

Ray and Katahn (1968) found significant correlations between locus of control scores and scores on the Manifest Anxiety Scale and the Mandler Test Anxiety Questionnaire (see Chapter 5, on anxiety). Factor analysis led them to conclude that the locus of control measure was not simply another measure of anxiety. However, as noted, several studies report positive, significant correlations between anxiety and externality.

Platt and Eisenman (1968) found that internals have a longer future-time perspective than externals have. That is, internals have an extensive view of time and externals have a restricted view of time. The notion of time as a framework for past, present, and future events is of paramount importance to achievement (I was there yesterday; I am here today; I will be there tomorrow). Those people who view time as present only are not likely to be high achievers. This finding suggests that externals might be less achievement oriented than internals are. This suggestion finds support from Valecha (1972) who administered an abbreviated version of Rotter's questionnaire to 2700 white males and 1000 black males between the ages of 16 and 26 years and related the resultant scores to work-relevant variables. White males who were internal had higher level positions, better knowledge of the world of work, had more stable work histories, worked more hours per week, had higher incomes, and received more additional training than white males who were external. These results generally were not significant for black males. Valecha suggests that the belief system in internality for blacks might not be transformed into behavioral manifestations as readily as it appears to be for whites.

Finally, externals, in contrast to internals, have been found to be more anxious, more aggressive, more dogmatic, less trustful, more suspicious of others, less confident, and less insightful (Joe, 1971).

The internal–external locus of control questionnaire devised by Rotter has been most extensively used in locus of control research. It is probably the best test available for use with adult populations, undergraduates, and upper high school students. Several other measures have been developed and will be discussed.

Crandall, Katkovsky, and Crandall (1965) developed a scale that is suitable for use with children from about 8 to 14 years of age. They call it the Intellectual Achievement Responsibility Questionnaire (IAR) and claim that it is more specific to academic achievement situations than is Rotter's questionnaire. The authors found the IAR to correlate significantly with academic achievement as measured by report-card grades and certain achievement tests. Other researchers have supported their findings (cf. McGhee & Crandall, 1968). The IAR produces three scores: the I+ score refers to the number of items selected that indicates acceptance of responsibility for one's successes; the I− score refers to the number of items selected that indicate acceptance of personal responsibility for one's failures; the I score is the sum of the I+ score and the I− score. Rhiengelheim, Bialer, and Morrissey (1969) prepared a modified version of the IAR. They shortened the scale and simplified its language to facilitate its use with mentally retarded children.

Gurin, Gurin, Lao, and Beattie (1969) administered Rotter's scale along with several additional items to black college students. They factor analyzed the results and obtained two major factors and two minor factors. The major factors were labeled *personal control* and *control ideology*. A perusal of the items in these factors suggests that a person might be internal with respect to his immediate personal life and at the same time be external with respect to the larger political system in which he lives. This two-factor analysis of locus of control found support in the research with black college students undertaken by Lao (1970). The results of more recent attempts to factor analyze locus of control suggests that a person's degree of internality might not be uniform across varied situations. Nonetheless, there is sufficient evidence to support the idea that a slight generalized tendency toward internal or external locus of control does exist, although situational factors might modify this finding.

Other tests of internal—external locus of control include the following:

- *The Children's Picture Test of Internal—External Control* (Battle & Rotter, 1963).
- *The Locus of Control Scale for Children*, an orally administered true—false scale (Bialer, 1961); and an alternate form prepared by Gozali and Bialer (1971).
- Historically, it might be noted that the *Phares Scale* (Phares, 1955) was the first formal attempt to measure the locus of control construct.

ATTRIBUTION OF RESPONSIBILITY

An area of investigation that is closely related to locus of control is the concept of attribution of responsibility. Researchers have attempted in various ways to measure the degree of responsibility that subjects attribute to themselves before and after various experiences (such as succeeding or failing at solving anagram puzzles).

Feather and Simon (1971) have assessed the degree of attribution of responsibility by asking subjects (after they had completed a task) to indicate the percentage of responsibility they would assign to themselves (for skill, effort, and so on) versus the percentage they would assign to other factors (luck, interference, and so on). This approach considers attribution of responsibility to be a dependent variable; it is after the fact and attempts to explain the outcome. Research in this area tends to ignore the possible influences of the subject's locus of control prior to his participation in the experimental task. Fanelli (1972) explored the relationship between locus of control and attribution of responsibility for their achievement in general. This score correlated moderately, but significantly, with their scores on Rotter's scale ($r = .31; N = 80; p < .01$). Then after performing on a task, the subjects assigned to themselves a percentage of responsibility for the outcome. The correlation between these scores and the Rotter scores was higher ($r = -.37$). There was a significant correlation between actual performance scores and the percentage of responsibility taken for the task ($r = .33$). Separate analyses of the behaviors of internals and externals indicated that the two groups reacted differently to performance scores and to success and failure treatments. For example, changes in self-ratings after success and failure related differentially to performance levels and to increases in performance scores for internals and externals. These findings suggest that there are two components to locus of control just as there are general and specific components to the expectancy factor in Rotter's original formulation. One component is the generalized tendency to attribute causality internally or externally across situations and the other component is the specific tendency to attribute causality internally or externally after results are known. Researchers who investigate attribution of responsibility after success and failure, therefore, might be advised to include a pretask measure of generalized locus of control.

Weiner, Heckhausen, Meyer, and Cook (1972) have attempted to reanalyze the concept of locus of control in terms of four elements: ability, effort, task difficulty, and luck. (A reading of Heider, 1958, serves as a strong foundation for this analysis.) The authors separate these four elements across two dimensions: locus of control and stability.

Table 3.1 indicates that effort and luck are perceived as variable, but one is internal and the other is external. Weiner *et al.* (1972) suggest that changes in expectancy depend not on the locus of control dimension but on the stability dimension. Some of the research dealing with locus of control

TABLE 3.1
Analysis of Attributes of Responsibility

	Locus of control	
Stability	Internal	External
Fixed	ability	task difficulty
Unstable	effort	luck

appears to be confounded, since the appropriate elements have not been separately analyzed. The authors conclude from their own research that in achievement-related contexts, affect is determined by the locus of control dimension. A person who places responsibility for success—failure on ability—effort (internal) feels more pride—shame than a person who places responsibility for outcomes on task difficulty or luck (external). It might be that extreme externality serves as a defensive measure against strong feelings of shame. However, this very defense against shame prevents the person from experiencing those feelings of pride and joy that result from successes for which he might be responsible.

The educational implication of these findings are as follows. Attempts to alter a person's level of externality by creating successful experiences for him are bound to suffer at least short-term failure for two reasons: first, the external might find it too painful to accept responsibility for the current "prideful" successes since the concomitant is that he accepts responsibility for past and present "shameful" failures; second, the fact that the instructor is actually setting up the success experiences might give support to the external's perception that the control of reinforcements resides in hands other than his own. Add the possibility that the external person can readily decide that a true success of his was in fact brought about by the teacher's contrivances, and the possibility of "cure" for the external seems to be low. Perhaps counseling might assist the extremely external person in his giving up of what might be an important psychological defense mechanism.

As with other "ailments," an ounce of prevention is worth a pound of cure. Unfortunately, neither preventative nor curative measures are clear-cut. Certain cultures seem to have predispositions to the development of externality, particularly among those that surround the Mediterranean Sea (Frankenstein, 1968). Coleman (1966) in a survey of equality of educational opportunity found that black children in the United States believed more than did white children that success was caused by luck rather than by hard work. Coleman found a strong relationship between these beliefs and the academic performance of black children. Black students who believed more in hard work had higher scores on a reading test than black children who believed in luck; black children who believed in hard work had higher verbal achievement scores than all children who believed in luck, regardless of their color or geographical origin.

Stephens (1972) administered three different locus of control scales to 575 black and white children in various types of second-grade classrooms. He was testing the hypothesis that the "open" classroom fosters development of internal locus of control. The results were inconclusive, partly because the three locus of control scales appeared to be measuring different variables. Stephens suggests the results indicate that the open classroom experiences might hve systematic effects on I—E variables. At any rate, the recent innovations in classroom styles tend to make the student more aware of the contingency between his behaviors and the resultant reinforcements.

Baker (1972) has devised a model for an instructional system that might help foster an internal locus of control among those community college students who have unrealistic aspirations, feelings of powerlessness, and low motivations. Baker suggests that the student's self-concept of failure might be transformed into a self-concept of mastery by the following process:

- Give the student obstacles (choices, for example).
- Judiciously reward the student for taking responsibility (for making choices, and so on).
- Build a pattern of success for the student.

Certain parental behaviors have been correlated with locus of control in children. Parents who encourage independence in their children and who are supportive and accepting of them, generally foster in them an internal locus of control. Parents who are hostile, rejecting, and punitive foster an external locus of control (Di Vesta & Thompson, 1970). Other factors that might play a role include the socioeconomic level of the parents, their educational level, and their religious beliefs. External children are found more often in poor, rather than wealthy, families; in ignorant, rather than educated, families; in dogmatic, rather than in liberal or reformed, religions. The preventive measures one might consider in light of this discussion include elevating the socioeconomic and educational levels of parents (and of future parents), and relaxing the rigidity of those dogmatic religions that usurp all individual autonomy.

LOCUS OF CONTROL AND
ACHIEVEMENT MOTIVATION

Achievement motivation research in the past two decades has dealt almost exclusively with the construct of need for achievement (nAch) particularly as measured by the Thematic Apperception Test (TAT). The research has been reviewed by Heckhausen (1967) and by Vidler (in Chapter 4 of this book). Investigators have used measures of anxiety along with the TAT to obtain what they call *resultant achievement motivation.* More recently, the relation between nAch and locus of control has come under consideration. Platt and Eisenman (1968) found that the behavioral correlates of those who are internal tend to resemble the behavioral correlates of those who are high in nAch. For example, both internal and high nAch subjects persist longer at tasks, prefer skill-determined rather than chance-determined tasks, and set their expected levels of attainment at moderately higher levels than their past performances. Both high nAch and internality correlate positively with socioeconomic status, with level of education, and with faster learning and greater attentiveness. The parental behaviors that seem to foster internality resemble those parental behaviors that seem to foster high nAch.

However, measures of locus of control do not correlate significantly with measures of nAch. Heckhausen (1968) attributes this finding to the generality of Rotter's scale with its "incorrect" presumption of consistency across diverse situations.[1] Heckhausen suggests that nAch will correlate with more specific measures of locus of control in achievement situations. An alternative explanation for the lack of significant correlations between locus of control and nAch is the notoriously low reliability of the TAT. The TAT score is readily influenced by the type of instructions given, and under the

---

[1] While this writer believes that there is a consistent generalized expectancy for internal or external locus of control, he does recognize that a weakness of the Rotter scale might lie in its definition of externality as attributing causality to fate, chance, luck, or powerful others as if each of these external attributions would have the same results. A person who believes in fate would have a more deterministic view of causality than would a person who believes in chance or luck. The former might choose his behaviors quite carefully so as not to "tempt fate"; whereas the latter person might act more precipitously to give his "luck" more "chances" for success. The believer in luck oscillates between good feelings and bad feelings depending on outcomes, whereas the believer in fate might more moderately accept all outcomes. Persons who attribute causality to powerful others will vary among themselves depending on the perceived (or actual) nature of the other.

most controlled circumstances, its test–retest reliability is low (McClelland, in Buros, 1970, reports $r = .22$).

Weiner and Kukla (1970) found that high nAch subjects, when given the choice of tasks with high, medium, or low probabilities of success, tended to select tasks that had a medium probability of success. This tendency was even greater for those high nAch subjects who accepted more responsibility for the outcomes of the tasks. Weiner and Kukla also found that a person's perception of his own responsibility influences the affect that might be associated with the attainment of a goal. Only when a person accepts responsibility for the outcomes of his behaviors will he fully enjoy success. But the person must also accept responsibility for failure. It might be the difficulty of accepting failure that results in the attribution of results to luck. The external person rejects responsibility for failure, but loses pride for success. The internal person enjoys pride by being responsible for success and failure. But rather than attributing failure to his own lack of ability, the internal ascribes failure to his own lack of effort. This tendency leads him to persist longer and more vigorously at the task. Other researchers have also found that internals (especially those who are high in nAch) persist longer at tasks than externals do.

Karabenick (1972) found that success and failure are more important to internals than to externals. He suggested that locus of control beliefs might be a moderator of affect in achievement situations. Breit (1969) had earlier suggested that the cognitive processes involved in achievement motivation might be mediated or not, depending on the nature of the person's beliefs regarding causality. His discussion suggests that achievement motivation might come into play only when success and failure are seen to be contingent on one's behavior. If a person characteristically attributes causality to external sources, then his level of achievement motivation would be low. Locus of control, then, might be the "gatekeeper" to the implementation of achievement motivation and a minimum degree of internality (threshhold level) would unlock the gate.

DeCharms (1968) points out that although the concept of personal responsibility is one of the major components of the achievement syndrome as presented by McClelland (1961), it is not a major element in the measure used in scoring nAch. And yet, much of what happens in training courses for increasing nAch are really attempts to increase the subject's feelings of personal causation. It appears that researchers who have been concerned with levels of nAch might also have been ("semiconsciously") concerned with personal causation.

School-Related Studies

Bryant (1972) explored teacher–student relationships as perceived by teachers and their internal and external students. She found that teachers tended to attribute more negative characteristics to external students and that external students described their teachers more negatively than did internal students. When teachers' and students' perceptions of teacher–student relationships were compared, it was found that external students had significantly more misperceptions of these relationships than did internal students. Students who were extremely external tended to have more disturbed relationships with their teachers than did students who were either moderately or extremely internal. External students, when compared to internal students, showed more misunderstandings and fewer understandings, showed more feelings of being misunderstood and fewer feelings of being understood. Assuming that students desire to maintain a shared sense of interpersonal experience with their teachers, Bryant concluded that students whose locus of control is external have more painful relationships with their teachers than do students whose locus of control is internal.

Hammer (1972) investigated the effects of differential teacher comments on the performance of internal and external undergraduate students. The results indicate that external students subsequently perform better after having received specified comments including their teachers' future expectations. Internal students performed better when no comments had previously been made. Hammer explains that individual differences in locus of control affect the responses because internals tend to resist outside influences, while externals welcome them. His findings suggest that teachers might profitably tailor the nature and frequency of their comments to the personality characteristics of each individual student.

Murray and Staebler (1972) investigated the effects of teachers' locus of control on their evaluations of a student's performances in ascending and descending patterns of improvement. They found that all teachers—regardless of locus of control—were more influenced by the initial performances of the student than by his more recent performances. This finding appears to contradict the expectation that more internal teachers would pay attention to relevant information. This discrepancy might be accounted for by the fact that there were no extreme externals in the sample of teachers. Nonetheless, the finding that teachers tend to evaluate a student more on the basis of his initial performance than on his recent performances carries implications for a need to reexamine the process of evaluation of students by their teachers.

Friend and Neale (1972) investigated the reactions of black and white fifth-grade children to success and failure experiences on a reading test. The major finding was that although the black children perceived their ability and effort levels to equal those of the white children, they rated these factors as being of less importance than did the white children. Perhaps because of this rejection of the importance of ability and effort, the black children also reported less pride after success than did the white children. These findings suggest that when children are raised with the belief that their levels of ability and effort are unimportant, they will feel less pride in successful accomplishment and, consequently, will feel less internal motivation to strive for further successes.

Fanelli (1972) found that in a series of clerical tasks given to college undergraduates, internals tended to improve their scores from trial to trial significantly more than externals did. He further found that those internals who reported a high value for achievement (determined by scores on the nAch category of the Edwards Personal Preference Schedule) got significantly higher scores on clerical tests than those internals who reported a low value for achievement. Fanelli concluded that the level of reported nAch may be secondary to locus of control with regard to predictions of scores on certain tasks. He suggested that one must be internal—that is, accept personal responsibility for outcomes—in order for the high level of reported nAch to effect both higher performance scores and greater improvement in performance from trial to trial.[2]

Crandall et al. (1965) used their Intellectual Achievement Responsibility Questionnaire to assess children's beliefs in reinforcement responsibility exclusively in intellectual—academic achievement situations. They obtained internality (I) scores of children in Grades 3, 4, and 5. They found very low correlations between this measure of internality and measures of social status and IQ. The highest and most consistent correlations were between I scores and report-card grades. Other significant correlations were obtained between I scores and scores on various achievement tests.

Masters and Peskay (1972) investigated the effect of socioeconomic status (SES) and race on the degree of reward children gave themselves under contingent and noncontingent success and failure conditions. All children gave themselves greater degrees of reward under noncontingent rather than contingent success or failure. That is, when the children were told to take what they "want" (rather than what they "deserve"), they awarded them-

---

[2] There appeared to be an optimal level of internality somewhat below the median Rotter I–E score where the level of nAch best predicted performance scores.

selves more prize tokens. Black and low-SES children showed greater degrees of self-reward than did white and high-SES children. The researchers suggest that black and poor children have greater needs for self-gratification than do white and high-SES children. It should be pointed out that maybe blacks and poor are hungrier!

Several hundred black and white ninth-grade students responded to the Crandall Intellectual Achievement Responsibility Questionnaire as part of a study (Entwisle & Greenberger, 1972) designed to investigate social class, internality–externality, and test anxiety. Black students had somewhat higher control scores than did white students. This finding, along with other recent findings that contradict the original results of Crandall *et al.*, suggests that blacks (in the United States) have recently become more internal. Entwisle and Greenberger found no consistent relationship between locus of control and social class, but did find evidence to suggest that IQ scores be controlled in research of this kind.

Phares (1968) compared internals and externals with regard to initial learning, retention, and correct utilization of information. With no significant differences between internals and externals regarding initial learning and retention, he found that internals were significantly better than externals in correctly utilizing the available information. He concluded that the evidence clearly points to the internal's greater potential for effectiveness in his environment.

Fanelli and Vidler (1970) measured the performance of internal and external high school students under two conditions of self-reinforcement. The supportive condition involved the silent rehearsing of self-referent positive statements; the challenging condition involved the silent rehearsing of negative statements. They found no differences in performance levels in the positive, supportive, condition. In the negative, challenging, conditions, the performances of externals were adversely affected. This depression of the performance level of externals was greatest when the task involved was novel rather than familiar. Since externals tend to be more anxious than internals and novel situations tend to be more arousing than familiar ones, it might be that the combination of novelty and challenging motivations produced sufficient anxiety in the external subjects to interfere with their ability to perform.

Garrett and Willoughby (1972) administered the Crandall Intellectual Achievement Responsibility Questionnaire to 162 black, urban fifth- and sixth-graders and found that these children tended to be somewhat more internal than the white children in Crandall's normative samples. This tendency held for the I+ scale, which scores the tendency to take responsibility for one's successes, but not for the I– scale, which scores the tendency to take responsibility for one's failures. The second aspect of Garrett and Willoughby's study was to measure performance in a series of learning trials involving concept discrimination. Subjects scoring in the upper quartile (internals) and in the lower quartile (externals) first experienced success or failure on an anagrams task. Other subjects served as a control group. In the control group, no differences in performance were noted between internals and externals. In the treatment groups, however, internals performed better than externals on the concept task after the success treatment, and externals performed better than internals after the failure treatment. The authors concluded that for the internal child, the experience of success is a powerful reinforcer, whereas for the external child success is less reinforcing because he does not accept responsibility for it. Failure, on the other hand, might be more debilitating to the internal child, since he feels responsible for it, and mildly arousing to the external, who simply would like to avoid failure but does not feel responsible for it.

Rotter (1966) summarizes research that indicates that when a subject perceives the task as controlled by chance, random conditions, or the experimenter, he is less likely to rely on his own past experiences; when the subject perceives a task to be under his own control, he is more likely to attend and to perceive better. Thus externals, who generally perceive control to be elsewhere than in themselves, might learn less, or worse, learn the wrong things. Externals tend to adjust their behaviors on the basis of what they perceive to be random or manipulated events having little to do with their own past experiences.

These findings suggest that in classrooms where the teacher is obviously in control, many students might become more external and then resort to guessing what it is that the teacher expects of them. No doubt this externalization of students occurs in many traditional classrooms, although it is not claimed that this process is the only, nor even a major, cause of externality. Ideally, the teacher must shift more and more responsibility to the student and carefully reward the student when he does accept responsibility for the outcomes of his behaviors.

The self-fulfilling prophecy explanation given by Schneider (1972) for the skill versus chance preferences of internals and externals suggests that attempts to alter a person's level of internality might involve the person's overall perception of himself. Feather (1969) found that a person's self-evaluation of confidence influences the degree to which he attributes responsibility to himself. Perhaps, therefore, increasing the self-assured confidence of students might make them more internal. Gibb (1970) summarizes a considerable number of studies that indicate sensitivity training is an effective method of increasing self-acceptance and confidence. The logical conclusion from the preceding thoughts is that sensitivity training might help a person become more internal. This change process is not immediate and might require temporary disruptive alterations in self-perception. However, the greater the instability of self-perception, the greater the potential for change, and the more likely is it that the desired behaviors will occur.

What Heider (1958) refers to as *naive psychology* influences many people—including teachers—in their perceptions of causality with regard to outcomes of behaviors. Heider developed the concepts of "can" and "try" as parallel to the psychological concepts of learning (ability) and motivation. The naive teacher says to his student, "You can do it if you try," because he assumes the task to be within the ability range of the student. When the student fails at this task, the teacher assumes that the student has not tried and urges him on more strongly. When failure occurs the second and third times, the teacher selects one of the following explanations: The student is stubbornly refusing to try; the student does not have the ability to do the task. Choosing the first explanation, the teacher will view the child in a negative light and might not reward future successes, since these confirm the teacher's notion that, initially, the child was not trying. Choosing the second explanation, the teacher might then attribute future successes to luck or chance. The finding by Murray and Staebler (1972) that teachers' evaluation of a student tends to be more influenced by the student's early performances than by his later performances lends support to this analysis.

The fact is, however, that the equational relationship—can (ability) plus try (effort) equals success—implied by the statement "you can do it if you try" is false. There are many examples of expert people who try very hard to succeed and who fail to do so in any particular attempt. For example, professional athletes who miss free throws in basketball or who fault first and even second services in tennis. While failure might result from many causes, a probable cause is the heightened anxiety that arises from a novel or challenging situation and from the uncertainty of the outcome. If teachers urge their students to try harder when the students are already trying hard, the increased arousal might interfere with the quality of the students' performances and cause continued failure. Certainly, teachers must be willing to take steps to reduce anxiety by avoiding shame-producing causal attributions particularly to anxious students and to externals, and especially in novel or challenging situations.

Perhaps altering the expression to "you *might* do it if you try" would not only lessen the impact of failure, but would also keep both teacher and pupil more in touch with the uncertainties of reality. This probabilistic statement allows for attribution of failure to chance or luck and permits the student to sustain hope for success. While extreme externality is pathologic in its posture of helplessness and avoidance of responsibility, extreme internality is potentially pathologic since it flaunts reality. The most mature position might be to have a generally internal locus of control with a slight admixture of externality and a recognition of uncertainty. Attaining this optimal level of internality might be the teacher's goal for herself as well as for her students. For if a teacher is 100% internal and does not recognize uncertainty, then she would feel unduly responsible for a pupil's success or failure. Her own image threatened by pupils' failures, she might then shift the burden of responsibility to them. Both teacher and pupil (ideally) must be optimally internal (realistic).

CONCLUDING REMARKS

Causality, itself, is an hypothesis. Events are seen to be related in some way—"after this, therefore, because of this"—and causality is inferred. Whole cultures might have erroneous views of causality, attributing events to fate, gods, taboos, or other similar factors. Consensual validation, of course, does not necessarily indicate having arrived at fact. This criticism applies with equal vigor to technologically advanced societies in whose sciences myth abounds (for example, the myths of energy, evolution, gravity, and inertia). Nonetheless, from the point of view of personal development and achievement, modern science appears to offer better predictability and wider cross-cultural consensual validation than do some traditional beliefs. And a minimum degree of internality appears to offer better chances of success in academic and entrepreneurial enterprises than does a maximum degree of externality.

A culture that hopes to foster optimal levels of internality among its members must anticipate that flexibility in the societal structure itself might be necessary to avoid fragmentation because of the alienation of its newly "internalized" individuals. On the other hand, the two-factor analysis of locus of control (Gurin *et al.*, 1969) suggests that a society's subjects may be appropriately external in a repressive society while being appropriately internal with regard to personal aspects of their lives. Therefore, a nation need not necessarily fear self-destruction by raising its citizens in ways that encourage them to accept greater personal responsibility for the outcomes of their actions. Gurin *et al.* (1969) and Lao (1970), who related the personal control and ideology factors of Rotter's scale of blacks' behavior, concluded that it is the personal control factor that differentiates motivation and performance. This finding suggests that members of minority groups, even in a repressive society, will perform better if they feel personally responsible in their immediate lives than if they feel powerless with regard to obtaining any reinforcements at all.

Based on the assumption that locus of control is a stable generalized expectancy for control of reinforcements, what is needed at present are research studies to explore the possibility of altering the levels of internal or external expectancies. Repeated measures of locus of control over long periods of time with various experiences given to large subject populations might be the indicated procedure. Along the lines of achievement training, programs might be devised to alter locus of control expectancies directly through educational means. Certainly, as a minimum undertaking, all personnel who are involved in the education of future generations must be well-versed in the implications of this concept.

ANNOTATED BIBLIOGRAPHY

Arnold, W. (Ed.). *Nebraska Symposium on Motivation.* Lincoln: University of Nebraska Press, 1968.
    The article by Heckhausen on achievement motivation research covers recent research with need for achievement and also discusses the relationship between need for achievement and locus of control.

de Charms, R. *Personal causation.* New York: Academic Press, 1968.
    De Charms discusses two modes of existence: beings as "origins" and beings as "pawns." These modes are described and related to several concepts including need achievement and locus of control.

Heider, F. *The psychology of interpersonal relations.* New York: Wiley, 1958.
    An important foundation for the study of causal attributions based upon what Heider refers to as *naive analysis of action.*

Joe, V. Review of the internal—external control construct as a personality variable. *Psychological Reports,* 1971, *28,* 619—640.
    A comprehensive survey of personality research involving the locus of control variable. It is organized into several areas such as ethnic group and social class differences, anxiety, achievement motivation, risk-taking, and adjustment.

Rotter, J. Generalized expectancies for internal vs. external control of reinforcement. *Psychological Monographs,* 1966, 80(1), 1—28.
    Rotter describes the theory and research that led to the development of his

internal—external locus of control questionnaire. The entire questionnaire and much reliability data are included in the monograph.

Throop, W., & MacDonald, H. Internal—external locus of control: A bibliography. *Psychological Reports*, 1971, *28*, 175—190.
This comprehensive survey of locus of control research covers the period from 1954 through 1969. It lists sources for 11 tests of internal—external control, and includes 169 published papers and books and 170 unpublished works.

Weiner, B., Frieze, D., Kukla, A., Reed, L., Kest, S., & Rosenbaum, R. M. *Perceiving the causes of success and failure*. New York: General Learning Press, 1971.
This book describes a model of achievement-related behavior in which causal ascriptions mediate between preceding conditions and responses that are achievement oriented. Discusses the assumption that causality might be attributed differentially across both a locus of control dimension and a stability dimension.

REFERENCES

Alpert, R., & Haber, N. Anxiety in academic achievement situations. *Journal of Abnormal and Social Psychology*, 1960, *2*, 207—215.
Baker, G. Toward internal locus of control in the community college student. *Educational Technology*, October 1972, 73—76.
Battle, E., & Rotter, J. Childrens' feelings of personal control as related to social class and ethnic group. *Journal of Personality*, 1963, *41*, 482—490.
Bialer, I. Conceptualization of success and failure in mentally retarded and normal children. *Journal of Personality*, 1961, *29*, 303—320.
Breit, S. Arousal of achievement motivation with causal attribution. *Psychological Reports*, 1969. *25*(2), 539—542.
Bryant, B. Student—teacher relationships as related to internal—external locus of control. APA *Proceedings*, 1972, *7*, 567—568.
Buros, O. *Personality: Tests and reviews*. Highland Park, N.J.: Gryphon Press, 1970.
Coleman, J., Hobson, C., McPartland, J., Mood, A., & Weinfeld, F. *Equality of educational opportunity*. Washington, D.C.: U.S. Government Printing Office, 1966.
Crandall, V., Katkovsky, W., & Crandall, V. Children's beliefs in their own control of reinforcements in intellectual—academic situations. *Child Development*, 1965, *36*, 91—109.
DeCharms, R. *Personal causation*. New York: Academic Press, 1968.
Di Vesta, F., & Thompson, G. *Educational psychology*. New York: Appleton, 1970.
Entwisle, D. R., & Greenberger, E. Questions about social class, internality—externality, and test anxiety. *Developmental Psychology*, 1972, *7*(2), 218.
Epstein, R., & Kemorita, S. Self-esteem, success—failure, and locus of control in Negro children. *Developmental Psychology*, 1971, *4*(1), 2—8.
Fanelli, G. The effect of need for achievement and locus of control on performance, level of aspiration behaviors, and self-rating changes. Unpublished doctoral dissertation, Columbia University, 1972.

Fanelli, G., & Vidler, D. The effect of supportive and challenging instructions on the performance of internals and externals. Unpublished manuscript, 1970.

Feather, N. T. Valence of outcome and expectation of success in relation to task difficulty and perceived locus-of-control. *Journal of Personality and Social Psychology*, 1967, *7*, 372–386.

Feather, N. T. Attribution of responsibility and valence of success and failure in relation to initial confidence and task performance. *Journal of Personality and Social Psychology*, 1969, *13*, 129–144.

Feather, N. T., & Simon, J. G. Attribution of responsibility and valence of outcome in relation to initial confidence. *Journal of Personality and Social Psychology*, May 1971, *18*(2), 173–188.

Frankenstein, C. *The psychodynamics of externalization.* Baltimore: Williams and Wilkins, 1968.

Friend, R., & Neale, J. Children's perceptions of success and failure: An attributional analysis of the effects of race and social class. *Developmental Psychology*, 1972, *7*(2), 124–128.

Garrett, A., & Willoughby, R. Personal orientation and reactions to success and failure in urban black children. *Developmental Psychology*, 1972, *7*(1), 92.

Gibb, J. Sensitivity training for personal growth. *Interpersonal Development*, 1970, *1*, 6–31.

Gozali, J. & Bialer, I. The locus of control scale for children—An alternate form. *Psychological Reports*, 1971, *28*, 175–190.

Gurin, P., Gurin, G., Lao, R., & Beattie, M. Internal—external control in the motivational dynamics of Negro youth. *Journal of Social Issues*, 1969, *25*, 29–53.

Hammer, B., Grade expectations, differential teacher comments, and student performance. *Journal of Educational Psychology*, 1972, *63*, 454–458.

Heckhausen, H. *The anatomy of achievement motivation.* New York: Academic Press, 1967.

Heckhausen, H. Achievement motivation research. In W. Arnold (Ed.), *Nebraska Symposium on Motivation.* Lincoln: University of Nebraska Press, 1968.

Heider, F. *The psychology of interpersonal relations.* New York: Wiley, 1958.

Hersch, P., & Scheibe, K. On the reliability and validity of internal—external control as a personality dimension. *Journal of Consulting Psychology*, 1967, *31*, 609–614.

Joe, V. Review of the internal—external construct as a personality variable. *Psychological Reports*, 1971, *28*, 619–640.

Julian, J., Lichtman, C., & Ryckman, R. Internal—external control and need to control. *Journal of Social Psychology*, 1968, *76*, 43–48.

Karabenik, S. A. Valence of success and failure as a function of achievement motives and locus-of-control. *Journal of Personality and Social Psychology*, 1972, *21*(1), 101–110.

Lao, R. C. Internal—external control and competent and innovative behavior among negro college students. *Journal of Personality and Social Psychology*, 1970, *14*(3), 263–270.

Masters, J., & Peskay, J. Effects of race, socioeconomic status, and success or failure upon contingent and noncontingent self-reinforcement in children. *Developmental Psychology*, 1972, *7*(2), 139–145.

McClelland, D. *The achieving society.* Princeton: Van Nostrand, 1961.

McGhee, P., & Crandall, V. Belief in internal–external control of reinforcement and academic performance. *Child Development*, 1968, *39*, 91–102.

Murray, H., & Staebler, B. Effects of locus of control and pattern of performance on teacher's evaluation. APA *Proceedings*, 1972, 7, 569–570.

Nowicki, S., Bonner, J., & Feather, B. Effects of locus of control on perceived therapeutic relationships. *Journal of Consulting and Clinical Psychology*, 1972, *38*(3), 434–438.

Phares, E. Changes in expectancy in skill and chance situations. Unpublished doctoral dissertation. Ohio State University, 1955.

Phares, E. Expectance changes in skill and chance situations. *Journal of Abnormal and Social Psychology*, 1957, *51*, 339–342.

Phares, E. Differential utilization of information as a function of internal–external control. *Journal of Personality*, 1968, *36*, 649–662.

Platt, J., & Eisenman, R. Internal–external control of reinforcement, time-perspective, adjustment, and anxiety. *Journal of General Psychology*, 1968, *79*, 121–128.

Ray, W., & Katahn, M. Relation of anxiety to locus-of-control. *Psychological Reports*, 1968, *3*, 1196.

Rhiengelheim, D., Bialer, I., & Morrissey, H. *The relationship among various dichotomous descriptive personality scales and achievement in the mentally retarded* (Project No. 6-2685). Washington, D.C.: U.S. Department of Health, Education and Welfare, 1969.

Rotter, J. B. *Social learning and clinical psychology.* Englewood Cliffs, N.J.: Prentice-Hall, 1954.

Rotter, J. B. Generalized expectancies for internal versus external control of reinforcements. *Psychological Monographs*, 1966, *80*(10), 1–28.

Schneider, J. Locus of control and activity preferences. *Journal of Consulting and Clinical Psychology*, 1972, *38*(2), 225–230.

Shybut, J. Time perspective, internal vs. external control, and psychological disturbance. *Journal of Clinical Psychology*, 1968, *24*, 312–315.

Stephens, M. Dimensions of locus of control: Impact of early educational experiences. APA *Proceedings*, 1972, 7, 137–138.

Strickland, B. Individual differences in conditioning and awareness. *Journal of Personality*, 1970, *38*, 364–378.

Valecha, G. Construct validation of internal–external locus of reinforcement related to work-related variables. APA *Proceedings*, 1972, 7, 455–456.

Weiner, B., & Kukla, A. An atributional analysis of achievement motivation. *Journal of Personality and Social Psychology*, 1970, *15*(1), 1–20.

Weiner, B., Heckhausen, H., Meyer, W., & Cook, R. Causal ascriptions and achievement behavior. *Journal of Personality and Social Psychology*, 1972, *21*(2), 239–248.

4

Achievement Motivation

DEREK C. VIDLER

Hunter College of CUNY

INTRODUCTION

Unlike more motivational constructs, the basic definition and the central concepts of achievement motivation (sometimes referred to as *need for achievement*, or *n-ach*) have not been in dispute. This consensus exists largely because the study of achievement motivation has been the work of a single school of thought and of a handful of theorists and researchers who have worked closely under the general leadership of D. C. McClelland. Since the initial studies two decades ago, the major researchers have branched out along somewhat different paths, exploring different aspects of the achievement motive. Through the steady and purposeful accumulation of research evidence over two decades, a large and relatively clear and consistent body of knowledge has gradually emerged.

The achievement motive is a pattern of planning, of actions, and of feelings connected with striving to achieve some internalized standard of excellence, as contrasted, for example, with power or friendship. Achievement motivation is not necessarily the same thing as the search for observable accomplishments, such as obtaining high test scores, socially approved positions, or a high salary. Though it involves planning and striving for excellence, it is the attitude toward achievement that is important, rather than the accomplishments per se. Achievement motivation may thus include a wide variety of activities, and express itself in jobs as widely different from each other, for example, as truck driver, accountant, or chimney sweep.

Research by McClelland and his associates began with initial explorations into the nature and measurement of the achievement motive. McClelland was from the beginning concerned with broad questions such as how achievement motivation showed itself both in the individual and in society, how the motives of individuals in a society reflected themselves in the dominant social values of that society, and how these values were related to factors like economic growth, political structure, and cultural patterns. Some of his early work, the scope and breadth of which were notable for its boldness in conception and far-reaching consequences, consisted of ingenious attempts to measure the achievement motive in societies past and present.

Reviewing traditional arguments that attempted to account for the rise and fall of civilizations and patterns of economic development, McClelland felt that a psychological factor, the general social motivational level of the people in a country, had been given less than its fair share of consideration. McClelland proposed that differences in the levels of motive for achievement were largely responsible for these patterns of economic growth and decline, and, in a series of unique studies, he set out to prove his proposition.

Thus, for example, one of the earliest pieces of research dealt with the ancient civilization of the Athenian Greeks (900 B.C.–100 B.C.). It is generally assumed that the rise of Athens was caused by and was not the cause of economic expansion, which created in its turn an achievement orientation in the people. McClelland argued that the reverse was true, that the level of achievement motivation created a psychological atmosphere in which subsequent economic expansion was made possible for Athens. Since Athenian prosperity was based on foreign trade, the area of trade formed a convenient index of economic growth. Athenian earthenware jars found at known locations provided an approximate index of the extent of trade at different periods. These jars were commonly used in trading, and their designs indicated the period in which they were made. Achievement motivation was measured from representative samples of Athenian literature and from the artistic patterns made on the jars selected from different periods. In this way, McClelland was able to show that the trade area rose from the early period to the period of maximal economic development and then gradually declined, and that the periods of economic rise and fall were preceded by corresponding rises and falls in achievement striving as reflected in the literature and art.

McClelland also sought to demonstrate a relationship between achievement motivation and economic development in more modern times, using different indices with a large number of countries. Amount of electrical power produced by a country relative to its population, for countries in the temperate zone, was used as the measure of economic growth. Achievement motivation was measured through children's reading books chosen from the periods around 1925 and around 1950. It was assumed that these readers reflected the relative emphasis on achievement striving in a given country, and stories were selected and scored for achievement themes. Analysis of this data showed that there was a positive relationship between the degree of achievement motivation in children's readers around 1925 and subsequent economic growth (based on electric power production comparisons from 1925 and from 1950). Countries that showed greatest increases in output also stressed achievement themes in their readers at an earlier date. This finding, therefore, again suggested that achievement striving preceded economic expansion.

PERSONALITY CORRELATES

In the years following McClelland's original research, a large number of studies were conducted to further explore the nature and effects of achievement motivation. Some of these studies investigated the personality characteristics of people with high achievement motivation, and discovered that such individuals tended to act in certain characteristic ways. As a result of considerable research over the years, a great deal has been discovered about the nature of the highly achievement-oriented person (Alschuler, 1973).

Individuals with high achievement motivation are interested in excellence for its own sake rather than for the rewards it brings. Those high in need for achievement will not work harder at a task just because money is offered as a reward (Atkinson & Reitman, 1956). They evaluate roles on the basis of the opportunities for excellence rather than those for prestige (Burnstein, Moulton, & Liberty, 1963). Their achievement concern is not affected by having to work for a group rather than for themselves (French, 1958). They pick experts rather than friends as work partners (French, 1956; McClelland & Winter, 1969). They prefer situations in which they can take personal responsibility for the outcomes of their efforts. They like to control their own destinies rather than leave things up to fate, chance or luck (French, 1958; McClelland, Atkinson, Clark, & Lowell, 1955; Heckhausen, 1967). They like to make independent judgments based on their own evaluations and experience rather than rely on the opinions of other people (Heckhausen, 1967).

Achievement-oriented people set their goals carefully after considering the probabilities of success of a variety of alternatives. Their goals tend to be moderate risks in which their efforts are neither doomed to failure nor guaranteed of success (Heckhausen, 1967). The goals are challenging ones in which the outcomes are most uncertain (McClelland, 1958; Atkinson & Litwin, 1960; McClelland, 1955; Atkinson, Bastian, & Litwin, 1960).

Individuals highly motivated toward achievement are more concerned with the medium-to-long range future. They have a longer future-time perspective (Ricks & Epley, 1960; Heckhausen, 1967), show greater anticipation of the future (McClelland et al., 1955), and prefer larger rewards in the future over smaller rewards in the present (Mischel, 1961). Perhaps because of this acute awareness of the passage of time, those with high need for achievement see time as passing rapidly (Green & Knapp, 1959; Knapp & Green, 1960), and do not feel they have enough time to get everything done (Knapp, 1962). In order to keep track of progress toward their goals, they like to get immediate, regular, concrete feedback on how well they are doing (French, 1958; Moss & Kagan, 1961).

ORIGINS OF ACHIEVEMENT MOTIVATION

Undoubtedly the development of the need for achievement is influenced by a number of factors. These would seem to include cultural values, social role systems, educational processes, peer-group interactions, and child-rearing practices. Of these, the most is known to date about the effect of child-rearing practices and cultural values.

In an early study of considerable importance, Winterbottom (cited in McClelland et al., 1955) studied the parents of 30 middle-class boys aged 8 to 10. She determined the strength of their need for achievement using the Thematic Apperception Test, and examined the child-rearing practices of the parents through an interview and questionnaire procedure. She found that the mothers of boys with high achievement motivation differed from those whose sons had low achievement motivation in three significant ways: They tended to set higher standards for their sons; they expected independence and mastery behavior to occur at an early age; and they more often rewarded their sons affectively (e.g., with kissing and hugging).

Additional support for this relationship between child-rearing patterns and level of children's achievement motivation was obtained in several other studies. Rosen and D'Andrade (1959) studied parents and children in six different American ethnic groups and varying social classes: French-Canadian, Italian, Greek, black, Jewish, and old American Yankee. Despite complex class differences, Rosen and D'Andrade found that self-reliance training promoted high need for achievement, provided that the training did not reflect generalized authoritarianism or rejection by the parents.

These results were taken a step further by Child, Storm, and Veroff (1958). They reasoned that child-rearing patterns reflected pervasive cultural values. To establish this relationship, ethnographic data were collected on child-rearing practices from 33 cultures. The measure of cultural values was obtained from an analysis of the folk tales told to children of the 33 cultures, since folk tales, it was argued, often are used to convey values to children. The authors found that cultures in which there was direct training in achievement orientation also had folk tales with high levels of achievement motivation. On the other hand, cultures characterized by rigid or restrictive child-rearing practices, such as punishing children for failure to be obedient and responsible, had folk tales with relatively low levels of achievement motivation.

Thus, it was found that certain cultural values are reflected in child-rearing practices that foster high achievement motivation in children. High achievement motivation in a child in turn often results in a particular set of behaviors in the adult, characteristic of what McClelland subsequently referred to as the *entrepreneurial personality*—the personality characterized by the set of traits of the highly achievement-motivated person, as described above.

MEASURING ACHIEVEMENT MOTIVATION

Thematic Apperception Test (TAT)

By far the most common technique employed in measuring the achievement motive has been an adaptation of the Thematic Apperception Test (TAT). This method of measuring individual differences in human motivation was based both on the methods of experimental psychology and on the insights of psychoanalysis. Psychoanalysts held that motivation is reflected in the fantasy lives of individuals, and that interpretation of dream fantasy is a principal method for revealing a person's motivations, hidden conflicts, and wishes. A widely used technique of eliciting fantasies in individuals is the TAT, originally devised by Henry Murray, which consists of a set of ambiguous pictures depicting a variety of common situations. McClelland (1961) integrated this approach with more rigorous psychometric techniques and thereby developed a modified version of the TAT.

In the typical administration of the TAT as modified by McClelland, a subject is shown a picture and given about five minutes in which to write a story about the picture. The picture is deliberately vague so as to allow for a wide degree of variation in interpretation and story production. One picture, for example, shows an adolescent boy sitting at a desk in a classroom. A book is open in front of him but he is not reading it. He rests his forehead on one hand, gazing pensively toward the reader.

Subjects are often told that they are taking a test of their "creative imagination," and are invited to make up a vivid and dramatic story. Four questions are usually asked—What is happening? What had led up to this situation? What is being thought? and What will happen? In the complete procedure, four pictures are presented, stories are written for each of them, and subsequently analyzed for content reflecting achievement motivation.

To illustrate the differences in story production between high and low achievement motivation, consider the content of the following two stories, written in response to the picture of the adolescent (Atkinson, 1958, p. 697).

High-motivation story
1. This chap is doing some heavy meditating. He is a sophomore and has reached an intellectual crisis. He cannot make up his mind. He is troubled, worried.
2. He is trying to reconcile the philosophies of Descartes and Thomas Aquinas—and at his tender age of eighteen. He has read several books on philosophy and feels the weight of the world on his shoulders.
3. He wants to present a clear-cut synthesis of these two conflicting philosophies, to satisfy his ego and to gain academic recognition from his professor.
4. He will screw himself up royally. Too inexperienced and uninformed, he has tackled too great a problem. He will give up in despair, go down to the G___ and drown his sorrows in a bucket of beer.

Low-motivation story
1. The boy in the checkered shirt whose name is Ed is in a classroom. He is supposed to be listening to the teacher.
2. Ed has been troubled by his father's drunkenness and his maltreatment of Ed's mother. He thinks of this often and worries about it.
3. Ed is thinking of leaving home for a while in the hope that this might shock his parents into getting along.
4. He will leave home but will only meet further disillusionment away from home.

The technique is based on the notion that the story productions of different persons can be analyzed for their content, which then might reveal facets of importance about the personalities of the storytellers. It is assumed that elements in the stories are indicative of matters of motivational concern and importance, which the story interpreter can analyze.

Initial studies with the TAT used deprivation of food, and checked TAT stories to see whether the stories reflected this motivating stimulus. Since the probable effect of deprivation of food on subjects' motivational states is known, it was possible to assess the degree to which the TAT reflected these motivational levels by checking to see whether the stories showed elements such as food-related imagery, or need for food. In some of the categories initially tested, the content of the stories did in fact seem to be responsive to the strength of the motive, and thus there was initial support for the TAT as a measure of a motivational state.

The manipulation of hunger was clearly an easier task than the manipulation of achievement. To assess the latter, an experiment was undertaken in which two situations, referred to as the "Aroused" and the "Relaxed" conditions, were arranged, differing in the degree to which they attempted to arouse motivation to achieve. The Aroused subjects were led to believe their performance on the TAT reflected important personal abilities. The Relaxed subjects were not given this impression. When TAT's were administered to both groups, it was found that those subjects in the Aroused condition had higher achievement motivation content in their TAT stories, again indicating that the TAT reflected differences in response to situational variation. Further, by comparing the two groups on categories such as general achievement imagery and instrumental activity, it was possible to determine those categories of the scoring system that showed differences between the groups in level of achievement motivation. These categories were then retained for subsequent use in assessment of the achievement motive (Brown, 1965, 430–432).

Level of achievement motivation was conceived as being both a relatively stable personality trait and as a state that was susceptible to the influence of situational conditions. So far, only the effect of the latter had been demonstrated. To show that need for achievement is an enduring personality characteristic, the TAT had to be administered on two separate occasions under conditions that were, as far as possible, neutral to the same group of individuals. Unfortunately, as we shall see below in the discussion of reliability, the stability of the score based on the TAT has been found to be rather low.

The scoring of the TAT is somewhat complex and time consuming. The fundamental decision to be made in the scoring is whether the story contains any reference to an achievement goal. The subcategories are not scored unless the story as a whole is judged to show achievement imagery, which is when some person in the story shows concern with competing successfully with some standard of excellence. If the story meets this requirement, it receives 1 point and the scorer looks for evidence for each of the subcategories, assigning +1 for each that can be scored.

The following categories are those commonly used.

Need: expression of a desire to reach an achievement goal. "He wants very much to solve the problem."

Hope of Success (HOS): stated anticipation of success in attaining a goal. "He hopes to become a great surgeon."

Fear of Failure (FOF): stated anticipation of failure of frustration. "He thinks he will make a mess of the job."

Success Feelings (SuF): stated experience of a positive emotional state associated with a definite accomplishment. "He is proud of his acceptance to graduate school."

Failure Feelings (FAF): stated negative emotion associated with failure to attain an achievement goal. "He is disgusted with himself for his failure."

Act: statement that something is being done to attain an achievement goal. "The man worked hard to sell more books."

World Obstacle (WO): statement that goal-directed activity is obstructed by something in the external world. "His family couldn't afford to send him to college."

Personal Obstacle (PO): statement that progress of goal-directed activity is obstructed by personal deficiencies. "He lacked the confidence to overcome his shyness."

Help: statement of someone's aiding or encouraging the person striving for achievement. "His boss encouraged him in his ambitions."

Achievement Theme: the major plot or theme of the story is achievement, rather than affiliation or power.

From a psychometric perspective, the TAT has been seriously challenged and criticized, since evidence for its reliability and validity has not been very satisfactory. Even in the early stages of research, for example, a test—retest study by Lowell (1950) over a 1-week period, using different sets of pictures, showed a correlation of only .22. This result was disappointingly low and did not suggest that the test was measuring an enduring personality characteristic, as claimed. However, the two sets of scores did agree to the extent of 72% in placing subjects above or below the median, so that while raw scores and relative rankings were not the same over a week, rough rankings of subjects above or below the median were maintained. From this evidence, it was assumed at the time, and frequently afterward, that high- and low-scoring groups could be justifiably identified and compared in a similar way.

Other studies have shown similar results. Birney (1959) showed the intercorrelation of scores for a set of subjects tested four times over 2 years varied from +.03 to +.56, but only two of the six correlations were significant. Kagan and Moss (1959), studying the stability of achievement motive scores on three occasions over 6 years, found that two of three such testings indicated stability. Though perhaps scores on the TAT do not have the kind of stability desirable in an index that presumes to measure a stable attribute of personality, most of the evidence suggests there is a small positive correlation between scores of the same individuals tested over different periods of time. The reliability among judges in scoring the TAT is considerably better, being usually in the 90s.

Moderate evidence for the validity of the TAT in measuring the achievement motive has slowly been accumulated.[1] The earlier experiment, for example, using "Aroused" and "Relaxed" conditions has been replicated (Angelini, 1955) in Brazil, with Portuguese-speaking subjects; and with Navajo Indian boys (Lowell, 1950) in New Mexico. Strodtbeck (1958) found that "overachievers" among a group of New Haven high school boys had higher scores on the TAT than "underachievers." Everett (1959) found that, among men in management positions, an index of occupational achievement had a low but positive relationship to McClelland's TAT measure. While other research has shown, as discussed earlier, a number of consistent findings, such as that high achievement-oriented individuals perform better in terms of long-term occupational and academic goals, and do better on brief immediate tasks when the reason for doing so is to satisfy some standard of excellence, there are unsolved problems with regard to measurement of the achievement motive. For example, researchers have largely been unable to devise techniques of assessment that are less onerous and time consuming to administer and score than the TAT. The TAT itself has, furthermore, never been shown to work with females (Veroff, 1950; Wilcox, 1951; Field, 1951).

The research on males has produced a body of data that is internally consistent and that contributes to a theory of achievement motivation in men. The few experiments that have used female subjects have yielded results that are not consistent with those that have used males and that are not always consistent with each other. Studies with males, for example, have

---

[1] With such low test–retest stability, validity indices could not be expected to be more than moderate.

consistently shown a greater number of achievement-relevant responses to projective measures under conditions that have appealed to their intelligence and leadership ability.

A study by French and Lesser (1964) attempted to resolve this long-standing paradox. French and Lesser hypothesized that female subjects would respond to arousal cues with increased achievement motivation when the cues were related to a goal that was achievement relevant to them, but not otherwise. The results of the study supported this notion. When the arousal condition provided cues that were relevant to social and marital success, as opposed to intellectual or leadership success, the female subjects tended to show higher achievement motivation scores.

French and Lesser explained their results as follows. For a man, the primary goal is almost universally success in his job area, and job success is not perceived as incompatible with achievement in other areas, such as political, social, and family relations. Thus, the arousal conditions that stress intelligence and leadership qualities would be expected to produce consistent increases in achievement motivation. A woman's situation is quite different. A woman's primary role in life has usually been to make a good marriage, be a good wife and mother, and make her family's life at home and in the community pleasant and comfortable. Leadership and intellectual pursuits have traditionally been less valued, as is still true for many women. Thus, arousal conditions that stress intellectual cues should not increase their level of achievement motivation. A heightened achievement motivation level should only show itself when the situation provides cues relating to social and marital success.

Other studies have expanded on the views put forward by French and Lesser, stressing differing aspects of the self-image and the societal role of women. Hoffman (1972), for example, reviewing research findings from child developmental studies, argues that what influences females most in their achievement motives and behavior is a high need for affiliation. Girls are less encouraged to be independent, are more protected, and are less pressured into establishing an identity separate from their mother. As a result, they do not develop adequate skills and confidence, and tend to remain dependent on others. Horner (1972) believes that the problem has been not so much that females have a lack of achievement motivation but that they are actually motivated to avoid success. Women develop a self-concept that regards competence, independence, competition, and intellectual achievement as qualities basically inconsistent with femininity. The expectancy that success in achievement-related situations will be followed by negative consequences arouses fear of success in women who might otherwise be achievement oriented and this fear inhibits their performance and level of aspiration. The strength of this fear of success is determined by such factors as age and educational and occupational level. At all events, it would seem reasonable to suppose that such factors are to some extent responsible for the observed differences between males and females on the TAT.

Tartan Test

Though adequate alternatives to the TAT have not been found, other measures of achievement motivation have been developed. Knapp (1958) constructed a Tartan Test and demonstrated that the preferences of high-achievement-motive people are quite different from those of low-achievement-motive people on the test. In this procedure, subjects examined a standard set of 30 tartans, indicating their preferences by grouping the tartans along a scale. The relations between rankings of individual tartans and motive scores were small, but the 10 tartans that had the strongest tendency to be liked by high scorers were in certain ways consistently different from the 10 that tended to be liked by low scorers. High scorers liked somber colors, low scorers light colors. High scorers also liked tartans with a good deal of blue in them, while low scorers liked red. In explanation, Knapp speculated that blue is a soft and background color, while red is a hard and imposing figural color. A high-motive person is intent on playing an active role, and on imposing his will on the environment. Such a person prefers a soft, unobtrusive, passive background. The low-motive person is himself the softer, more passive element and thus favors a hard, imposing color.

Knapp points out that subdued and conservative dress characterizes North European Protestant cultures, where the achievement motive seems to be stronger than it is in Catholic Mediterranean cultures, where dress is more colorful. He notes also the sobriety of taste characteristic of the Puritans, whose achievement motivation appears to have been very high. This suggestion, furthermore, agrees with evidence suggesting that a higher level of achievement motivation prevails among the middle class than the lower class, and, in the United States today, middle-class dress still favors a duller look than lower-class dress.

Knapp's conception of the high-motive person led him further to suppose that to such a person time might be seen as exceptionally valuable and as moving rapidly. Knapp devised an ingenious way of discovering how high scorers thought of time. Ideas like time can be conceived in many ways, and individual preferences in ways of thinking about time may reveal something about an individual's perspective in this regard. Knapp and Green

(1960) provided subjects with a collection of 25 metaphors for time and asked them to judge the appropriateness of each one. There was a striking difference between the metaphors preferred by high scorers and those preferred by low scorers. High scorers liked, for example, a "dashing waterfall," a "galloping horseman," and a "winding spool." Low scorers liked, for example, a "quiet motionless ocean," a "stairway leading upward," and a "vast expanse of sky." The former group contain action and speed, the latter passivity and peace. The metaphors liked by the high-motive people suggested mostly directionality, purposiveness, and haste, which thus lent support to the author's theoretical position.

Graphic Method

Another attempt to measure the achievement motive is that of Aronson (1958). Aronson found that the scribbles or doodles of high-motive people are different from those of low-motive people. In particular, he found stylistic consistencies that distinguish doodles of one person from those of another. He assumed that patterns drawn on paper that are a record of free expressive movement might have corresponding correlates in personality.

In his initial experiment, subjects were presented with a complex design, to be glanced at for only a fraction of a second. Having glanced at it, they were asked to reproduce it to the best of their ability, drawing what they thought they saw. In presenting the design, which contained the different kinds of scribbles or doodles people typically make, Aronson ensured that the exposure time was brief enough to exclude the possibility of an exact copy, and assumed that subjects would select doodles that reflected aspects of themselves. On examination, it was found that the drawings of high scorers and low scorers differed in the following ways.

1. *Discreteness versus fuzziness:* High scorers made a preponderance of single, unattached, discrete lines while low scorers produced mostly fuzzy, overlaid lines.
2. *Unused space:* High scorers left a smaller margin at the bottom of the page than did low scorers.
3. *Diagonal configurations:* High scorers produced more diagonals than did low scorers.
4. *Multiwave lines:* High scorers made fewer multiwave lines (lines consisting of two or more crests in the same direction) than low scorers.

This *graphic measure,* as it has been referred to, had several qualities not possessed by the other measures. It allowed access to subjects who could not otherwise be reached, such as children below the age of about 8, with whom the TAT does not work well, and to a broad variety of different cultural groups. It also made possible the assessment of achievement motivation in the ancient cultures of Greece, Egypt, and Peru, since designs on pottery from these respective cultures could be scored for the characteristics outlined above.

Nevertheless, neither the Tartan Test nor the doodle technique have been employed extensively and seem to have been largely neglected in recent years. Only the TAT has been consistently used, and remains in effect the single means through which the achievement motive is assessed.

Self-Report, Paper-and-Pencil Questionnaires

The most commonly used test of achievement motivation in this category is the Edwards Personal Preference Schedule (Edwards, 1959). This schedule presents 225 pairs of items and measures other constructs (e.g., autonomy, affiliation, and aggression) as well as need for achievement. The subject is asked to choose one of each pair of statements to indicate which is more characteristic of what he likes or feels (e.g.: (A) I like to talk about myself to others; (B) I like to work toward some goal that I have set for myself). The pairs assessing need achievement can be pulled from the total set. The Edwards Schedule is a more reliable measure than the projective techniques described above, but its validity is open to question. Obviously, its purpose is much more transparent and this factor allows subjects to "fake" their responses.

METHODS OF INCREASING
ACHIEVEMENT MOTIVATION

In recent years, extensive achievement motivation training programs in educational contexts have been undertaken. Alschuler and his associates (1973) and McClelland (1965) have outlined the various principles of operation of such courses and more specifically delineated a series of steps to be followed in carrying them out.

Achievement motivation training encourages commitments to basic social values, such as independence, acceptance of personal responsibility for the consequences of one's actions, and actively attempting to master the environment according to standards of excellence (Dreeben, 1967). Entrepreneurial role responsibility is developed through clarifying and labeling the cluster of achievement thoughts by teaching the element of achievement planning; through relating these thoughts to the expressive style (moderate risk taking, initiative, using concrete feedback, planning ahead carefully); and through tying these thoughts and actions to appropriate life contexts (entrepreneurial-type situations).

These goals may be accomplished in various ways (McClelland & Winter, 1969). Participants can be taught to score their own TAT stories, and subsequently to code their own spontaneous thoughts, as well as to code newspaper editorials, folk tales, and conversations. The critical task is to clearly conceptualize and label achievement motivation thoughts. The expressive style is taught through game simulations in which the actions are adaptive and valuable. Participants can practice and see the results of acting according to the required expressive style in situations where the real-life consequences are relaxed enough to allow experimental learning without threat to the learner. Group discussions help to clarify how and why these actions are natural outgrowths of the achievement thought pattern. Through the analysis of case studies, lectures by successful men, and discussions of the student's own life situation, achievement ideas and actions are tied to real-life contexts.

Such techniques, which have a good deal in common with so-called "psychological education" courses, normally consist of four characteristic types of procedure. Subjects are encouraged to fantasize about doing things exceptionally well and are taught how to differentiate between achievement imagery and task imagery. Later in the course, these achievement images are tied to reality through careful planning and undertaking of projects. These procedures often bring previously ignored aspects of personality within awareness.

Second, nonverbal action, meditation, and the exaggeration of spontaneous body movements are encouraged through a variety of games. Understanding psychological concepts is often facilitated when such concepts are learned motorically rather than simply comprehended intellectually. For example, in achievement motivation courses, the concept of moderate risk taking is taught through a dart game in which the subject must bid on his performance and only wins when he makes a bid. A very low bid earns few points, while a very high bid is nearly impossible to make. The game experience is subsequently generalized to other life situations.

Third, individual emotional responses to the outside world are explored. How people feel is considered to be more important than what they think and strong group feelings are developed to help support the individual in whatever he chooses to do well. This approach is based on the idea that affective involvement increases meaningful learning, and that the capacity for the full range of feelings is a crucial human potentiality often underdeveloped in adults.

Fourth, the importance of living fully and intensely here and now is emphasized. Courses may be held in retreat settings which cut people off from past obligations. The isolated resort settings dramatize the here-and-now opportunities to experiment with new behaviors. Less emphasis is given to past personal history as an explanation for behavior, and references to the past and future are considered escapes from the present opportunity. The assumption is that if a person cannot change in a situation where the conditions for growth are optimal, he is not likely to continue growing outside and after the course.

Such techniques in general aim at the growth of a "healthier, more sensitive, multi-level communication, the integration of irrational fantasies into constructive responses, and greater capacity for ecstatic emotional experience. A person who has developed sensitive non-verbal communication is less likely to express himself hatefully or violently" (Alschuler, 1973, p. 14–15).

These general procedures are elsewhere translated into more specific guidelines. Alschuler, Tabor, and McIntyre (1970) present and explain six basic steps to be followed in teaching achievement motivation. These, considered in turn, are as follows:

1. Focus attention on what is happening here and now.
2. Provide an intense, integrated experience of new thoughts, actions and feelings.
3. Help the person make sense out of his experience by attempting to conceptualize what happened.
4. Relate the experience to the person's values, goals, behavior, and relationships with others.
5. Stabilize the new thought, action and feelings through practice.
6. Internalize the changes.

Getting attention is mainly a question of creating moderate novelty, avoiding extremes of old routines and extremely unusual experiences. In one situation, this environment was achieved through recruiting subjects from the full spectrum within a school, thus suggesting that the program was something new. Sometimes only a portion of volunteers are selected, to give the program added value by making it appear special. In recruitment, typical results of achievement motivation training, testimonials of respected people, and stressing the characteristics of highly achievement-motivated people all help to create favorable, moderately novel expectations. Efforts are made to avoid allowing the training program to become just another lesson, such as by having the class meet at a special time, using special labels for the group, avoiding traditional-looking classrooms, and making use of retreat-like situations that create separateness and that are conducive to warm interpersonal relationships. Although significant personal change is difficult to induce, if the moderately novel situation can be created, the course experiences are more likely to be intense and personally meaningful and are more likely to stand apart from normal school learning.

The only way to know achievement motivation is to experience it. Descriptions and presentations fall short of the experience of goal setting, planning, risk taking, and so on. Only after a concrete experience of these kinds can a person make a knowledgable choice about whether or not to practice and strengthen his achievement motivation. This experience may be provided through a variety of games like "Ring-Toss," "Darts-Dice," and "Origami." For most people, involvement in the games means working for achievement goals, such as improving personal performances or coming out ahead of others. Since the games are strongly geared towards achievement motivation, the players learn through experience what achievement motivation is like.

Their experience is often an opportunity for self-confrontation—people frequently discover something of particular value to them. The games encourage individual goal setting in a context that encourages achievement goals. The participant is free to determine his own goals measured objectively against the performance of others or some other stated criterion. The scoring system encourages moderate, carefully calculated risk taking. The situation is complex enough to include the thoughts, actions, and feelings associated with the motive and is challenging enough to make players care about winning or losing. Yet the content is sufficiently different from everyday activities to allow nonthreatening experimentation with one's own behavior.

Once subjects have intensely and thoroughly experienced the motive, it is then appropriate to help them make sense out of what happened. Labeling the elements of achievement planning, feelings, and action strategies makes it easier to discuss what happened in the games and to locate for individuals gaps that exist in their need for achievement. For instance, a pattern of low risk taking is more understandable when a person discovers he seldom has hopes of success or success feelings. Learning the achievement vocabulary makes the course experience easier to remember and to use in everyday life situations.

Increased achievement motivation is appropriate for a person to the degree that it helps him get along in his world, enhances his view of himself, and is consistent with his basic values. When a person knows what need for achievement is, and has words with which to talk about it, he can more easily assess the desirability of developing the motive.

Since it is important that the person be convinced, for himself, of the value of this personal change, the course should present opportunities to help the student evaluate how the change will affect his own life style and personality. For example, a way to help subjects see that achievement motivation is consistent with the demands of reality is to help them to distinguish between situations where achievement behavior is valuable and where it is a hindrance, such as by discussing the variety of areas that reward achievement goal setting and those that do not. Similarly, the recognition of how need for achievement enhances self-image and is compatible with basic values can be pursued through discussions of the goals and motivations of the participants, of related literature, and analysis of games and their outcomes.

An integral part of any need-for-achievement course is to have subjects practice using the motive by carrying out a goal-setting project. A cognitive awareness of the motive is not sufficient. The crucial feature is a concern for excellence and emotional involvement, so that the success or failure will have meaning. Once a subject has settled on a goal, the next step is to specify it and to devise concrete methods of feedback and measuring progress, to imagine and devise a specific concrete goal with intermediate goals and checkpoints. Support for continued strong achievement motivation must be gradually transferred from external sources to the person's own inner resources—not too soon, because guidance is still needed as in the early phases, and not too late, because delay retards essential self-reliance. Within this broad framework, the phased withdrawal has to be determined, in given situations, by the teacher himself. Support should continue for some time after the formal course is over. Follow-up reports are usually made to encourage record keeping and to show continued interest in the subject's progress, and reunions are usually held at periodic intervals after the course is completed.

STUDIES IN AN EDUCATIONAL CONTEXT

Although, as a result of extensive and continuous research investigations over a period of more than 20 years, a great deal is now known about the achievement motive, there has been very little research that is directly school related. Those few studies that have been conducted have on the whole been only moderately successful in showing the importance of this motive in school settings. There is evidence that the achievement motive shows some relationship to school performance. A small positive relationship was found between need for achievement and grades of college students (McClelland *et al.*, 1955); between achievement motivation and academic performance of superior high school students (Uhlinger & Stephens, 1960); between achievement motivation and grades among equal-ability-grouped students (Morgan, 1966); and between low achievement motivation and "underachievement" (Burgess, 1957; Gebhart & Hoyt, 1958).

A number of attempts have been made to develop achievement motivation in school-age students and to observe the effect of such training on their behavior in and out of school. McClelland and Winter (1969) report a study of unmotivated high school boys, for whom all other techniques of parental or school counseling seemed to be failing. A group of potential high school dropouts of 16 or 17 years of age were taken to a retreat country setting for a 5-day course. Half of the boys soon dropped out of the course, thereby following the same pattern they had been showing in school; but among those who stayed, the changes in behavior a year and a half later were quite marked. Seven out of nine showed a notable improvement in grades, as contrasted with three out of nine of their matched controls. Further, in an interview some time afterward, all of them reported thinking very seriously about their vocational plans.

Another achievement motivation training course for high school students was given to a group of eight underachieving boys enrolled in an intensive, remedial, summer-school program at Brown University (Kolb, 1965). Of the 57 boys, 20 were chosen randomly to receive the additional motivational training. The remaining 37 boys served as the control group. Kolb demonstrated that adolescents' striving for excellence could be increased for relatively long periods of time. The effects of the training were most pronounced for high-SES boys because, it was claimed, they returned to environments that supported and encouraged the achievement values they had learned.

The general findings of research on achievement motivation in educational contexts are complicated by the fact that, since no strong relationships are typically found between increased achievement motivation and performance in school, the results are generally discussed from other perspectives. This fact is evident, for example, in a useful summary provided by McClelland (Alschuler, 1973).

Achievement motivation courses have been given to students in Boston, St. Louis, and California under the control of two separate, though allied, research projects at Harvard and at Washington University, St. Louis. No very convincing evidence is provided by the Harvard studies to show that achievement motivation training improves grades or test scores. The findings so far as academic performance is concerned are inconsistent, small, and not impressive (McClelland & Alschuler, 1971).

On the other hand, the St. Louis group has reported quite dramatically different results. Ryals (1969), for example, arranged for achievement motivation courses to be given to eighth-graders on four different weekends, either on school grounds or in a camp in the mountains. He found that while there were no effects of training on grade-point average, or social studies test scores, training did seem to improve science and math performance quite significantly in the year after training. Further, the gains on the average were larger for students coming from a high school containing a high proportion of minority groups (Blacks and Chicanos) than for students coming from a middle-class high school. The chief difference between these brief training courses and those sponsored by the Harvard group was that the St. Louis subjects were taught by their own teachers, who had received achievement motivation training already.

As regards the effects of such training programs on non-school activities, the findings are more consistent. Nearly all groups receiving full achievement motivation training reported 8 to 18 months later in an interview that they were spending their time in more achievement-related ways. For example, when the trained potential dropouts were asked to state the most important thing they do and think about, all mentioned doing well in school or in their work as it related to a future career.

Whereas research on achievement motivation training for students provides little evidence for increased grades in school, such training most often seems to result in more purposeful planning and action outside of school, where students are more clearly in charge of their lives. Since the ultimate purpose of schooling is to teach students knowledge, skills, values, and feelings that help them live more effective, mature adults lives, this is generally considered to be a most encouraging finding (Alschuler, 1973). This finding is also consistent with the typical and most appropriate applications of need-for-achievement training to entrepreneurial situations, such as jobs, athletics, administrative activities, and some learning situations.

As a final point, the ethical side of attempts to enhance achievement motivation deserves attention. Programs whose goal is to increase achievement motivation are built on the premise that this outcome is desirable. This premise is sometimes taken for granted by researchers bent on other objectives. Yet, although such questions are important, they are clearly not simple to answer and in the end must necessarily remain a question of value judgment. Objections have been raised against the notion that all students can benefit from increased achievement motivation and that it is always a desirable goal to strive for in education. In this light it is instructive to consider a statement provided by Alschuler *et al.* (1970, pp. 10–11), which addressed itself directly to the central point.

> Need-for-achievement training is appropriate for those individuals who need and want increased achievement motivation so that they can respond more fully effectively, joyfully and judiciously in entrepreneurial situations. This could include nearly all of us, since according to research findings, most people have fairly low achievement motivation, and thus providing the opportunity for such training is a legitimate responsibility of public schooling. As teachers become familiar with Psychological Education techniques, it will be easier to introduce need-for-achievement training in schools and more difficult to avoid the responsibility for directly educating other aspects of healthy adult functioning as well. Since living effectively in a pluralistic society requires a broad range of psychological experience, a repertiore of personal skills, and a variety of strong motives, public education might well offer many different Psychological Education courses. Learning to give achievement motivation training is the first step towards introducing Psychological Education courses in schools, and, therefore, it is also a step toward realizing the ultimate aim of education.

ANNOTATED BIBLIOGRAPHY

Alschuler, A. S., Tabor, D., & McIntyre, J. *Teaching achievement motivation.* Middletown, Conn.: Educational Ventures, 1970.
This book aims to help the classroom teachers directly. It is a "do-it-yourself" book based on the assumption that an average experienced teacher can learn the techniques it describes. The book describes new techniques, presents theoretical background for such techniques, and explains how their effects on pupil performance can be measured. It does not prescribe the single "best way" that every teacher should follow. Rather, it aims to encourage those characteristics in teachers—such as achievement motivation, curiosity, and adaptability—that most teachers would like to create in their students. The emphasis throughout is on teaching general principles that each teacher can apply in his own way. [Paraphrase of the authors' preface, p. xiii]

Alschuler, A. S. *Developing achievement motivation in adolescents.* Englewood Cliffs, N.J.: Educational Technology Publications, 1973.
Part 1 of the book reviews the origins of psychological education, and the history and impact of achievement motivation. Part 2 presents the findings of research studies dealing with achievement motivation training, and Part 3 outlines achievement motivating systems. A useful appendix includes a discussion, by D. McClelland, of the effects of achievement motivation training in schools.

REFERENCES

Alschuler, A. S. *Developing achievement motivation in adolescents.* Englewood Cliffs, N.J.: Educational Technology Publications, 1973.

Alschuler, A. S., Tabor, D., & McIntyre, J. *Teaching achievement motivation.* Middletown, Conn.: Educational Ventures, 1970.

Angelini, A. L. *Um novo método pata avaliar a motivação humana.* Unpublished doctoral dissertation, Universidad de São Paolo, Brazil, 1955.

Aronson, E. The need for achievement as measured by graphic expression. In J. W. Atkinson (Ed.), *Motives in fantasy, action, and society.* Toronto: Van Nostrand, 1958.

Atkinson, J. W. (Ed.). *Motives in fantasy, action, and society.* Toronto: Van Nostrand, 1958.

Atkinson, J. W., & Feather, N. T. (Eds.). *A theory of achievement motivation.* New York: Wiley, 1966.

Atkinson, J. W., & Litwin, G. H. Achievement motive and test-anxiety conceived as motive to approach success and motive to avoid failure. *Journal of Abnormal Psychology,* 1960, *60,* 52–63.

Atkinson, J. W., & Reitman, W. R. Performance as a function of motive strength and expectancy of goal attainment. *Journal of Abnormal Psychology,* 1956, *53,* 361–366.

Atkinson, J. W., Bastian, J. R., & Litwin, G. H. The achievement motive, goal-setting, and probability of preference. *Journal of Abnormal Psychology,* 1960, *60,* 27–36.

Birney, R. C. The reliability of the achievement motive. *Journal of Abnormal Psychology,* 1959, *58,* 266–267.

Brown, R. Social psychology. In *The achievement motive.* New York: Free Press, 1965. Pp. 423–476.

Burgess, L. Personality factors of over- and under-achievers in engineering. *Journal of Educational Psychology,* 1957, *47,* 89–99.

Burnstein, E., Moulton, R., & Liberty, P. Prestige vs. excellence as determinants of role attractiveness. *American Sociological Review,* 1963, *28,* 212–219.

Child, I. L., Storm, T., & Veroff, J. Achievement themes in folk tales related to socialization practice. In J. W. Atkinson (Ed.), *Motives in fantasy, action, and society.* Toronto: Van Nostrand, 1958.

Dreeben, R. The contribution of schooling to the learning of motives. *Harvard Educational Review,* 1967, *37*(2), 211–237.

Edwards, A. L. *Manual for the Edwards Personal Preference Schedule.* New York: Psychological Corporation, 1959.

Everett, J. L. *Motivation and job success.* Unpublished master's thesis, School of Industrial Management, Massachusetts Institute of Technology, 1959.

Field, W. F. *The effects of thematic apperception on certain experimentally aroused needs.* Unpublished doctoral dissertation, University of Maryland, 1951.

French, E. G. Motivation as a variable in work partner selection. *Journal of Abnormal Psychology,* 1956, *53,* 96–99.

French, E. G. Effects of the interaction of motivation and feedback on task performance. In J. W. Atkinson (Ed.), *Motives in fantasy, action, and society.* Toronto: Van Nostrand, 1958.

French, E. G., & Lesser, G. S. Some characteristics of the achievement motive in women. *Journal of Abnormal Psychology*, 1964, *68*, 119–128.

Gebhart, G. G., & Hoyt, D. P. Personality needs of under- and over-achieving freshmen. *Journal of Applied Psychology*, 1958, *42*, 125–128.

Green, H. B., & Knapp, R. H. Time judgment, aesthetic preference, and need-for-achievement. *Journal of Abnormal Psychology*, 1959, *58*, 140–142.

Heckhausen, H. *The anatomy of achievement motivation.* New York: Academic Press, 1967.

Hoffman, L. W. Early childhood experiences and women's achievement motives. *Journal of Social Issues*, 1972, *28*, 129–155.

Horner, M. S. Toward an understanding of achievement related conflicts in women. *Journal of Social Issues*, 1972, *28*, 157–175.

Kagan, J., & Moss, H. A. Stability and validity of achievement fantasy. *Journal of Abnormal Psychology*, 1959, *58*, 357–364.

Knapp, R. H. Non-achievement and aesthetic preference. In J. W. Atkinson (Ed.), *Motives in fantasy, action, and society.* Toronto: Van Nostrand, 1958.

Knapp, R. H. Attitudes toward time and aesthetic choice. *Journal of Social Psychology*, 1962, *56*, 79–87.

Knapp, R. H., & Green, H. B. The judgment of music-filled intervals and non-achievement. *Journal of Social Psychology*, 1960, *54*, 263–267.

Kolb, D. Achievement motivation training for under-achieving high school boys. *Journal of Personality and Social Psychology*, 1965, *2*, 783–792.

Lowell, E. L. *A methodological study of projectively measured achievement motivation.* Unpublished master's thesis, Wesleyan University, 1950.

McClelland, D. C. (Ed.) *Studies in motivation.* New York: Appleton, 1955.

McClelland, D. C. Risk-taking in children with high and low needs for achievement. In J. W. Atkinson (Ed.), *Motives in fantasy, action, and society.* Toronto: Van Nostrand, 1958.

McClelland, D. C. *The achieving society.* New York: Free Press, 1961.

McClelland, D. C. Toward a theory of motive acquisition. *American Psychologist*, May 1965, *20*, 321–333.

McClelland, D. C., & Alschuler, A. S. The achievement motivation development project. *Final report to USOE project No. 7-1231*, Bureau of Research, April 1971.

McClelland, D. C., and Winter, D. G. *Motivating economic achievement.* New York: Free Press, 1969.

McClelland, D. D., Atkinson, J. W., Clark, R. A., & Lowell, E. L. *The achievement motive.* New York: Appleton, 1955.

Mischel, W. Delay of gratification, need for achievement and acquiescence in another culture. *Journal of Abnormal and Social Psychology*, 1961, *62*, 543–552.

Morgan, T. N. The achievement motive and economic behavior. In J. W. Atkinson & N. Feather (Eds.), *A theory of achievement motivation.* New York: Wiley, 1966.

Moss, H. A., & Kagan, J. Stability of achievement and recognition-seeking behaviors from early childhood through adulthood. *Journal of Abnormal Psychology*, 1961, *62*, 504–513.

Murray, E. J. *Motivation and emotion.* Englewood Cliffs, N.J.: Prentice-Hall, 1964.

Ricks, D., & Epley, D. Foresight and hindsight in the TAT. Paper read at a meeting of the Eastern Psychological Association, New York, April 1960.

Rosen, B. C., & D'Andrade, R. G. The psychosocial origin of achievement motivation. *Sociometry*, 1959, *22*, 185–218.

Ryals, K. R. Achievement motivation training for average ability underachieving eighth and tenth grade boys. Unpublished doctoral dissertation, Washington University, St. Louis, Missouri, 1969.

Strodtbeck, F. L. Family interaction, values, and achievement. In D. C. McClelland, A. Baldwin, U. Bronfenbrenner, & F. L. Strodtbeck (Eds.), *Talent and society*. Toronto: Van Nostrand, 1958.

Uhlinger, C. A., & Stephens, M. W. Relation of achievement motivation to academic achievement in students of superior ability. *Journal of Educational Psychology*, 1960, *51*, 259–266.

Veroff, J. *A projective measure of achievement motivation in adolescent males and females.* Unpublished honors thesis, Wesleyan University, 1950.

Wilcox, S. *A projective measure of the achievement motivation of college women.* Unpublished honors thesis, University of Michigan, 1951.

5

Anxiety

RICHARD A. HANSEN

City College of CUNY

DEFINITIONS

Almost every individual has had the experiences of general uneasiness, a sense of foreboding, a feeling of tension, in situations where the cause of the tension was not readily apparent. We have come to associate the term *anxiety* with these kinds of phenomena. In the broadest sense, anxiety can be associated with a variety of physiological and emotional states. When a child is reluctant to go to school on the morning of an examination, we may attribute the child's reluctance to feelings of anxiety concerning performance. When an athlete is unable to eat before an important competition, we may suggest that such behavior is a result of anxiety. Similarly, when a child chooses a course of study that is obviously not challenging for him, we may suggest that the choice is a consequence of fear of failure or anxiety. Obviously, there are a variety of sources of anxiety and many ways in which it may be displayed. Anxiety may result in certain physiological symptoms similar to those generated by the emotion of fear. It may result in a decrement in performance on a particular complex intellectual task or it may facilitate performance on a simpler task. It may result in irrational choice behavior or it may result in the individual's withdrawing from activities that induce anxiety.

While speculation concerning the sources and meaning of anxiety has been a concern of theologians and philosophers for centuries, Freud is often credited with the first psychological investigation of the phenomena. For Freud, anxiety has three components: "(1) a specific unpleasurable character, (2) efferent or discharge phenomena, and (3) a perception of these." Freud (1949) stated in somewhat more general terms that anxiety is unpleasant and is associated with the emotion of fear, and it is consciously perceived by the individual. Sullivan (1948) clarified the distinction between fear and anxiety. For Sullivan, anxiety is a reflection of an internal tension, while fear is a mechanism for dealing with external and presumably more realistic dangers. For most of the researchers in the psychoanalytic tradition, fear is usually presumed to be a reasonable and sometimes helpful response to an objectively dangerous situation. Anxiety, on the other hand, is presumed to be less rational and usually a more harmful, debilitating response to a situation that is not necessarily objectively threatening.

At a surface level, the distinction between fear and anxiety is easy to make but, in practice, some confusion may occur. It is almost impossible to observe either pure anxiety or pure fear. For this reason, the terms *fear* and *anxiety* are often used interchangeably since an observer usually can only record a fusion of both.

Even if it were possible to resolve the distinction between fear and anxiety, there would still remain some confusion concerning the source of the anxiety. Thus we find discussions on many kinds of anxiety, which are distinguished on the basis of source: for example, "separation anxiety," "interpersonal anxiety," "social anxiety," "instinctual anxiety," "oral anxiety," and "anal anxiety." Not only the degree of uncertainty concerning the *source* of the anxiety, but also the *effects* of anxiety on the behavior of the individual are also difficult to determine. For example, individuals typed as highly anxious on the basis of a score on a particular questionnaire may vary considerably in their behavioral reactions—some showing great energy in overcoming obstacles, and others showing considerable passivity.

In view of the great variety of ways in which the emotion of anxiety can be triggered and expressed, it may be useful to restrict attention in this chapter to anxiety that is aroused in schools and in school-related situations. While there is a long psychoanalytic tradition of concern with anxiety, this tradition will not be the focus of the present discussion. (Fischer, 1970, offers an excellent summary of the psychoanalytic theories of anxiety.)

Even within the school setting, there are many sources of anxiety. A child may be anxious about the opinions of the teacher. A teenager may be concerned about relationships with the opposite sex. A football player may be anxious about the next school game. Consequently, we will further restrict our attention to the anxiety aroused by achievement-related situations in schools.

The difficulty in making a clear distinction between fear and anxiety is seen in the fact that, even when restricted to achievement related situations in school, various labels have been used. Sarason, Davidson, Lighthall, Waite, and Ruebush (1960) use the term "test anxiety," to describe the anxiety induced by the experience of having to take a test. Alpert and Haber (1960) speak of "achievement anxiety," anxiety aroused in situations where the individual must demonstrate some individual skill. Atkinson and Feather (1966) use the term "motive to avoid failure"; Taylor (1953) talks of "manifest anxiety"; and "fear of failure," is used by Birney, Burdick, and Teevan (1969). Test anxiety is frequently used as a measure of general achievement anxiety, since it is in the test situation that a child's achievement is estimated in schools. The supposition is made that such specific anxiety will be reflective of a general anxiety about achievement situations.

The major concern here is with anxiety that is associated with situations where the individual is required to demonstrate his achievement of academically related goals. This achievement anxiety is presumably a relatively enduring attribute of personality. Spielberger (1966) has recently emphasized a distinction, made earlier by Cattell and Scheier (1961), between anxiety as a transitory state or condition of the organism and anxiety as a relatively stable personality trait. The term *state anxiety* refers to feelings of apprehension and heightened autonomic nervous system activity that vary in intensity and fluctuate over time. A student going off to high school for the first time would exhibit state anxiety. The term *trait anxiety* refers to individual differences in anxiety proneness. That is, some individuals respond with different levels of anxiety to situations that are perceived as threatening. A person with high trait anxiety would tend to be highly anxious in most situations and a person with low trait anxiety would tend to be low in anxiety, even in relatively threatening circumstances. Our primary concern in this chapter will be with the more stable aspect of anxiety that Spielberger describes as *trait anxiety.*

Another factor to be considered in a study of anxiety is presented by Alpert and Haber (1960). They have made a distinction between facilitating anxiety and debilitating anxiety. They claim that there are aspects of fear or anxiety that improve the performance of individuals in certain achievement-related situations, while other aspects of anxiety are actually a hindrance. While most workers in the field have focused on the debilitating aspects of anxiety, there is some evidence that certain kinds or levels of anxiety may facilitate performance. If anxiety is considered to be one aspect of level of activation, then a minimal level of activation or anxiety is certainly helpful in stimulating performance. Rather than emphasizing the distinction between debilitating and facilitating aspects of anxiety, this review will consider anxiety as a kind of activating force, in which intensity rather than type will be the primary determiner of the effects.

MEASURES IN USE

There are a variety of techniques in use that yield measures of anxiety. They range from relatively unstructured projective techniques to forced-choice questionnaires; from relatively covert measures such as those developed by Cattell to obvious questions concerning subjective emotional states.

Many of the global instruments designed to provide measures of several aspects of personality or interests also can be scored to yield estimates of anxiety. The Holtzman Inkblot Technique (Holtzman, 1961) uses a modification of the Rorschach technique to measure several aspects of personality including anxiety. Cattell and Warburton (1967) have developed a variety of tests that all yield measures of anxiety. Included among their instruments are the Institute for Personality and Ability Testing (IPAT) Anxiety Scale, the IPAT Music Preference Test of Personality, the Children's Personality Questionnaire and the Early School Personality Questionnaire. Many other major general personality and interest tests can be scored so as to give measures of anxiety. For example, Janet Taylor (1953) developed the Manifest Anxiety Scale from the items of the Minnesota Multiphasic Personality Inventory (MMPI). Garman and Uhr (1958) have developed a scoring key for the Strong Vocational Interest Inventory that will estimate the degree of anxiety in the respondent.

Since the major concern of this paper is with anxiety that has been related to achievement in school settings our discussion of measuring instruments will be restricted to those that have been used in this context.

One projective technique that has been widely used is the Thematic Apperception Test (TAT). Used by McClelland (1961) as a measure of need for achievement (nAch), it has also been used as a measure of anxiety. In one particular use of the measure, subjects were given an achievement-related task that is designed to induce feelings of failure. The subject is then shown a series of pictures and is instructed to make up a story about each of the pictures. The story is then scored on the basis of the extent to which the story reveals "hostile press." Those individuals who tell stories with a high degree of hostile press are scored as anxious (Birney *et al.,* 1969). Bellak (1954) has described a Children's Apperception Test that is used with young children.

Many instruments have been designed to measure only one personality trait, that of anxiety. Mandler and Sarason (1952) have developed an instrument designed to measure the test anxiety of older students. Sarason *et al.* (1960) have also developed a Test Anxiety Scale for children, which is a series of 30 questions that are read aloud to groups of children. Included in the questions are items like "Are you afraid of school tests?" to which the child is instructed to answer "yes" or "no."

Alpert and Haber (1960) have developed a general Achievement Anxiety Test, which provides separate measures of facilitating and debilitating anxiety. Similarly Spielberger, Gorsuch, and Lushene (1970) have developed a State Trait Anxiety Inventory, which has been used on investigations of aptitude–treatment interaction. Spielberger claims that the two dimensions, facilitating and debilitating (anxiety), are sufficiently independent to justify separate scores.

In some studies, a combination of instruments has been used to assess the extent to which the individual is fearful in achievement-related situations. Atkinson, for example, uses a combination of the Thematic Apperception Test and a standard anxiety questionnaire such as the Alpert and Haber (1960) instrument. The Thematic Apperception Test is scored for need for achievement on the basis of the scoring system developed by McClelland. Atkinson defines the failure-threatened individual as that individual who scores low on the need-for-achievement measure and high on the anxiety questionnaire. For Atkinson, the relative strength of these two motives is more important than the absolute level of either one.

While there are a variety of other measures of anxiety, the instruments described above have been used most frequently in educational research studies. In particular, the Taylor Manifest Anxiety Scale and the Mandler–Sarason Test Anxiety Questionnaire are the most frequently used measures of anxiety in the school setting.

CORRELATES OF ANXIETY

The statement that an individual has a tendency to be anxious has implications for the performance of the individual in a variety of settings. However, since our concern is with school and achievement in school-related settings, we will restrict our attention to those correlates of anxiety that have immediate consequences for education. We begin with a discussion of some of the studies that have related anxiety to intellectual aptitude. Subsequently, we will consider the relationship of anxiety to school performance, to success in problem solving, to the relative efficacy of various methods of instruction, and, finally, to the kinds of choices made by the individual. It should be mentioned at the outset that this review is not comprehensive. Studies that are important and representative of those in the literature have been selected to make the major points.

The Relationship between Anxiety and Intellectual Aptitude

Most of the studies show a negative relationship between anxiety and performance on measures of intellectual aptitude. Sarason *et al.* (1960) reported significant negative correlations between test anxiety and intelligence. Using the Thurstone Primary Mental Abilities Test as a measure of intelligence and the Test Anxiety Scale for Children as the measure of anxiety, Sarason obtained negative correlations between each of the subscales of the Thurstone instrument and the anxiety measure.

In a similar study with a more selected group, Mandler and Sarason (1952) found a similar relationship. Using the Mandler–Sarason Test Anxiety Questionnaire and using the Henmon–Nelson Test of Mental Ability as a measure of intellectual aptitude, a correlation of −.21 was obtained among a group of Yale students. Sarason concluded, from these and other, similar studies, that the negative correlations could best be explained if test anxiety were presumed to be the *cause* of poor performance on measures of intellectual functioning rather than presumed to be the *result* of poor test performance. This conclusion was, in part, based on the finding that the negative correlations were obtained even in groups that were high in intellectual ability. Students in these groups were not marked by poor performance in any absolute sense, but some students were high in anxiety and these tended to have poorer relative performance on the ingelligence scale. While anxiety is the more probable cause of poor performance on an intelligence test in these circumstances (rather than vice versa), it should also be remembered that the negative relationship, although statistically significant, and therefore believable, is not large. Thus, the relationship exists, but it is not an overwhelming one. Given a correlation of about −.3 between anxiety and intellectual performance, we know that about 10% of the variability on the ingelligence test can be accounted for by scores on the anxiety scale.

The Relationship between Anxiety and School Performance

There have been conflicting findings on the relationships between anxiety and school achievement. Although a majority of the studies in the literature report negative correlations between anxiety and achievement, there have been studies where anxious students performed better. On the one hand, for example, McCandless and Castaneda (1956) found that, of 30 correlations they reviewed between measures of anxiety and academic performance, all but two were negative. They also suggested that performance in arithmetic was most susceptible to interference by anxiety. On the other hand, Lynn (1957) reported that anxiety was significantly and positively related to achievement in reading, but not in arithmetic. Hansen and Demel (1969) report a study that computed correlations between anxiety and scores on standardized tests of achievement. All of the correlations between achievement and anxiety were negative in this group of high school students. The correlations between arithmetic skills and anxiety were larger than the correlations with other academic areas. The correlations were significant even when the correlations between intelligence and achievement were partialed out.

There are several possible explanations that might account for the conflicting relationships that have been reported. We have noted already that certain kinds of anxiety facilitate performance, while other kinds hinder academic achievement. It is also possible that certain kinds of tasks are susceptible to interference by anxiety, while other tasks are aided. A third possibility (related to the previous one) is that there is a curvilinear relationship between anxiety and performance. Up to a certain point, anxiety serves to arouse the individual and consequently leads to improved performance, but if the level of anxiety increases beyond that point, the performance is hindered.

Alpert and Haber (1960) argue for the first explanation—for two distinct kinds of anxiety. Walsh, Engbretson, and O'Brien (1968) have used the Alpert and Haber Achievement Anxiety Test to study the relationship of anxiety to performance on classroom tests. A positive relationship was reported between facilitating anxiety and performance and a negative relationship between debilitating anxiety and performance.

The second explanation is related to the nature of the material. While anxiety may interfere with the performance of individuals on complex tasks, it may facilitate performance on less complex and more familiar materials. If you wish a student to memorize a list of words, inducing a high degree of anxiety may improve the performance. On the other hand, the development of an original proof in geometry is not likely to be assisted by a high degree of anxiety. Casteneda, McCandless, and Palermo (1956) offer an example of this phenomenon. In studying the performance of highly anxious and less anxious fifth-grade children on both easy and complex learning tasks, the highly anxious children performed better on the easier components, while the less anxious students performed better on the more difficult aspects of the problem. Thus, for a task of a given level of complexity, there is a level of anxiety that is optimal for performance at that task. This principal was first presented as the Yerkes–Dodson law and is often referred to as such in the technical literature (Young, 1936).

The Relationship between Anxiety and Problem Solving

The literature on problem solving and anxiety may provide some additional clues regarding the relationship between anxiety and achievement. Since the kinds and complexity of problems to be solved in various school subjects vary considerably, the differing relationships between anxiety and achievement may be a function of the different kinds of problems to be solved.

Janet Taylor, for example, has done a series of studies on the relationships between anxiety and performance on a variety of problem-solving tasks. Her findings are congruent with the results reported for the relationships between anxiety and school achievement. On tasks of low complexity or on tasks where the individual is already a skilled performer, anxiety may facilitate performance; on tasks of high complexity or in task situations where individuals are not well practiced, anxiety may serve to lower the level of performance.

A number of studies have related performance on an eyelid conditioning task to extreme scores on the Taylor Manifest Anxiety Scale. In the majority of cases, a positive relationship is found: The more anxious subjects learn the response more rapidly. As one proceeds to more complex problem-solving tasks, the direction of the relationship changes. Taylor and Spence (1952) report that, in a kind of serial maze learning task, more anxious subjects performed less well. Similarly, Spence (1953) has reported a study relating serial learning to scores on the Manifest Anxiety Scale. He found that, when the degree of association between each of the elements in a paired association learning task was strong, anxiety was facilitating. When the relationships between the elements of the learning task were less strong and when there were competing response tendencies, anxiety hindered performance. Thus, the simple rote learning of multiplication tables may be facilitated by relatively high degrees of anxiety; but the more complex learning of how to add fractions would most likely be impeded by high degrees of anxiety.

Given the interaction between the nature of the task and the influence of anxiety on the performance of that task, there still remains the problem of organizing material for optimum learning in children. One of the more interesting areas of research in recent years has been in using anxiety as a moderator variable in studies of aptitude—treatment interaction. Implicit in this approach is the notion of designing the particular style of presentation of learning material (treatment) to the specific traits of the individual learner. It has been argued that learners with high anxiety require different treatments from those with low anxiety. Although there may be little we can do to modify the level of anxiety of students, it may well be possible to provide the individual student with instructional materials that are appropriate for his or her level of anxiety.

There has been research on the relative efficacy of different methods for presenting materials to individuals who differ in their level of anxiety. Spielberger, O'Neil, and Hansen (1972) compared the proportion of errors, the number of avoidance responses, and anxiety scores for seventh-grade students working on a science curriculum that was taught either in a laboratory setting by teachers or by computer-aided instruction (CAI). The results of the study indicated that the laboratory setting evoked more avoidance responses, higher state anxiety, and a greater proportion of errors. Of further interest was the finding that the high-anxiety group made more avoidance responses in the lab setting than when using CAI. This finding might suggest that CAI is a more appropriate mode of instruction for highly anxious students than one in which teachers are primarily involved.

Much of the research on the relationship between anxiety and modes of presentation of material has dealt with programed instruction. This emphasis might be attributed to the fact that in the programed instructional setting the experimenter has greater control over the specific activities of the student than he does in more conventional modes of presenting information. When a student is working on a computer-aided instructional unit, it is usually possible to get a better estimate of what he is attending to than in a conventional classroom, where he may be listening to the teacher or daydreaming and looking out the window. Campeau (1968) reported a significant interaction between feedback and anxiety in programed instruction. High-anxiety girls achieved more than low-anxiety girls when concrete reinforcements were provided during a program. When the reinforcements were removed, the low-anxiety girls scored higher than the high-anxiety girls.

Similar effects on boys were not found. Similarly, Tobias and Abramson (1971) studied the effects of three response modes, two stress conditions, and two types of anxiety on achievement in a linear program containing both familiar material and technical material. While Taylor would have predicted interactions between the type of materials and the effects of anxiety, no interactions were found.

In a recent review, Tobias (1972) suggests that the failure to obtain the predicted relationships between anxiety and the treatment variables may be an artifact of the experimental situation. Given that most investigations are carried out with materials that are experimental, and given the voluntary nature of participation in most experiments, it may well be that the situations simply do not arouse sufficient anxiety. Tobias suggests that it would be more fruitful to use state anxiety rather than trait anxiety as an experimental independent variable.

In another review, Birney et al. (1969) provide a reasonable summary of the research findings relating anxiety to performance in achievement-related situations. They suggest that in unfamiliar, speeded, and threatening situations the student who highly fears failure student is at a distinct disadvantage. He does not master such situations rapidly. Competition does not seem to aid his performance. On the other hand, on tasks where such a student receives encouragement from authority figures, he tends to do better. The anxious student seems to perform better in situations that are cooperative rather than competitive. He performs better on familiar and less complex tasks.

Anxiety and Choice Behavior

The highly anxious student is clearly at a disadvantage in learning complex materials in the context of a highly competitive classroom. His disadvantage is compounded by the kinds of choices he makes when allowed the freedom to choose his own course of action.

Most of the studies relating anxiety to the risk-taking behavior of individuals have indicated that those low in anxiety prefer moderate risks, while the more anxious tend to extremes (very high or very low) of risk taking. A moderate-risk task is one in which the probability of success for the individual is about 50%; extreme-risk tasks have very high (90%) or very low (10%) probabilities of success.

In many of these studies, anxiety is described as motivation to avoid failure. Motivation to avoid failure is usually measured by one of the test anxiety questionnaires and by a projective measure of need for achievement. Individuals are described as high in motivation to avoid failure when they are high in anxiety and low in need for achievement. Brody (1963) found that students low in motivation to avoid failure would make choices at intermediate levels of difficulty, while more anxious students would make choices at either very high or very low levels of difficulty. This tendency of individuals low in motivation to avoid failure to prefer moderate risks seems to occur in situations where the outcome of the event is under the control of the individual taking the risks. (Note that, if you are highly anxious and you choose a very easy task, you probably will readily accomplish it. Thus, your anxiety is not increased. If you choose a very difficult task and you fail at it, as also seems likely, you can always explain it away by saying it was too difficult anyway. However, in moderately difficult tasks a real challenge and threat is present and the highly anxious person tries to avoid this kind of situation.)

To the extent that the individual student has a freedom in choosing his own materials, this tendency of the highly anxious student to choose the extremes of difficulty will tend to place him at an even greater disadvantage in schools. Since progress in school subject areas such as reading partly depends on choosing materials that are challenging to the student but not impossible to master, the highly anxious student is at a disadvantage. High anxiety will tend to lead him to choose a book that is either too easy or too difficult for his level of mastery. In either case, his progress relative to the low-anxiety student is impeded.

Given the freedom to choose outside reading materials, another choice is open to the highly anxious child. That choice is to not read at all. Since school-related factors are the source of some of his anxiety, his choice may be to escape the source of his anxiety completely by not reading at all.

The highly anxious student often reacts to the experience of success or failure in less than a rational fashion. This irrationality has consequences for areas closely related to the classroom. Mahone (1960) studied the relationship between motivation to avoid failure and the realism of vocational choice. Students were asked to provide information concerning their vocational choices. These choices were then classified as either realistic or unrealistic on the basis of such criteria as: *(a)* the judgments of clinical psychologists, based on the discrepancy between the students' measured ability and the ability required by the vocation; *(b)* the discrepancy between the student's estimate of his own ability and his estimate of the ability required by the vocation; and *(c)* the discrepancy between the student's interest pattern and his vocational aspiration. On each criterion, significantly more students high in motivation to avoid failure were classified as having unrealistic vocational choices.

Atkinson has presented perhaps the most comprehensive theory relating both anxiety and need for achievement to a large number of dependent variables. In his model (Atkinson, 1966), fear of failure or anxiety is called *motivation to avoid failure.* It is measured by one of the standard measures of anxiety such as the Alpert and Haber instrument (1960). A second major motivational variable is the motivation to achieve, which is measured by a variation of the Thematic Apperception Test using scoring criteria established by McClelland (1961).

The total motivation operating on a particular individual is considered to be the sum of the total motivation leading the individual to approach success and the total motivation leading the individual to avoid failure. The motivation to achieve success M_s is operationally defined in terms of the need for achievement scores on the Thematic Apperception Test. The positive product of the M_s times the incentive value of success (I_s) times the probability of success (P_s) $(M_s \times I_s \times P_s)$ is called the *tendency to achieve.* This is interpreted as the tendency to undertake an activity that is expected to lead to success. The negative product of motivation to avoid failure (M_{af}) times the incentive value of failure (I_f) times the probability of failure (P_f) $(M_f \times I_f \times P_f)$ is called *tendency to avoid failure* and should be interpreted as a tendency to avoid undertaking an activity that is expected to lead to failure. As was noted, M_{af} is measured by one of the test anxiety questionnaires. According to Atkinson, this motivation to avoid failure should always be considered to be inhibitory in nature and leads to a tendency to oppose, resist, or dampen the motivation to achieve success.

The total motivation in any situation can be assessed if one makes the simple assumption that the probability of failure is one minus the probability of success $(P_f = 1 - P_s)$ and that the incentive value of success is indirectly related to the probability of success $(I_s = 1 - P_s)$. For individuals in whom the motivation to succeed is greater than the motivation to avoid failure $(M_s > M_{af})$, the resultant motivation is greatest when the probability of success is intermediate. For individuals dominated by the motivation to avoid failure $(M_{af} > M_s)$, the highest motivation results when the probability of success is either relatively high or relatively low. As we have seen, these predictions from the Atkinson model are borne out empirically.

Using this model as a guide, Atkinson and his co-workers have done a great deal of research. They draw the following picture of the individual high in fear of failure.

> He is dominated by the threat of failure, and so resists activities in which his competence might be evaluated against a standard or the competence of others. Were he not surrounded by social constraints he would never voluntarily under-

take an activity requiring skill where there is any uncertainty about the outcome. When forced into achievement-oriented activities, he is most threatened by what the other fellow considers the greatest challenge. Constrained, but given a choice, he will defend himself by undertaking activities in which success is virtually assured or activities which offer so little real chance of success that the appearance of trying to do a very difficult thing (which society usually applauds) more than compensates for repeated and minimally embarrassing failures. . . . This fellow's general resistance to achievement-oriented activity opposes any and all sources of positive motivation to undertake the customary competitive activities of life. Thus he suffers a chronic decrement in achievement tests. His long history of relative failure means he will view his chance in new ventures more pessimistically than others unless there is specific information to contradict a simple generalization from past experience. Most startling, perhaps, are the erratic changes in level of aspiration which take place when the least likely outcome occurs. Should this fellow fail at a task he undertook as a reasonably safe venture, he might respond with a startling increase in his level of aspiration instead of his persistence at the initial activity. Should be begin to succeed at a task initially conceived as very difficult he might exhibit a dramatic decrease in his level of aspiration, a retreat to the safest ventures. [Atkinson, 1966, p. 369]

In most of the studies reviewed, anxiety has been shown to have a negative effect on performance. While there are certain circumstances under which anxiety can lead to improved performance, these conditions are of lesser importance in education. Yet, from a theoretical perspective, one would expect a curvilinear relationship between anxiety and performance at certain tasks, the optimum level of anxiety being higher for simpler tasks and lower for more complex tasks. The fact that most of the empirical work has shown a simple negative relationship may in part be caused by the nature of the measuring instruments. The questions on most of the instruments relate to extremes of emotional response, usually extremes that have a negative influence on performance. A child who is completely relaxed in a classroom may be sleeping. A certain minimal degree of emotional arousal may be necessary to keep him attentive. Nevertheless, while a certain minimal level of anxiety may facilitate performance in the classroom, the child who is prone to high anxiety is a student operating at a disadvantage in the typically competitive, achievement-oriented classroom.

THE GROWTH AND DEVELOPMENT OF ANXIETY IN CHILDREN

Given that anxiety is frequently less than helpful in most school settings, it may be useful to investigate the beginnings of anxiety in children.

There are two major general theories of how children develop a fear of failure or anxiety in school. On the one hand, there is a learning theory explanation proposing that the conditioning of school or achievement situations elicits the emotional reactions of anxiety. In this conception, the child specifically learns to be anxious or fearful in school by a number of associations of school with unpleasant happenings. The other view that will be presented is the more classic psychoanalytic position on anxiety. For the psychoanalyst, the school may be the specific trigger for attacks of anxiety, although school is not the direct cause. Anxiety is an emotion that could be triggered by a variety of stimuli. The basic cause of the emotion is internal; the school is simply one stimulus that may trigger the response.

Freud (1949) provides a psychoanalytic explanation of the phenomenon. Anxiety is conceived of as a defensive reaction to conflicts deriving from the phallic stage of psychosexual development. In one sense, the phobic reaction is a projection of an internal, instinctual danger or conflict on some external object that can be more clearly perceived by the individual. In general, the phobic reaction to a specific object or situation becomes established only after the child has experienced anxiety while interacting in some way with the particular object or situation. The specific circumstances may be experienced in a direct physical way or may be experienced only vicariously. In either case, anxiety is triggered when an underlying conflict threatens to become conscious.

In the classical Freudian formulation, anxiety is therefore an unconscious process. The individual is never aware of its real source. The price that the individual pays for inhibiting the fear response to a particular stimulus is that the anxiety response comes to be provoked by other stimuli. Consequently, anxiety that has its roots in early childhood experiences may come to be associated with school or achievement settings. The anxiety manifested toward the school is nothing more than a general anxiety that is only triggered by school. There may be no direct cause of the emotion within the school setting. Therefore, in dealing with such anxiety, we must consider not only the conditions within the school that are only the trigger for the emotion, but also the early experiences of the child that are the most probable source of the anxiety.

The fact that most of the measures of specific anxiety correlate with each other lends some empirical support to this view. If test anxiety is nothing more than a particular manifestation of a general anxiety, one would expect that test anxiety would correlate with other, more general, measures of anxiety.

A second approach to the development of anxiety is presented by the learning theorists. One can easily explain much of the anxiety associated with school on the basis of simple classical conditioning. Certain children perform poorly on a particular kind of task. Their poor performance tends to earn them the disapproval of their teachers and their peers. Poor performance leads to scolding and other unpleasant, anxiety-provoking situations. Gradually, through the mechanism of classical conditioning, the child learns to become anxious whenever similar situations are presented. The classroom thus becomes a conditioned stimulus for fear.

In some ways, this argument would reverse the cause—effect relationship between anxiety and performance postulated earlier. Poor performance tends to place the child in situations where teachers and others show disapproval of his performance. This disapproval leads to anxiety, which comes to be associated with the achievement-related setting. It might be possible to interfere with this learning of anxiety by not expressing disapproval or provoking the anxiety of children in situations where they perform poorly. Making the classroom a pleasant rather than an unpleasant place to be certainly should reduce anxiety in the classroom.

Another aspect of the learning theory approach to anxiety in school is that students arrive at school with self-concepts and attitudes developed in their homes. If their parents have made them feel inadequate or given them to believe that overly high expectations are held for their performance in school, then the children will tend to be anxious in the school setting. This phenomenon is harder for the teacher to deal with. In a real sense, it is the parent and not the child who needs counseling. Usually the home is more powerful than the school in influencing the child, but the school can try to counteract high anxiety by giving the child experiences of success and providing him with some responsibility that he can readily handle.

It is possible that a kind of interactive effect accounts for the relationship between anxiety and achievement. To an extent, children learn to be anxious in situations where they perform poorly. This anxiety may then lead to even worse performance in future situations, leading to even more anxiety. A combination of a Freudian explanation and a learning theory explanation can probably best account for anxiety in the school. There are, to be sure, circumstances external to the school that lead children to be anxious. The school may simply be a new trigger for old anxiety. On the other hand, there is abundant evidence that schools place most children in situations where anxiety could potentially be aroused. Much of school anxiety can probably be explained on the basis of this kind of learning.

IMPLICATIONS FOR EDUCATION

Even if one begins with the premise that the relationship between anxiety and achievement in schools is curvilinear and that certain small amounts of anxiety may facilitate performance, most school settings pose problems because they engender too much rather than too little anxiety in students. While there may be schoolrooms where the primary problem is a lack of sufficient anxiety to lead to optimum performance, the modification of this classroom setting is well within the limits of our present knowledge of classroom practices. In most cases, however, the educator faces the problem of minimizing the aversive effects of too much anxiety.

There are two broad approaches available to the educator in dealing with the problems of anxiety. The first would be to modify educational procedures so as to minimize anxiety. If one takes a learning theory approach to the development of anxiety in children, then one would conclude that the school should not be organized in such a way as to teach children to be anxious. Since it is the experience of failure within the school that is often associated with increased anxiety, the school should be organized to minimize the opportunities for failure and to give each child opportunities for feelings of success. Materials should be prepared in such a way that each child is usually successful in mastering them. This approach may involve some effort to individualize instruction in at least some subjects. Competition should be discouraged when it leads to failure in a consistent fashion for a particular child or group of children. If competition is retained, it should be within groups of similar ability or where the child is competing against his own previous performance. Most of the early school experiences of children should be experiences of mastery and success. The open classroom approach to education seems to emphasize these features. By allowing the student latitude to pursue particular aspects of the curriculum that he finds most interesting and with which he is successful, the trauma and anxiety associated with failure in the schools are minimized.

This particular approach will be successful if schools are in fact the main determiners of anxiety in children. The approach offers less for the child who has already learned to be highly anxious or for the child whose anxiety in school is a reflection of an emotion that was generated outside the school. In short, the problem remains of what should be done with the child who is already anxious before he arrives in school.

There is some evidence that a child who is anxious will not do his best on standardized tests of achievement or aptitude. If a particular child is identified as test anxious, then some less competitive method for assessment may lead to a more accurate estimate of true performance. Similarly, the observation of such a child in competition with other children is not likely to give an accurate picture of the child's potential.

The kinds of tasks presented to the highly anxious child should be different from the kinds of tasks given to the less anxious child. Tasks with a high probability of success are likely to arouse less anxiety and lead to better performance. Since anxiety may lead to increased performance on simple concrete tasks and in learning highly structured materials, these kinds of learning might be stressed. Materials perceived as difficult or moderately difficult are likely to pose problems for the highly anxious child.

The child high in anxiety is also likely to be in need of extra guidance in making academic and career decisions. The tendency of the anxious student to make extreme probability choices combined with relatively unrealistic assessments of his own abilities may lead to inappropriate choices of both curriculum and vocational goals. This child may need considerable assistance in modifying his vocational and educational plans so as to be more congruent with his actual needs and abilities.

The child high in anxiety may perform better when instruction is given in less competitive situations. One possible approach mentioned earlier is the approach of the British Infant Schools. Although the lack of competition in such classrooms may facilitate the performance of highly anxious children, the tendency of highly anxious children to choose tasks at an inappropriate level of difficulty is likely to lead to somewhat slower progress in mastering cognitive goals. While this approach might reduce the overt anxiety of children, it may not be as successful in improving the cognitive performance of children.

Programed instruction, especially programed instruction with low error rates, would seem to be a promising approach to the instruction of the anxious child. The concrete nature of the materials, as well as the success experience in mastering them, would contribute to improved performance on the part of the highly anxious child.

One idea that is not usually pursued is to group children who have debilitatingly high anxiety into the one classroom and provide a teacher for them who can put them at their ease through a "low-key" teaching approach. The hope would be to have these children return to their regular classrooms eventually as they learned to cope with their anxiety, to understand its origins, and to realize that they have "nothing to fear save fear itself."

It is realized that all these suggestions are somewhat culture bound. In every society, the school is a servant of that society. In some societies, the schools serve to filter an academic elite. Many would like to join that elite but, by definition, few are chosen. Such conditions beget a fierce competitiveness and only the most able (and that usually includes those who can cope with the pressure) survive. Such societies—and many economically developing countries have such a situation—should perhaps recognize that much-needed talent may be lost if anxiety levels are so high as to spoil performance. If we really want to choose the most talented, high anxiety may defeat our purpose.

For economically developed countries, the situation may be reversed. The phenomenon of talented children who are now sufficiently aroused to learn in school is a common one. Anxiety levels are low because school will have little effect on their lives. Inherited wealth, a sense of comfort without working for it, and, if racism occurs, a sense that nothing matters anyway, will all serve to create low levels of anxiety in school and poor performance. It is not surprising that, in the international study of mathematics performance (Husén, 1967), Japan, a recently emerging and fast-developing country, had the highest performing level for children and that the United States and Sweden (developed countries) had two of the lowest performing levels at any given grade level. Therefore, as in the other chapters in this monograph, it would be well for the reader to interpret and adapt the information provided so that it can be properly used to improve the educational system of each country.

REFERENCES

Alpert, R., & Haber, R. N. Anxiety in academic achievement settings. *Journal of Abnormal and Social Psychology*, 1960, *61*, 207–215.

Atkinson, J. W., & Feather, N. T. *A theory of achievement motivation.* New York: Wiley, 1966.

Bellack, L. *The Thematic Apperception Test and the Children's Apperception Test in clinical use.* New York: Grune and Stratton, 1954.

Birney, R. C., Burdick, H., & Teevan, R. C. *Fear of failure.* New York: Van Nostrand–Reinhold, 1969.

Brody, N. N achievement, test anxiety and subjective probability of success in risk taking behavior. *Journal of Abnormal and Social Psychology*, 1963, *66*, 413–418.

Campeau, P. L. Test anxiety and feedback in programmed instruction. *Journal of Educational Psychology*, 1968, *59*, 159–163.

Castaneda, A., McCandless, B. R., & Palermo, D. J. Complex learning and performance as a function of anxiety in children and task difficulty. *Child Development*, 1956, *27*, 327–332.

Cattell, R. B., & Scheier, I. H. *The meaning and measurement of neuroticism and anxiety.* New York: Ronald Press, 1961.

Cattell, R. B., & Warburton, F. W. *Objective personality and motivation tests.* Urbana: University of Illinois Press, 1967.

Fischer, W. F. *Theories of anxiety.* New York: Harper & Row, 1970.

Freud, S. *Inhibitions, symptoms and anxiety.* London: Hogarth Press, 1949.

Garman, G. D., & Uhr, L. An anxiety scale for the Strong Vocational Interest Inventory. *Journal of Applied Psychology,* 1958, *42,* 241–246.

Hansen, R., & Demel, A. Reliability and validity of a multidimensional motivation scale. Paper presented at the annual meeting of the National Council for Measurement in Education, Los Angeles, March, 1969.

Holtzman, W. H. *Inkblot perception and personality: Holtzman Inkblot Technique.* Austin, Tex.: University of Texas Press, 1961.

Husén, T. (Ed.) *International study of achievement in mathematics: A comparison of twelve countries.* New York: Wiley, 1967.

Lynn, R. Temperamental characteristics related to disparity of attainment in reading and arithmetic. *British Journal of Educational Psychology,* 1957, *27,* 62–67.

Mahone, C. H. Fear of failure and unrealistic vocational aspiration. *Journal of Abnormal and Social Psychology,* 1960, *60,* 253–261.

Mandler, G., & Sarason, S. B. A study of anxiety and learning. *Journal of Abnormal and Social Psychology,* 1952, *47,* 166–173.

McCandless, B. R., & Castaneda, A. Anxiety in children, school achievement and intelligence. *Child Development,* 1956, *27,* 379–382.

McClelland, D. C. *The achieving society.* Princeton, N.J.: Van Nostrand, 1961.

Sarason, S. B., Davidson, K. S., Lighthall, F. F., Waite, R. R., & Ruebush. B. H. *Anxiety in elementary school children.* New York: Wiley, 1960.

Spence, K. W. Current interpretations of learning data and some recent developments in stimulus response theory. In *Learning theory, personality therapy and clinical research: The Kentucky Symposium.* New York: Wiley, 1953.

Spielberger, C. D. (Ed.) *Anxiety and behavior.* New York: Academic Press, 1966.

Spielberger, C. D., Gorsuch, R. L., & Lushene, R. E. *The State Trait Anxiety Inventory.* Palo Alto, Calif.: Consulting Psychologists Press, 1970.

Spielberger, C. D., O'Neil, H. F., & Hansen, D. N. Anxiety, drive theory, and computer assisted learning. In B. Maber (Ed.), *Progress in experimental personality research.* Vol. 6. New York: Academic Press, 1972.

Sullivan, H. S. *The meaning of anxiety in psychiatry and life.* Washington, D.C.: William Alanson White Foundation, 1948.

Taylor, J. A. A personality scale of manifest anxiety. *Journal of Abnormal and Social Psychology,* 1953, *48,* 285–290.

Taylor, J. A., & Spence, K. W. The relationship of anxiety level to performance in serial learning. *Journal of Experimental Psychology,* 1952, *44,* 61–74.

Tobias, S. Anxiety, attribute treatment interactions, and individualized instruction. Paper presented at the annual meeting of the American Psychological Association, Honolulu, Hawaii, September, 1972.

Tobias, S., and Abramson, T. The relationship of anxiety, response mode, and content difficulty to achievement in programmed instruction. *Journal of Educational Psychology,* 1971, *62,* 357–364.

Walsh, R. P., Engbretson, R. O., & O'Brien, B. A. Anxiety and test taking behavior: Alpert–Haber Achievement Anxiety Test. *Journal of Counseling Psychology,* 1968, *15,* 572–575.

Young, P. T. *Motivation of Behavior.* New York: Wiley, 1936.

6

Attitudes

DEREK H. GREEN
The Psychological Corporation

DEFINITION

No single definition of attitude can be found that will satisfy all those who study the topic. This fact is largely a consequence of the broadness of the concept, which permits various definitions reflecting the theoretical point of view of the individual student of attitudes. Nevertheless, a certain commonality is apparent when we examine some of the more widely held definitions. Secord and Backman (1964) express the view that attitude "refers to certain regularities of an individual's feelings, thoughts and predispositions to act towards some aspect of the environment" (p. 97). Sherif, Sherif, and Nebergall (1965) emphasize the evaluative aspect of attitudes and, like Secord and Backman, note the regularity of this evaluative disposition. Also pointing to the relative permanence of attitudes, Krech, Crutchfield, Ballachey (1962) offer this definition—"enduring systems of positive or negative evaluations, emotional feelings, and pro or con action tendencies with respect to social objects" (p. 139). Reflecting a somewhat different theoretical orientation, Doob (1967) defines an attitude in the language characteristic of behavioristic psychology. For him, an attitude is "an implicit, drive-producing response considered socially significant in the individual's society" (p. 43). Doob's definition draws attention to an aspect of attitudes that will be seen later to be of considerable significance, namely the social context that serves to maintain or modify the individual's attitude.

It is important to realize that attitudes are not directly observable but are inferred from behavior. In some sense, then, an attitude is an "invention" of the observer. Such conceptual "inventions" are common in the behavioral sciences and are called *hypothetical constructs.* Because of this fact, the concept of attitude can be and has been challenged on the ground that it is an unnecessary complication of matters that can be dealt with simply by considering the behaviors themselves from which these attitudes are inferred. Such criticisms are most relevant when considering the problem of attitude change. In general, it is useful to infer attitudes, for these inferences help us to understand behavioral consistencies and inconsistencies. In education, they help particularly in the motivational domain, because they provide explanations of why some students avoid, while others approach, educational tasks. If we learn how to develop positive attitudes in students, we can presumably increase the approach behavior and lessen the avoidance behavior.

MEASUREMENT

Indulgence in introspection will serve to confirm that when an attitude exists, it seems to be associated with direction and intensity. In other words, attitudes represent a tendency to act positively or negatively toward some object and, furthermore, this response tendency may be more intense toward some aspect of the environment than toward others. For example, it is certainly possible to be favorably or unfavorably disposed toward people from a particular country, but this disposition need not be of equal intensity toward all people from that country. Different attitude objects may, then, be located at different points along a dimension. To grasp this idea is to recognize the fundamental characteristics of an attitude scale. In the scientific enterprise, it is often of major importance to be able to quantify whatever is being studied. The concept of magnetic attraction is an example from the physical sciences. Quantification facilitates the transition from the theoretical and philosophical to the empirical. This rule has been no less true in the study of attitudes.

An early but major contribution to the measurement of attitudes was made in the late 1920s by Thurstone (see Fishbein, 1967) when he developed a scale for studying attitudes toward religion. It is interesting to note that Thurstone's original interests were in the area of psychophysics, which was primarily concerned with the determination of sensory discriminations among physical stimuli. This application of the methods of psychophysics to an area

generally thought at that time to be unmeasurable constituted a break-
through.

The Thurstone scale is basically a paper-and-pencil task requiring the
subject to select from a series of attitude statements those statements with
which he agrees. The construction of the scale requires that each statement be
assigned a numerical value representing the degree of its favorableness or
unfavorableness toward the attitude being investigated. A person's attitude
score is then taken as the mean of the values of those items selected.

A second major methodological contribution to attitude measurement
was provided by Likert (1932). Unlike the Thurstone scale, the attitude
statements presented in the Likert scale are not assigned numerical values
prior to administration. Rather, the respondent is required to rate each
attitude item on a 5-point scale (5 = strongly agree, 4 = agree, 3 = undecided,
2 = disagree, 1 = strongly disagree) and the attitude score is represented by
the sum of scores on all the statements. This method eliminates the elaborate
procedures necessary for predetermining scale values in the Thurstone
method. (See Stanley & Hopkins, 1972, or Lemon, 1973, for further details
of these techniques.)

Guttman's scalogram represents yet another technique for the measurement of attitudes (Stouffer, Guttman, Suchman, Lazarsfeld, Star, & Clausen,
1950, pp. 46–90). As with the measures previously discussed, people are
asked to respond to opinion statements relating to the attitude being measured. However, the statements are ordered according to their difficulty of
acceptance. Thus a continuum is represented, ranging from those statements
most easy to accept to others that will be accepted by very few, if by any.
The acceptance of later scale items presuppose the acceptance of items
preceding it. The respondent's attitude is determined by the pattern of
statements that he is willing to accept.

Osgood's semantic differential (Osgood, Suci, & Tannenbaum, 1957)
was developed to measure the meaning of words and concepts and its use has
been extended to the measurement of attitudes. The theoretical assumption
behind this measure is that the meaning that a word or concept has for an
individual can be conceptualized as a particular location in a semantic space.
This location can be determined by obtaining ratings of the concept on
several bipolar dimensions (e.g., large–small, good–bad, fast–slow) scaled on a
7-point continuum passing through a neutral point. Factor analysis has
determined that these ratings fall into three major clusters (factors) that
define the coordinates of this hypothetical semantic space. These clusters are
the evaluative factor (e.g., good–bad), the potency factor (e.g., strong–weak),

and the activity factor (e.g., active–passive). The semantic differential, then, presumes that attitudes constitute part of the meaning system of an individual, and is loaded heavily on the evaluative dimension. An example of the use of the semantic differential in order to assess attitudes toward countries follows (Anderson, Ball, & Murphy, 1975, pp. 37–38).

On each of the following pages there is the name of a country. It is followed by pairs of opposite words. Between each of the pairs of opposites are 7 dashes. Put a check on the dash that indicates how you feel about that country. (An example would then be given.) What is wanted is your first impression. There are no right or wrong answers. Make only one check for each pair of words. Do not skip any pairs of words or any countries.

AUSTRALIA

good	—	—	—	—	—	—	—	bad
passive	—	—	—	—	—	—	—	active
small	—	—	—	—	—	—	—	large
strong	—	—	—	—	—	—	—	weak
democratic	—	—	—	—	—	—	—	undemocratic
aggressive	—	—	—	—	—	—	—	peaceful
rich	—	—	—	—	—	—	—	poor
unified	—	—	—	—	—	—	—	divided
liberal	—	—	—	—	—	—	—	conservative

(Then the same pairs of adjectives would be used for other countries to enable comparisons to be made between countries.)

As other examples, students in a program could be asked to fill in a semantic differential on their teacher, the program itself, or themselves in the program. For any one of these, scores can be averaged across students in the program, for each set of adjectives, in order to obtain a global impression of the students' attitudes.

In addition to these paper-and-pencil, self-report measures that have been described here briefly, there are two other major techniques that may be used to assess attitudes. One is to use observation techniques, formal or informal, and then have the observer make ratings. The other, to be presented later in this chapter, is to use unobtrusive measures. However, first let us examine observation techniques.

If we want to know if a student has a positive attitude toward school or if, for example, he enjoys mathematics, a useful technique is to get the teacher or instructor to rate the student on these dimensions. The assumption here is that the teacher has had sufficient experience with the student's behavior to be able to make correct inferences about the student's attitudes. A reasonable method is to give the teacher a 5-point scale, with the points carefully delineated. An example of a descriptive-graphic rating scale follows (Anderson, Ball, & Murphy, 1975, p. 34).

Directions: Make your ratings on each of the following attitudes by placing an X anywhere along the line. If you have insufficient knowledge of the person to make a particular rating, put a check mark in the margin and go on to the next rating.

Attitude toward reading lessons:

1	2	3	4	5
Acts bored, slow to take out materials, strongly prefers other activities.		Seems about as eager as other class members in reading lessons.		Asks teacher for reading activities, becomes happy and excited when reading lessons begin. Often is seen reading.

People using the teacher rating technique to assess the attitudes of students should be aware of certain problems that persistently occur:

- Some teachers tend to use only one position on a scale to rate all the students in their classes. They may be oversevere, overcautious, or overgenerous. Whatever their reason for using mainly one section of the scale, the result is that each student has about the same score. Thus, it is usually impossible to use the assessments for their intended purposes—for example, to find the students who need special help, or to see what programs create the most positive attitudinal impacts. Therefore, a teacher should be encouraged to use all of the scale unless the class members are atypically uniform in their attitudes.
- Most teachers tend to be influenced in their ratings by their overall impression of the student. If the teacher likes a student, he tends to rate the student high across all the attitudes being assessed. This halo effect obscures the strengths and weaknesses of a student's structure. It can be mitigated, though probably not eliminated, by warning teachers about this tendency.
- Sometimes ratings are invalidated, because the rater feels that the ratings of students or trainees will in some way be used to evaluate the rater himself. For example, suppose he hears that the school principal evaluates a teacher in part by the proportion of children in his class who have poor attitudes. Is the teacher now likely to rate

his students generously? The rater will provide valid ratings mainly if he realizes there will be no personal consequences to his ratings.

To avoid the last problem, an independent observer may be introduced into the classroom to rate the students' attitudes. This procedure may involve a large commitment of time on the rater's part if all students in the class are to be rated. Even if only one student is to be rated, it may be some time before the situation offers an opportunity for the relevant behavior to occur so that the observer can make inferences about the student's attitudes. As a partial answer to this problem, a third rating technique may be used—that of rating the student under simulated conditions. It is time consuming to follow a student around in a classroom for a long enough period to allow an independent observer to be able to infer his attitudes, for example, toward school and specific school-related activities. An observer with some training in clinical techniques could set up a room or corner of a room to simulate, say, a training environment. By setting up situations for the student in this simulated situation, by directing conversations, and by observing reactions, the observer can cut the time required to make usefully accurate ratings of the student's attitudes. This means of assessing attitudes is not recommended unless a skilled observer with special training is available.

So far we have presented some self-report techniques and some observational (rating) techniques for assessing attitudes. A third possibility is to use unobtrusive measures (Webb, Campbell, Schwartz, & Sechrest, 1966). There are two major types of unobtrusive measures: physical traces and archives. Physical trace measures include such varied indicators as the rate of floor tile replacement around instructional exhibits, wear on library book pages (or dust on a particular collection of books), consumption of scratch pads or other program-related materials, and number of different fingerprints on a training device (to find out how many different students practiced with it). Some of these are examples or erosion measures (based on selective wear on some materials) and others are examples of accretion measures (based on deposits on materials).

The kinds of archives or records that would be of use in attitude assessment include such things as records of class attendance; records of books checked out of the library; requests for transfer; numbers of dropouts; and number of promotions after training. Of course, as with more conventional measures, a good case must be made for the relevance and relative unambiguity of the meaning of any unobtrusive measures used.

The most persuasive argument for using unconventional measures such as those discussed here is to supplement other measures of the same variables. Almost all measures leave something to be desired, and it is at best naive to put all of our faith in any single measure of a phenomenon. Social scientists call the process of using multiple measures that overlap in theory but not in inferential weaknesses *triangulation.* If we think of a variable as occupying some logical space, the problem is to locate (explain) that variable as precisely as possible. Any single measure, subject as it is to error and contamination, is likely to miss the mark and leave us with an incomplete or erroneous explanation.

Because an attitude is only one aspect of the forces operating to determine behavior, it is not surprising that measures of attitudes often do not correlate highly with the behaviors that one might associate with them. An excellent example of this discrepancy appears in a study carried out by La Piere in 1934 (see La Piere, 1967). He accompanied a young Chinese student and his wife on a tour covering several thousand miles. They sought and obtained accommodations in a wide variety of establishments from hotels to trailer camps. Nevertheless, 6 months following the experimental journey, La Piere sent a questionnaire to the managements of all the establishments that he had visited in the company of his Chinese friends asking whether they would be willing to accept members of the Chinese race as guests in their establishments. The replies came in with 90% of those replying indicating that they would not be willing to permit such guests to stay in their hotels. Clearly, since the couple had already been accommodated at all these places, the attitudes expressed in the replies to the author's query were at variance with their actions. Therefore, these expressions of attitude toward Asians could not have been predictive of behavior under the given circumstances. Action toward attitude objects is not determined simply by the attitudes toward those objects. The context within which the object is perceived serves to modify, sometimes drastically, the behaviors predicted from simple attitude measures. Furthermore, single, isolated attitudes do not exist in reality. A person's attitudes interact with and modify each other. Within any given situation, an individual determines how valuable the outcome of each of a set of particular actions might be and also considers the dictates of a set of attitudes. In the cases described in the La Piere study, the managements might have preferred not to accommodate Asians, but they may also have had quite negative feelings about showing prejudice in a face-to-face confrontation and about running a hotel at low occupancy rate, and they may have had favorable attitudes toward students and married couples without children. These other attitudes might readily overcome the negative attitudes to Asians.

Indeed, we shall see that the fact that people often behave in ways contrary to certain attitudinal dispositions is a basis for at least one theory of attitude change.

DEVELOPMENT OF ATTITUDES

Let us examine the development of attitudes using the ideas of Katz and Stotland (1958) as a starting point. These authors have argued that the affective (feeling, emotional) aspect of attitudes serves as the avenue through which attitudes are acquired. A similar view is held by Staats (1967), who holds that an attitude is an emotional response to a stimulus that is usually of social significance. Other aspects of attitudes usually recognized by other writers, namely the cognitive (knowledge that one has about the attitude object) and the behavioral (response tendency implicit in the attitude), receive less consideration.

Katz and Stotland exhibit what might be called a *functional* approach to the study of attitude formation. Their major premise is that attitudes develop in the process of the organism fulfilling some need. Three types of attitudes may be developed—proximal, object instrumental, and ego instrumental.

The development of the first of these, the proximal attitude, may be demonstrated in the following example. A student studying mathematics is rewarded and encouraged by his teacher in an environment that the pupil finds pleasant. As a consequence of these feelings of pleasure associated with the study of mathematics, the student develops a positive attitude toward this subject. (No statement is made about whether he does well at mathematics or not. It would be expected, however, that proficiency would further intensify the attitude.) Thus, proximal attitudes are formed as a result of associations between the object of the attitude and particular affective conditions associated with it. Proximal attitudes may also be formed if the object satisfies some need directly.

Object-instrumental attitudes, on the other hand, come into being in a somewhat more remote fashion. They are acquired when the affect associated with a goal becomes attached to those events or objects instrumental to the attainment of that goal. Let us look at our student again; but now he is laboring over his chemistry problems and being relentlessly prodded by a stern teacher. Later we find him in medical school, where the laborious chemistry sessions have begun to pay off. It is likely that his attitudes toward his chemistry teacher and chemistry are likely to be positive ones because of their instrumentality in attaining success in medical school.

It would be fair to say that every individual has some idea about the kind of person he is or would like to be or wants others to think he is. This knowledge or idea concerning the self is one aspect of what is called the *ego* and may serve as the means through which attitudes are developed. People who view themselves as "intellectuals," for example, may express attitudes they consider to be in keeping with those of the intellectual community. This attitude serves to strengthen the reality of illusion of the perceived membership in the class "intellectuals." Such attitudes are referred to as *ego instrumental* by the authors. A relationship between this concept and the psychoanalytic one of identification is evident. People tend to adopt the views of those for whom they have a strong positive attraction.

Although Katz and Stotland have not addressed themselves to the role of knowledge or information in this description of attitude development, it is clear that it does play a role. Clearly we may acquire attitudes toward certain individuals if we are given information concerning aspects of their behavior or even their attitudes.

In subsequent sections, we will examine some of these ideas in the context of attitude change and the role of attitudes in relation to school achievement.

ATTITUDE CHANGE

Attempts at influencing and changing attitudes are a part of everyday living. The total socialization process of which schooling is a fundamental part includes a continuing process of attitude formation and change. On a more formal level, the activities of advertising, political campaigning, and wartime propaganda are clearly recognized as overt attempts at influencing attitudes. Central to all these activities is the idea that communication, primarily verbal and visual, can serve as the vehicle for the desired change.

The consequences of certain communications for attitude change have been extensively studied for many years (Hovland, Janis, & Kelly, 1953) in an attempt to determine the effect of various dimensions of the communication process. Zimbardo and Ebbesen (1970) have outlined some of the process variables found to be of significance for the change process. Among these variables are: the characteristics of the source of the communication (communicator), primarily his credibility, expertise, and trustworthiness; the communication itself, (the order of presentation of arguments and content of the communications have been found to be relevant); and the characteristics of the audience, which include such variables as intelligence, personality traits, and motivational level.

Theoretically, the findings obtained from the systematic study of attitude change have been interpreted in the light of what Brown (1965) has called the *principle of cognitive consistency*. This theory holds that the human mind strives (is motivated) toward consistent relationships and that attitudes will change in an attempt to restore a state of equilibrium or balance to a disrupted cognitive organization. The idea of consistency implies that individuals expect certain ideas, feelings, or actions to be related to or to follow from others. For example, we generally expect our friends to enjoy the same things that we do. Or, given the opportunity to buy a certain item that we dislike, we would not choose to buy it. If in a given situation the assumed relationships do not hold, a state of imbalance is created and we set about to restore prior balance.

Three major consistency theories are recognized and will be briefly described. These are the congruity, balance, and cognitive dissonance theories.

Congruity theory has been formulated by Osgood, Suci, and Tannen-baum (1957), whose work we have already discussed in connection with the use of the semantic differential in the measurement of attitudes. In describing attitude change mechanisms, a 7-point scale is employed that is similar to that used in the semantic differential. Attitude objects may be placed at points on the scale from -3 through 0 to $+3$. These points represent the values these objects assume for the individual respondents. In addition to rating attitude objects, this theory postulates a set of elements called *bands* or *linkages*. These elements are verbal or other behavioral indications either of approval or disapproval. The theory holds that equilibrium exists where there is an associative bond linking objects that have identical values with the same sign (e.g., $+2$, $+2$). Equilibrium also exists where there is a dissociative bond between objects with identical values but of opposite sign (e.g., $+2$, -2). Any other arrangement consitutes incongruity and motivates change. If, for example, a boy received a new bicycle for his birthday and if this gift has a maximum positive value ($+3$) for him, and if his best friend ($+3$) expresses a liking ($+3$) for the bicycle, then there exists a state of balance. This rule would also hold true if his least liked peer (-3) expressed a hatred (-3) for the highly valued bicycle. On the other hand, if his best friend ($+3$) expresses a dislike (-2) for the liked object, a state of imbalance would exist and a consequent change in the evaluations of the bicycle and/or the friend would result.

One of the significant features of the congruity model is that it makes specific quantitative predictions of the direction and amount of change anticipated under conditions of inconsistency.

Balance theory has had a long history and is primarily associated with Heider (1944, 1958). As Brown (1965) has pointed out, there are several similar formulations and, following him, the one treated here is an adaptation of a version proposed by Abelson and Rosenberg (Rosenberg, Hovland, McGuire, Abelson, & Brehm, 1960). The congruity and balance theories are in fact quite similar, one major difference between them being the absence of any numerical values assigned to the cognitive elements (attitude objects). The elements have either positive (+), negative (−), or zero (0) value and the relations between them may be positive (p), negative (n), or null ($\bar{0}$) signifying no relationship. Balance exists where elements of the same sign are linked by positive or null relations (+p+, −p−, +$\bar{0}$+, −$\bar{0}$−), or where elements of opposite sign have negative or null relations (+n−, +$\bar{0}$−). Unlike the congruity formulation, no distinction is made between relative positions of elements that are either positive or negative; thus, there is a loss in precision of prediction relative to the congruity model.

Abelson and Rosenberg (Rosenberg *et al.*, 1960) propose that the condition of imbalance is not in itself sufficient for motivating attitude change. It is essential that the elements be recognized as being unbalanced. That is, the individual must be aware of the relationship in question. (Note that awareness is not required of congruity theory.) Furthermore, the authors recognize several means by which balance can be restored to an unbalanced situation. As in the congruity situation, changes may be made either in the sign of one or more elements or in the relations between them. Any of these adjustments to restore cognitive balance would constitute a change in attitude. On the other hand, there is an alternative to attitude change, called *differentiation*, which works in the following manner. Let us take our lad with his new bicycle. Instead of changing his attitude toward either friend or bicycle when he learns of his friend's dislike for his bicycle, he may decide that in truth this friend is a particular type of friend, one that is certainly of high intellectual ability but who does not know much about bicycles anyway. In this way, a kind of dissociation between the two attitude objects is achieved. This differentiation process is also considered important in cognitive dissonance theory.

Cognitive dissonance theory owes its existence to Festinger (1957), who, along with his associates, has performed many interesting experiments that have been interpreted in light of the theory. Although many criticisms have been advanced concerning the interpretation of experimental findings based on the theory, it has nevertheless become one of the most influential concepts in psychology, perhaps because of the non-obvious outcomes that it predicts.

In outline, the theory defines a state of cognitive dissonance to be a condition of psychological tension that motivates an individual's attempts to revert to a state of consonance. Two cognitive (knowledge, opinion, or belief) elements are dissonant if one implies the negation of the other. Cognitive elements are consonant if the one implies the other. Here is an example of two cognitive elements that are dissonant, taken from an experiment by Festinger and Carlsmith (1959): (1) "I found this task extremely tedious" and (2) "I volunteered for this task." Note that the terms *consonance–dissonance* are roughly equivalent to the terms *balance–imbalance* and *congruity–incongruity*.

One of the most important aspects of cognitive dissonance theory is its concern with the consequences of action for attitude change. This consideration is not adequately covered, if at all, by the other two theories presented. Dissonance theory predicts that attitudes are likely to change if a person is made to act in a way contrary to the dictates of his attitude orientation. A condition of dissonance is thus introduced between the elements, (1) attitude toward a set of objects and (2) action toward a member of that object. Most interestingly, the theory holds that the degree of dissonance, and hence the likelihood of change, is greater when there is less inducement for performing the dissonant act. This surprising prediction has been demonstrated in several experiments, including the Festinger and Carlsmith (1959) study previously cited. In this experiment, subjects spent some time working on a rather insignificant and boring task. Subsequently subjects were paid either $5 or $2 to report to other fellow students that the task was in fact an interesting one. This report was clearly contrary to the view they actually held concerning the task. Later their evaluation of the task was determined in an unobtrusive fashion and it was found that those individuals receiving the smaller reward reported significantly more positive attitudes toward the task than those in the higher reward condition.

The three cognitive consistency theories discussed above seek to handle attitude change data by focusing on different aspects of the attitude structure. Congruity and balance theory seem most relevant with regard to the affective and, to some extent, cognitive (or knowledge) component of attitudes. It is not surprising that these formulations seem most appropriate in discussing the effect of persuasion communication, which of necessity bases change strategy on these two aspects of attitude.

Cognitive dissonance theory, on the other hand, has more to say about the changes that may be induced via the behavioral component of the attitude. This facet of dissonance research points, if somewhat obliquely, to another type of attitude change technique that seems more "natural" in light of the discussion of attitude development introduced earlier in this chapter.

CONDITIONING TECHNIQUES

Among investigators interested in the study of attitudes, there is a group whose concern is not primarily with the internal organization of attitudes but rather with the behavioral and environmental factors with which attitudes are associated. Emphasis on the behavioral aspect of attitudes has led to experimental modifications of attitudes through conditioning procedures.

Two types of conditioning that are recognized are classical and instrumental. The basic paradigm of classical conditioning is that a temporal association of two objects or events causes behavior spontaneously elicited by one stimulus (the unconditional stimulus) to be elicited by the other (the conditioned stimulus). Instrumental conditioning, on the other hand, depends for its effect on the operation of reinforcements or reward. In general, if a person performs an act that is either rewarding in itself or is followed by a verbal or material reward, the act is likely to be repeated. (See Chapter 1 of this volume.)

Staats and Staats (1971) have demonstrated the use of classical conditioning in the acquisition of attitudes. In this experiment, the investigators were able to create negative or positive evaluations of names by pairing them verbally with words that had either positive or negative connotations.

An experiment by Scott (1971) demonstrates the use of reinforcement in inducing attitude change. Students in a debating course were required to debate an issue about which attitudes among them varied. They were unaware that the experiment was concerned with attitude change and several of them volunteered to support a point of view contrary to the one they currently held. Scott found that significant attitude change took place in those situations where the outcome of the debate could be considered rewarding, that is, where the participant won the debate.

An extreme behaviorist would deny the utility of the concept of attitude in cases such as those described above. In his view, what is important would be the behavior and its consequences for the individual, rather than any central organization. Further, attitudes as expressed by scores on attitude measures would be but one type of response, a verbal or written one, and the consequences of this type of response behavior are different from those obtained under other response conditions. Considering this viewpoint, one can again understand why prediction about one response category cannot always be made from knowledge of another. Nevertheless, at this stage in the development of psychology, both conceptual approaches to attitude study appear useful to explain given sets of data and to derive hypotheses for further study.

ATTITUDES AND EDUCATION

Because of the rather broad conceptual framework within which attitudes can be studied, several of the other variables considered in this monograph may be considered in the light of attitude research.

Consider, for example, need for achievement, which can be restated and examined as attitude toward achievement or success. As we have seen, need for achievement appears to be quite firmly rooted in the parents' attitudes toward achievement and their behavior toward their offspring in achievement situations (Rosen & D'Andrade, 1959). Children's attitudes toward achievement may be said, then, to develop from the positive outcomes that follow their performance on achievement-oriented tasks, namely warm parental approval and encouragement. Although the research attempting to establish correlations between need for achievement and scholastic achievement is not definitive, there do appear to be some positive relationships between scholastic attainment for pupils exhibiting high achievement motivation (Robinson, 1965).

Similarly, locus of control is another personality variable that may be viewed as a general attitudinal orientation. This orientation develops through the outcomes an individual experiences during interactions with the environment. The Coleman Report (Coleman, 1966) has documented the profound differences in "attitude toward their environment" that exist between disadvantaged children in large northern United States cities and their counterparts from more advantaged backgrounds. The environment factor has been hypothesized to have important consequences for academic achievement, the consequences being quite deleterious for the disadvantaged groups. The report indicates that these attitudes toward environment account for the greatest amount of variation in achievement between these two groups. The social structure of the school is hypothesized to exert great influence on the maintenance and modification of attitudes, since Coleman states that "attributes of other students account for far more variation in the achievement of minority group children than do any attributes of school facilities" (Dentler, 1970, p. 195). Further evidence of the effect of group membership on the attitudes of students comes from a report by Siegel and Siegel (1957). Their results imply that the individual's social group exerts an influence on his attitudes, modifying them in the direction of conformity to the group norm. These findings surely imply that integrating children who exhibit attitudes considered detrimental to success with those children who show more success-related attitudes could prove advantageous to the school achievement of the potential failures. The importance of this view can be further appreciated if we consider another finding by Siegel and Siegel. They state that individuals seek to associate themselves with those who have similar attitudes. This homogeneity serves to reinforce the attitudes already held. But where these attitudes are maladaptive—in a school setting, for example—the total educational enterprise suffers.

Backman and Secord (1968) have reviewed a number of studies that deal with pupils' attitudes toward themselves (an aspect of the self-concept) and its possible relationship of attitude and school success. They concluded that there is indeed a positive correlation between high self-regard and academic success. They emphasize a 3-year longitudinal study by Brookover, La Pue, Erickson, and Thomas (1965), which indicates that changes in self-concept in students from seventh through the tenth grades have been related to changes in their academic performance.

Hamachek (1971) has indicated how parental behavior can have a considerable effect on the self-concept of children, with presumed consequences for achievement. Children learn to perceive the attitudes of influential people (parents and teachers) toward them, their achievements and potential, and come to accept these evaluations as true. An interesting finding related to this issue is documented by Katkovsky, Preston, and Crandall (1964). They found a strong cross-sex relationship between parents' achievement attitudes and their behavior to their offspring. Mothers' values were associated more often with their behavior to their sons than to their daughters and the opposite was true for fathers.

When considering the possible effects of certain attitudes, particularly the self-concept, on the success or failure of students, it is important that we keep the following in mind. It is almost always impossible to say which comes first, positive attitude toward self or higher academic achievement. Almost all of the evidence bearing on this subject is derived from correlational studies from which no causal inferences can be made. Quite possibly, success and failure could determine the quality of the self-concept.

These personality-related attitudes have been the most extensively studied in the context of school-related areas. Neale and Proshek (1967) found that elementary school children from low socioeconomic backgrounds did not show marked negative attitudes toward school-related words or concepts such as "my school building," and "books." This finding is supported by Coleman (1966), who also found that, on attitudes toward school and academic work generally, there were insignificant differences between white and black twelfth-grade students. In an attempt to relate the general attitude toward school to achievement in school, Jackson and Lahanderne (1967) studied a population of sixth-graders and found no significant correlation between these two variables.

CONCLUSION

Our brief excursion through the domain of attitudes indicates a wealth of formal research and theory that does not appear to have been brought to bear in any appreciable way on the educational enterprise. The predominant emphasis in the field of education has been on the attitude dimensions of larger personality variables as they relate to overall school achievement. Although very little information is available concerning attitude toward specific school subjects, it seems clear that the outcomes that students experience as they attempt to grapple with their school courses have significant consequences for their attitudes toward those subjects and for their orientation toward success or failure in general.

An important point to keep in mind is that without further experimentation it is virtually impossible to determine cause-and-effect relationships between attitudes and school achievement. Specific, controlled experiments are necessary to claarify these relationships. One can readily recognize the difficulty of achieving this control in a school setting, however; every attempt should be made to carry out such investigations. If researchers were to focus on how positive attitudes develop and if proper research designs were employed, we would learn more about the extent of the school's ability to change the attitudes of students, the techniques appropriate to various age levels, and the effects these changes would have on school performance. At present, the evidence hints strongly that the school has the greatest impact on young children's attitudes and that the peer group becomes a more salient factor with older children (see Chapter 8). It would also seem that attitudes, especially attitudes to one's self, are related to school performance, and that these attitudes can be affected by the use of learning principles such as those found in reinforcement theory, associative learning, imitation learning, and classical conditioning.

ANNOTATED BIBLIOGRAPHY

Backman, C. W., & Secord, P. F. *A social psychological view of education.* New York: Harcourt, Brace and World, 1968.
One of the few treatments of the educational process from the vantage point of social psychology. Deals with some of the attitude variables having educational consequences.

Brown, R. *Social psychology.* New York: Free Press, 1965.
Is perhaps one of the most readable books in psychology, while at the same time providing excellent treatment of important topics in social psychology.

Fishbein, M. (Ed.). *Readings in attitude theory and measurement.* New York: Wiley, 1967.
A collection of many of the theoretical and experimental writings of important figures in the study of attitudes.

Hamachek, D. E. *Encounters with the self.* New York: Holt, 1971.
A well-written and interesting examination of the concept of self. A good portion of the book is concerned with the self-concept as it relates to academic achievement.

McGinnies, E., & Forster, C. B. (Eds.). *The reinforcement of social behavior.* Boston: Houghton Mifflin, 1971.
Here is collected a rich sample of experimental work on attitudes and other social behavior within the framework of behavioristic psychology.

Zimbardo, P., & Ebbesen, E. B. *Influencing attitudes and changing behavior.* Rev. ed. Reading, Mass.: Addison-Wesley, 1970.
A very terse account of what is known about attitude change. The emphasis is on practical applications of attitude change principles.

REFERENCES

Anderson, S. B., Ball, S., & Murphy, R. T. *Encyclopedia of educational evaluation.* San Francisco: Jossey-Bass, 1975.
Backman, C. W., & Secord, P. F. *A social psychological view of education.* New York: Harcourt, Brace and World, 1968.

Brookover, W. B., La Pue, J. M., Erickson, E. L., & Thomas, S. *Definitions of others, self-concept and academic achievement: A longitudinal study.* Paper presented at meeting of the American Sociological Association, Chicago, August 1965. Reported in C. W. Backman & P. F. Secord, *A social psychological view of education* (New York: Harcourt, Brace and World, 1968).

Brown, R. *Social psychology.* New York: Free Press, 1965.

Coleman, J. S. *Equality of educational opportunity.* Washington, D.C.: U.S. Government Printing Office, 1966.

Dentler, R. A. Equality of educational opportunity—A special review. In M. W. Miles & W. W. Charters, *Learning in social settings.* Boston: Allyn and Bacon, 1970.

Doob, L. W. The behavior of attitudes. In M. Fishbein (Ed.), *Readings in attitude theory and measurement.* New York: Wiley, 1967.

Festinger, L. *A theory of cognitive dissonance.* New York: Row, Peterson, 1957.

Festinger, L., & Carlsmith, J. M. Cognitive consequences of forced compliance. *Journal of Abnormal Social Psychology,* 1959, *58,* 203–210.

Hamachek, D. E. *Encounters with the self.* New York: Holt, 1971.

Heider, F. Social perception and phenomenal causality. *Psychological Review,* 1944, *51,* 358–374.

Heider, F. *The psychology of interpersonal relations.* New York: Wiley, 1958.

Hovland, C. I., Janis, I. L., & Kelly, H. H. *Communication and persuasion.* New Haven, Conn.: Yale University Press, 1953.

Jackson, P. .W., & Lahanderne, H. M. Scholastic success and attitude toward school in a population of sixth grades. *Journal of Educational Psychology,* 1967, *58,* 15–18.

Katkovsky, W., Preston, A., & Crandall, V. J. Parents' attitudes toward their personal achievement and toward the achievement behaviors of their children. *Journal of Genetic Psychology,* 1964, *104,* 67–82.

Katz, D., & Stotland, E. A preliminary statement to a theory of attitude structure and change. In S. Koch (Ed.), *Psychology: A study of a science.* Vol. 3. New York: McGraw-Hill, 1958.

Krech, D., Crutchfield, R. S., & Ballachey, E. L. *Individual in society: A textbook of social psychology.* New York: McGraw-Hill, 1962.

La Piere, R. T. Attitudes versus actions. In M. Fishbein (Ed.), *Readings in attitude theory and measurement.* New York: Wiley, 1967.

Lemon, N. *Attitudes and their measurement.* New York: Wiley, 1973.

Likert, R. A technique for the measurement of attitude. *Archives of Psychology,* 1932, *22*(140).

Neale, D. C., & Proshek, J. M. School-related attitudes of culturally disadvantaged elementary school children. *Journal of Educational Psychology,* 1967, *58,* 238–244.

Osgood, C. E., Suci, G. J., & Tannenbaum, P. H. *The measurement of meaning.* Urbana: University of Illinois Press, 1957.

Robinson, W. P. The achievement motive, academic success and intelligence test scores. *British Journal of Social and Clinical Psychology,* 1965, *4,* 93–103.

Rosen, B. C., & D'Andrade, R. G. The psychosocial origin of achievement motivation. *Sociometry,* 1959, *22,* 185–218.

Rosenberg, M. J., Hovland, C. I., McGuire, W. J., Abelson, R. P., & Brehm, J. W. *Attitude organization and change.* New Haven, Conn.: Yale University Press, 1960.

Scott, W. A. Attitude change by response reinforcement: Replication and extension. In E. McGinnies & C. B. Forster (Eds.), *The reinforcement of social behavior*. Boston: Houghton Mifflin, 1971.

Secord, P. F., & Backman, C. W. *Social psychology*. New York: McGraw-Hill, 1964.

Sherif, C. W., Sherif, M., & Nebergall, R. E. *Attitude and attitude change: The social judgment-involvement approach*. Philadelphia: Saunders, 1965.

Siegel, A. E., & Siegel, S. Reference groups, membership groups and attitude change. *Journal of Abnormal and Social Psychology*, 1957, *55*, 360–364.

Staats, A. W. An outline of an integrated learning theory of attitude formation and function. In M. Fishbein (Ed.), *Readings in attitude theory and measurement*. New York: Wiley, 1967.

Staats, A. W., & Staats, C. K. Attitudes established by classical conditioning. In E. McGinnies & C. B. Forster (Eds.), *The reinforcement of social behavior*. Boston: Houghton Mifflin, 1971.

Stanley, J. C., & Hopkins, K. D. *Educational and psychological measurement and evaluation*. Englewood Cliffs, N.J.: Prentice-Hall, 1972.

Stouffer, S. A., Guttman, L., Suchman, E. A., Lazarsfeld, P. F., Star., S. A., & Clausen, J. A. *Measurement and prediction: Studies in social psychology—World War II*. Vol. 4. Princeton, N.J.: Princeton University Press, 1950.

Webb, E. J., Campbell, D. T., Schwartz, R. D., & Sechrest, L. *Unobtrusive measures: Nonreactive research in the social sciences*. Chicago: Rand McNally, 1966.

Zimbardo, P., & Ebbesen, E. B. *Influencing attitudes and changing behavior*. Rev. ed. Reading, Mass.: Addison-Wesley, 1970.

7

Interests

LANGBOURNE W. RUST

Langbourne Rust Research

The present chapter discusses what we mean when we refer to a child's *interests* and outlines some common ways of measuring interest strength. It reviews several research strategies in the light of their ability to uncover the general properties of stimulus items that children find interesting and discusses a number of ways in which teachers can use and change students' interests.

WHAT IS AN INTEREST?

The term *interest* is used in many ways. Sometimes it is assessed by the amount of time someone spends at an activity without being forced to: The child who spends hours reading history books of his own free will may be said to be interested in them. Sometimes interest is assessed by the frequency of a spontaneously occurring behavior: We might say that the child who often goes on nature walks in his free time is interested in that activity. And occasionally interest is assessed by the relative reinforcement value he finds in an activity: The student who works harder than anyone in the class to get good marks may be said to be more interested in grades than the others are.

The term has been used for between-group comparisons (boys and girls are said to have different interests); for between-person comparisons (different individuals have different interests); and for between-behavior comparison

131

within groups or persons (a child or a group of children may be more interested in one activity than in another).

In all of these uses, however, the term *interests* refers to patterns of choice among alternatives—patterns that demonstrate some stability over time and that do not appear to result from external pressures. The patterns, in other words, appear to result from characteristics of the chooser and from the attributes of his alternatives. Thus, to say that someone has an interest in something is to say that, other things being equal, he is apt to favor it over its alternatives.

HOW INTERESTS CAN BE SEEN IN BEHAVIOR

Compared to many of the topics in this monograph, interests are not very abstract. Indirect tests, experimental settings, or self-reporting procedures, though they can be used, are not essential to discover or measure them. One can learn a great deal about a child's interests just by watching him over a period of time in his everyday world, by noting the things with which he spends more or less time and the things that he does more or less often.

The data from which interests are inferred are directly observable, frequently occurring, and tend to be quite reliable. Teachers who choose to be sensitive to their students' interests are thus able to proceed with readily available information. Psychology, concerned with the everyday behavior patterns of people, can profit from a serious study of interests.

Aside from convenience, however, interests are constructs that permit a variety of predictions about people's behaviors. If one can determine what someone's interests are, one can predict which items or activities he will favor among a set of alternatives, how long he will spend with them, how frequently the behaviors will occur, and how much (if any) external reinforcement will be necessary to sustain a particular activity.

What at first glance appears to be a weakness of the concept of interest—the many and varied operational definitions—turns out to be the source of one of its greatest strengths. Duration, frequency, and reinforcement value are measured in very different ways, but they tend to correlate highly with each other in a variety of circumstances. These circumstances can be characterized by terms like *free choice, free play, open environment,* or *free operant conditions.* Much of a child's everyday life can be characterized this way, and knowledge of his interests opens one up to a deeper understanding of much of his everyday behavior.

A number of studies support the contention that duration, frequency, and reinforcement value tend to intercorrelate. K. M. B. Bridges (1927) compared frequency and duration measures of different types of play by preschoolers in Montessori classrooms and reported a close correlation between the two. Because frequency was a somewhat more convenient measure for him to use, he used it as a measure of interest, but it was clear from his work that interest patterns discovered from frequency measures could be used to predict duration patterns with considerable confidence. Similarly, in a study of visitor interest in different museum displays, Goins and Griffenhagen (1957) found frequency and duration measurements to correlate highly (r = .79). Moreover, Premack (1965) reported that those behaviors that were most frequent in the free operant behavior of rats tended to have the highest reward value when the experimenter used them to reinforce other responses under instrumental conditioning conditions. And Rust (1966) found a close relation between the amount of time different people spent trying to unscramble sentence and the frequency with which they referred to verbal mastery tasks in written responses to the items in a projective test.

These examples suggest the variety of topics that can come under the heading of interests and illustrate that the various measures of interest strength tend to intercorrelate under a variety of circumstances. However, it is appropriate at this point to note some important qualifications.

Between- versus Within-Person Interests

One source of ambiguity has already been hinted at: It is often unclear whether a statement that someone is interested in something refers to a between-person or a within-person comparison. The difference is critical. A child may be interested in hieroglyphics in comparison to his classmates but be relatively uninterested in it in comparison to his other interests. A discussion of interests should keep this distinction in mind.

FREEDOM OF CHOICE:
PREFERENCES VERSUS INTERESTS

Caution must also be exercised in judging whether or not a particular choice has actually been a free one on the part of the chooser. If it was primarily a function of the specifics of the particular choosing situation it might be thought of more appropriately as a preference. J. W. Getzels (1966) discusses this distinction between interests and preferences. He notes that "the child faced with a choice of subjects already available in school may admit to a *preference* for one subject over the other, but he may have no *interest* in either." The difference is that "a preference is to *receive* one object as against another," while an interest induces us to *"seek out* particular objects and activities" (p. 97).

One can see another distinction, implicit in Getzel's analysis, related to the number of alternatives available to a child when a choice is made. If a subject were given only a few alternatives, the chances are (s)he would be expressing a preference. If (s)he were given a vast selection to choose among, the chances are (s)he would be expressing an interest.

Preference and interest need not be seen as pure and distinct categories. One might better see them as defining a continuum of choice situations that parallels the degree of freedom that the chooser has when making his choice.

At the most restricted end of the continuum, the chooser is required to make a choice and has only one alternative. This arrangement is only one step away from where the subject is compelled to do a particular thing: where an act is required and only one type of act is permitted. Forced-choice comparisons, so often used in psychological testing, are clearly at this end of the continuum. At the other end of the continuum, with maximum freedom of choice, an unlimited number of alternatives is available and the chooser is not required to do anything at all if he does not wish to. Whatever he does under those circumstances could be interpreted as directly reflecting his interests. Such pure freedom of choice, of course, is impossible to realize, but the idea defines the limit of the continuum along which real situations do occur.

The difference between preference and interest is stressed here because, while the two are often used interchangeably, they are not functionally equivalent. Predictions of how people will respond in new situations are apt to be more accurate when they are based on the choice patterns they have exhibited among a wide variety of alternatives than they are when they are based on more limited preference data. The more a researcher restricts his subjects, and the more a teacher restricts her students, the less they can find out about them, and the less they will be able to predict their behavior when the restrictions are no longer in effect (as, for example, when the students leave the classroom). To be sure, by restricting his subjects, a researcher can more confidently compare his results with findings from similarly restricted circumstances. It is partly for this reason that restricted situations have been used so often for research. One can learn a great deal about one's own conceptual structures, and one can predict behavior from one controlled setting to the next quite accurately. But, as a consequence, once can neither learn much about the subjects' conceptual structures nor make consistently successful predictions to the domain of everyday life.

One of the problems in interpreting choices made among a limited number of alternatives is determining whether the choice was made *for* one of the alternatives or *against* the others. The fewer the number of alternatives, the harder this problem is to resolve. In the extreme case, where only two alternatives are provided and one of the two must be chosen, there is no possibility at all of determining whether one was sought out, whether one was avoided, or both.

Young children do not respond as consistently to the abstract properties of the items in their worlds as do adolescent children and adults. The particulars of the choosing situation, the affective state of the child at the time of the choice, and the immediate perceptual contrasts among their alternatives all have an influence on his behavior. Consequently the restrictions imposed by teachers or researchers on a young child's choosing situation have even more of a distorting effect on the child's choices than they have on the choices of older persons. Paired comparison procedures for ranking children's interests, being based on forced-choice preferences between pairs of alternatives, have not worked very well with young children. Both Clifford (1968) and Borstelmann (1961) have expressed doubt that this procedure works at all with preschoolers.

MEASURES OF PREFERENCE AND INTEREST

A variety of techniques has been used to assess children's interests for research purposes. For more detailed information on these techniques, the reader may wish to refer to one of the comprehensive reviews of the literature in this area. Witty (1961) covers a particularly broad range of studies. Terman and Tyler (1954) is a useful reference to the early research into sex typing of interests. A generalized review of the research into the vocational and occupational interests of teenagers and adults can be found in Tyler (1965).

A list of some of the more widely used measurement techniques follows. All share the strategy of using a comparative frequency, duration, or reinforcement measure as an index of interest level.

Open-ended inquiry: Children are asked, in a questionnaire or interview, to name their interests.

Interest inventories provide more structure than the open-ended approach. Children are asked to indicate their interests among a number of alternatives. First and last choices are often asked for. This approach has been frequently used where standardized data have been sought. The Strong Vocational Interest Inventory uses this approach: Respondents are asked to respond to a large number of activities by indicating whether they like, dislike, or feel indifferent to each one.

Forced-choice preferences have also been used for standardized measurements. The Kuder Preference Record and the Minnesota Vocational Interest Inventory use this basic method. Respondents are asked to express their preferences among a limited number of alternatives (usually two or three).

Teacher ratings of behavior frequency: A classroom teacher is asked to keep a running record of the frequency of various behaviors performed by the students (Hattwick, 1937).

Observation of free play in classrooms: A passive observer records children's activities in classrooms that provide some degree of choice to the child. Frequency of choice has been the most common measure of interest, although amount of time spent with toy has also been used. Farwell (1930) and Rust (1971) are examples.

Study of children's artistic productions: The frequency with which different themes are represented in children's painting, drawing, or modeling is tabulated. Terman and Tyler (1954) review several studies of this type.

Library selection studies: The books that children withdraw from the library are recorded. Frequency of withdrawal is the usual index of interest used (Smith, 1962).

Attentiveness, or resistance to distraction, is used as a measure of audience interest in television material. While a subject views a program on a television set, distracting stimuli in the form of slides projected on a second screen are presented at regular intervals. The proportion of total program time during which the subject maintained eye contact with the television set is the measure of his interest in that program (Palmer, Crawford, Kielsmeier, & Inglis, 1968).

TWO STRATEGIES

Whatever the setting employed, and whatever the measure of interest strength, the research in this area has tended to employ one of two basic strategies: Either it has looked at children's reactions to discrete items, or it has examined their choices among preestablished categories of items. Both strategies have been limited in their ability to reveal what children really are interested in. The following discussion is presented in quite general terms. A more detailed analysis, with discussions of particular studies that have employed these strategies, is included in Rust (1971).

Problems of the Pre-Set Category Approach

It has proven most difficult to study children's interests in terms of pre-set categories. Different researchers have often used incompatible categories, and so when apparent discrepancies between studies have occurred (as they often have), it has been impossible to interpret the differences meaningfully. One study, which used "blocks" (Vance & McCall, 1934), reported a low interest by boys, while another study that looked at "building materials" (Farwell, 1930) reported the opposite. It is tempting to conclude that the discrepancy resulted from differences in the samples of children used in these two studies, but that may not be the reason. Boys may favor some feature that is present in many building materials (thus producing the Farwell finding) but that is not present in blocks. And, conceivably, the "building" aspect of the items that Farwell called "building materials" have been irrelevant to the boys' preference for many of these items.

Studies that are based on categories rigidly defined by the investigator before the study is begun run a distinct risk of using ones that poorly reflect those categories actually used by the subjects.

Researchers typically structure their data into highly formalized taxonomies made of hierarchically organized sets of mutually exclusive categories. In everyday life, however, children are apt to see some things as belonging to several categories, to see some things as pertaining to only one category, and to see others as not belonging to any category. Yet the choices the children make are often analyzed as if the children categorized exactly as the researcher does.

Most of the problems of the pre-set category approach boil down to the fact that there are at least two points of view to consider in any choosing situation: that of the chooser and that of the observer. The grosser and more rigid the observer's categories, the greater is the risk that they will not parallel the chooser's. And unless the observer's and the chooser's categories are parallel, the observer will not know how the chooser will respond to something that is in any way new.

Problems of the Straight Item-Testing Approach

At the opposite extreme from these studies are those that have kept strictly to the study of children's reactions to particular items. These studies have typically produced more accurate predictions than have the category studies—but, of course, one is extremely limited in the predictions that can be made. If one finds out, for example, that a sample of children frequently chooses to play with Lego Blocks, then the best one can do with that information is to predict that similar groups of children will respond similarly to Lego Blocks. But the finding would not help one to predict how even the original sample of children would respond to alphabet blocks or Tinker Toys. Data that is restricted to item choices is of little help to persons who seek guidance in the selection or design of new toys. Item testing can only reveal what children are already interested in, it cannot, by itself, reveal why.

GENERALIZING FROM ITEM DATA

It is true that many researchers who have studied item choices have reported, in discussion sections, their impressions about the general categories into which the item data appeared to fall. But, in practice, these generalizations from item data were seldom treated like formal research findings and were not subjected to the same scrutiny that the item data typically received. The categories were seldom expressed in operation or measurable terms, so they are most difficult to evaluate empirically. Moreover, since the derivation of the generalizations is seldom discussed, one may wonder whether they are the result of a rational weighting of all the item data or whether they are unsystematic observations of a small number of the potentially salinet contrasts within those data. The basic strategy of beginning with item data and then generalizing from them promises both flexibility and precision. But the generalizing phase has typically been done so unsystematically that the categories suggested are probably best seen as thought-provoking speculations.

A Refinement of This Approach

In a study on the differences between boys' and girls' interests in various educational materials, Rust (1971) began with item response data and then derived operational definitions of the attributes that most consistently differentiated the boy-favored and the girl-favored items from each other.

The item choice data were based upon observations of 24 boys and 24 girls (aged 3 and 4) in four open preschool classes. For each classroom item, the frequency of boy and girl choices were tabulated.

By contrasting the most strongly-boy-favored items with the girl-favored ones, prototype ideas about the attributes that were being responded to were generated. These prototype definitions then underwent systematic modifications in an attempt to refine them to the point at which they accounted most broadly and consistently for the item preferences of the children among all the items in the classrooms.

Attributes favored by boys

Boys' interests fell into six major categories. The attributes defining them are presented below:

Linking building: including hard materials that can be used for building larger units by linking the elements rigidly together.

Blocklike-unstructured: including rectangular prisms or cubes or rigid construction by not including physical constraints or guidelines to pattern the way they are put together.

Learning about animals: animals or materials that tell about or picture single kinds of animals.

Numerals and letters (unstructured): focusing on letters or involving numerals in a relatively unprogramed manner.

Dry food: involving food, but not involving liquid or sticky substances.

Climbing—no walking: apparatus conducive to climbing or sliding on, but on which walking or sitting would be most difficult.

Attributes favored by girls

Girls tended to favor materials embodying one or more of the following six attributes:

Art, arts, and crafts: including art or arts and crafts materials: materials for drawing, painting, tracing, collage, ornament making, and so on.

Clothing related (not masculine): related to clothing that is not exclusively masculine.

Pourables: items involving direct interaction with freely pourable substances.

Cleanliness-related: including materials for achieving or maintaining cleanliness or dryness.

One solution (excepting picture puzzles): materials offering structures or problems to which there is only one correct response or solution, excepting picture puzzles.

Climbing and walking: apparatus conducive to climbing on, and on which walking and sitting is easily done.

The interest patterns revealed by these attributes were quite pervasive. Of the 437 items, 70% in the four classrooms were identified as possessing at least one sex-typed attributed. Children chose to play with items that had attributes favored by their own sex twice as frequently as they chose items that had attributes favored by the other sex. The children responded very similarly to the attributes from class to class and from school to school, even though the particular items that embodied the attributes were often different.

It is unclear just how broadly these attribute findings can be generalized. In the particulars of their definitions, some of them may be quite restricted. In general ways, most of them seem to reflect quite broad interest patterns.

Direct precedents for five of the attributes were found in a literature search. Although the findings were occasionally mixed, several studies reported boys being interested in building materials, in blocks, and in science (presumably including animals). Girls have often been reported to be interested in artistic activities.

Indirect evidence can be found to support the other attributes. Research on sex differences in the perception and fear of failure is consistent with the findings that girls favor one-solution materials and that boys and girls show interest in different kinds of climbing apparatus. Boys have often been reported to be messier than girls and to clean up with greater reluctance. This pattern may lie behind girls' relative interest in cleanliness-related and pourable materials and it may account for boys' avoidance of wet and sticky foodstuffs.

Since most of the precedents that were found had been based on the study of middle-class white American children, it is clear these interest patterns cannot be generalized to other populations. More research is needed and it should be carried out within each culture and subculture. Interests are determined by social and educational influences interacting with the natural talents of the child. Obviously, each culture will generate different interests in its children. Finally, the effects of the choosing environment on the choice patterns that occur within them require serious and systematic study.

These unresolved issues suggest that the attribute definitions reported here be thought of only as an example of what can be done to study interests and thereby to generalize to new activities in different settings.

APPLICATIONS OF THE FINDINGS ON CHILDREN'S SEX-TYPED INTERESTS

The first practical application of the findings did give some suggestion of their potential value. After the attributes had been defined, an examination of the classrooms in which the data had been colected revealed them to have many more materials with strongly girl-appropriate attributes than with boy-appropriate ones. It was suggested to one of the teachers that she use the attribute definitions to select more boy-appropriate toys. She followed the recommendation and introduced a number of such toys into her classroom. She reported an immediate change in the behavior of the boys in her class. Previously they had presented serious discipline problems. Now they gave her no trouble at all. They worked as quietly and intensively with the classroom materials as the girls had ever done (Rust, 1971).

The findings were also subjected to a more formal test of their validity. The attributes were used to predict the sex-favoredness of 49 untested materials that had been added to one of the classrooms. Subsequent observations on 18 children over a 3-day period confirmed the predictions for 39 of the materials. Most of the 10 remaining items were chosen about equally by both sexes.

ATTRIBUTES OF CHILDREN'S TELEVISION INTERESTS

Children's interests in different kinds of television material were examined in a study of second- and third-graders' responses to different scenes in the television program "The Electric Company" (Rust, 1972). The primary measure of interest strength was the distractor method developed by Palmer *et al.* (1968), described earlier. Different scenes in a sample of tested television shows were analyzed in terms of their distractor scores, and the attributes with the most consistently high and low interest value were defined. These definitions were tested by using them to predict how new samples of children would respond to new television material: predicting high scores when high-interest qualities were present in a scene and low scores when there were low-appeal qualities. The predictions proved not only to be more accurate than chance, but also, with certain limitations, to be more accurate than the predictions made by writers and researchers who had worked on the show. These findings about the program have been of considerable value in the writing and production of new television material. The attributes that most consistently hold children's interest can be focused on, while the attributes that turn them away can be avoided.

SOME IMPLICATIONS FOR EDUCATION

Getting Children to Do Things That Don't Interest Them

It is sometimes necessary to get students to do things in which they have no current intrinsic interest. Cultures require many learnings of children, and not all of these learnings have elements that are intrinsically interesting. The teacher confronting such a situation can still be aided by a knowledge of what it is that most interests students. Interesting activities can be incorporated with the content to be learned that has neutral or negative interest. Following an instrumental conditioning model, the teacher who wants students to translate Latin into English might get those students involved in some interesting activity that requires Latin-to-English translation. Such an activity was found at Culver Military Academy where the Latin classes participated in building working replicas of Roman catapults. They staged rock-hurling contests as a climax to their project. For students to participate in this project and to learn how to build and operate the catapults, it was necessary for them to do translations. And they did so, one can image, with fewer motivational problems that are conventionally encountered in Latin courses. While teachers and students may not always be able to devote the nonacademic time and effort that are involved in catapult building, the example serves to illustrate the principle. Students will involve themselves in an otherwise uninteresting activity if it gives them a chance to do something that does interest them.

The more interesting the reinforcing activity is to a child, the more effective it will be as a reinforcer. The problem of the teacher may not be solved, however, just be finding a reinforcer of high interest value. If the learning task is a very difficult one, the child may lose sight of the intended reinforcer entirely. This phenomenon was pointed out by Piaget (1952) in a discussion of the development of intelligent behavior in young children. A child will not be able to subordinate one activity (chair pushing, for example) as instrumental to another (getting to the cookie jar), until the first activity has been learned for its own sake first. Although Piaget had been observing very young children, the principle continues to operate throughout life. The poor reader to whom the tasks in an advanced workbook are nearly incomprehensible is apt to lose sight of any promised rewards once he is immersed in the exercises themselves, and he may then lose all drive whatever to continue working on them.

Some reinforcers are more eadily kept in mind than others. Haim Ginott, in a book of practical advice to parents (1965), repeatedly stresses the need to offer children alternatives or rewards in concrete terms. An abstract suggestion is not as effective as a concrete one. Children can picture a future state of affairs more clearly, and respond to it more securely, if they can picture it in real, substantial, and concrete terms. Telling a child who likes to play baseball that he will be free to do anything he would like to do as soon as he finishes his present task will not be as effective as telling him he can go out to play baseball when he is through. He is far more apt to lose sight of the former reinforcer then the latter.

To summarize this discussion: The instrumental conditioner model provides one way in which teachers can employ the interests of students to get them to do things that otherwise hold no interest to them. The teacher who has a sound knowledge of students' interests will be able to reinforce uninteresting behaviors more effectively. The instrumental conditioning strategy is not uniformly effective. If the task being reinforced is not clearly understood by the student, he may lose sight of the reinforcement that had been promised him. And some reinforcers are most easily lost sight of than others. In general, given rewards of equal interest value, the one that is pictured more concretely will be the more effective one.

Developing New Interests

A teacher can employ a child's interests not only to sustain uninteresting behaviors, but also to make such behaviors self-sustaining and interesting in their own right. The classical conditioning model may thus be a useful one for a teacher to consider when the goal is to develop an interest in a new activity. Children who come to associate previously neutral activities with highly interesting ones are apt, in time, to develop a greater interest in the former. It is likely that some of the Latin students who get involved in catapult building developed new interests out of that experience. The instrumental activity, Latin translation, may have sparked an independent interest in a few of the students. Others may have developed new interests in the technology or tactics of warfare, for example, or in ballistics, or in Roman history, or in woodworking, even though these activities may have only been tangentially associated to the interests that got the students involved in the first place.

The teacher who wishes to instill a new interest should try to associate the students' existing interests with the intended one. The relationship between algebraic equations and automobile trips, though they may be associated in mathematics workbooks, is not an obvious one. A child is not apt to develop a sustaining interest in the former, no matter what the interest value of the latter, just because they are artificially coupled in such restricted circumstances. In the larger sphere of most children's lives, algebraic equations and automobile trips might as well be mutually exclusive phenomena: A child never does one when he is doing the other.

On the other hand, the relationship between playing an instrument and listening to music is much closer. While one can certainly do one without the other (rank beginners may never hear themselves play any music, and many muscially appreciative persons play no instruments), the relationship is there, nonetheless. Similarly, there is an intrinsic, though not necessary, relationship between, for example, reading and storytelling or politics and social gatherings. A teacher can greatly influence the development of a child's interests by the *judicious* pairing of neutral with interesting activities.

The teacher can shape a child's interests in still another way: through identification and modeling. The actual learning process involved may be classical conditioning, or it may involve components of instrumental conditioning, but the phenomena typically involved differ from those used in the previous examples. Observational learning, learning that takes place through imitation and identification, has been the subject of less research than have the processes of classical and instrumental conditioning, but it apparently plays an important role in the development of young children, and can directly influence their interests. Bandura has done much of the pioneering work in this area and the interested reader should refer to his writings (Bandura, 1962; Bandura & Walters, 1963).

Children tend to identify with certain models more than others. In general, it appears that if the model is an admired one, is liked by the child, and is warm to him in return, and if the child perceives the model to be somewhat similar to himself while at the same time perceiving the model to be in control of reinforcers that the child finds desirable, then that model is apt to elicit strong identification from that child. Next to parents, teachers probably constitute the strongest adult models to most children's identification learnings. The interests that a warm and respected teacher manifests in class can profoundly influence the interests that his students develop.

Selecting Materials

If a teacher knew those attributes of educational materials that held the highest and lowest interest to students and knew the attributes that best differentiated the choices of the different groups of children within a class, then the teacher could approach the setting up of classrooms and curricula with considerably more confidence than is now generaly possible. We related previously that the teachers of several preschool classrooms had unwittingly shortchanged the boys in their classes by not providing enough materials of interest to them. Research of the kind described here, which identifies children's interests, can diagnose problems of this kind and can give teachers the direction they need to correct them. Research can also be used to minimize the chance of such problems ever arising in the first place. Had these teachers been aware of the properties of toys that held unique interest to young boys, they could have structured a more balanced educational environment for their classes, and their chronic problems of trying to keep the boys under control might never have become so severe.

Precisely defined attributes that can also give teachers flexibility in their selection of classroom materials can provide the kinds of guidelines that only a few teachers are able to develop entirely on their own. With materials that offer more assurance of catching and holding children's interest, the teacher can be freed to devote more attention to promoting desirable kinds of learning experiences. The need for external controls and reinforcements, for rewards and punishments and contingencies in the classroom can be reduced.

Whether classrooms are organized along open or traditional lines, getting students interested in their work is one of the most common problems of teachers. The scientific study of what it is that interests children may help those teachers to solve that problem.

ANNOTATED BIBLIOGRAPHY

Getzels, J. W. The problem of interests: A reconsideration. In H. A. Robinson (Ed.), *Reading: Seventy-five years of progress* (Suppl. Ed. Monographs), 1966, *96*.
Getzels presents an in-depth discussion of the concept of interests and points out some salient distinctions between interests and preferences.

Rust, L. W. *Attributes that differentiate boys' and girls' preferences for materials in the preschool classroom: A system design approach.* Doctoral dissertation, Teachers College, Columbia University, 1971. University Microfilms No. 3258.
Reviews the literature on children's sex-typed interests and evaluates the strengths and weaknesses of the research strategies that were employed. An alternative procedure is presented an an empirical study is reported that employed this procedure to discover and define the categories into which children's sex-typed interests tend to fall.

Tyler, L. E. *The psychology of human differences.* New York: Appleton, 1965.
Chapter 8 gives a good review of the research done on the interest preferences of adults, especially with respect to occupational interests. Many of the studies reported included high school and college students.

Witty, P. A study of children's interests: Grades 9, 10, 11, 12. *Education*, 1961, *82*, 39–45, 100–110, 169– 74.
This is a comprehensive review of the research literature on children's interests. It gives some coverage of the research methods that were used.

REFERENCES

Bandura, A. Social learning through imitation. In M. R. Jones (Ed.), *Nebraska Symposium on Motivation*. Lincoln: University of Nebraska Press, 1962. Pp. 211–269.

Bandura, A., & Walters, R. H. *Social learning and personality development*. New York: Holt, 1963.

Borstelmann, L. J. Sex of E and sex-typed behavior in young children. *Child Development*, 1961, *32*, 519–524.

Bridges, K. M. B. Occupational interests of 3-year-olds. *Pedagogical Seminary*, 1927, *34*, 415–433.

Clifford, E. Ordering of phenomenon in a paired comparisons procedure. *Child Development*, 1968, *39*, 237–247.

Farwell, L. Reactions of kindergarten, first- and second-grade children to constructive play materials. *Genetic Psychology Monographs*, 1930, *8*, 431–562.

Getzels, J. W. The problem of interests: A reconsideration. In H. A. Robinson (Ed.), *Reading: Seventy-five years of progress* (Suppl. Ed. Monographs), 1966, *96*.

Goins, A. E., & Griffenhagen, G. B. Psychological studies on museum visitors and exhibits at the U.S. National Museum. *The Museologist*, 1957, *64*, 1–6.

Ginott, Haim. *Between parent and child*. New York: Macmillan, 1965.

Hattwick, L. A. Sex differences in the behavior of nursery school children. *Child Development*, 1937, *8*, 343–355.

Palmer, E. L., Crawford, J. J., Kielsmeir, C. J., & Inglis, L. *A comparative study of current educational television programs for preschool children* (Cooperative Research Project #1120). U.S. Office of Education, 1968.

Piaget, J. *Origins of intelligence in children*. New York: International Universities Press, 1952.

Premack, D. Reinforcement theory. In M. R. Jones (Ed.), *Nebraska Symposium on Motivation*. Lincoln: University of Nebraska Press, 1965. Pp. 123–180.

Rust, L. W. A test for intellectual motivation. Unpublished masters' thesis. Teachers College, Columbia University, 1966.

Rust, L. W. *Attributes that differentiate boys' and girls' preferences for materials in the preschool classroom: A systems design approach*. Doctoral dissertation, Teachers College, Columbia University, 1971. (University Microfilms, No. 3258).

Rust, L. W. *Attributes of "The Electric Company" that influence children's attention to the television screen*. In-house research report, Children's Television Workshop, New York, N.Y., 1972.

Smith, R. E. Children's reading choices and basic reader content. *Elementary English*, 1962, *39*, 202–209.

Terman, L. M., & Tyler, L. E. Psychological sex differences. In L. Carmichael (Ed.), *Manual of child psychology*. New York: Wiley, 1954.

Tyler, L. E. *The psychology of human differences*. New York: Appleton, 1965.

Vance, T. F., & McCall, L. T. Children's preferences among play materials as determined by the method of paired comparisons of pictures. *Child Development*, 1934, *5*, 267–277.

Witty, P. A study of children's interests: Grades 9, 10, 11, 12. *Education*, 1961, *82*, 39–45, 100–110, 169–174.

8

Social Motivation
in the Classroom

MARGARET NANCY WHITE

Northeastern University

INTRODUCTION

The study of the relation of education and society has a long history in the philosophy of education. John Dewey (1915, 1916) was one of the strongest advocates of viewing education in the context of society and, as he pointed out, education and society are linked in a variety of ways. Education, as embodied in schools, is an institution of the larger society. As such, it reflects the larger society in perpetuating society's values. At the same time, however, education can be viewed as a refined model of society. It is an institution in its own right, because it has a social system peculiar to itself. And education can also be viewed as a vehicle for changing society. But of most importance here is the fact that education and its agent, the school, as a microcosm of society, influences the growth and development of the child. The school determines through the classroom, teacher, and classmates, the kind of motives that will operate in the classroom and helps determine the kind of motives that will influence the child as he learns in schools.

The classroom can be regarded as a microcosm of society and the pupil can represent the individual. But how does viewing education in this way help the educator? What is the advantage of looking at the classroom in social terms? A sociological and social psychological perspective of the classroom may help the teacher look at the classroom differently from before. Yet, will seeing things in a new way enable the teacher to change and make improvements? The purpose of this chapter is to provide a background on social motivation that will enable educators to choose social incentives to aid them in their own classrooms.

Through a sociological analysis, the teacher can identify activities that occur in the classroom. For instance, pupils can be described as peer-group subcultures that form and develop characteristics of their own. Conformity, persuasion, and suggestibility operate in creating norms and standards for groups and roles for individuals. Teachers and pupils play their own particular roles. As wielders of rewards and punishments, teachers exhibit various kinds of power in the classroom and thus set the classroom climate. The climate is tempered by other variables such as the socioeconomic background of the pupils and teachers and the organization of the school. All these social factors—group behavior, social roles, systems of power, and school organization—have a strong influence on the learning behavior and achievement of the pupil, since school learning occurs in this social setting. Now, it is assumed that one of the teacher's goals is to create a climate conducive to learning in order to maximize achievement. Toward this goal, a social analysis of the classroom can do more than identify the variables in a particular classroom. Since a significant amount of theory and research on the classroom already exists, outcomes of certain variables can be predicted. For example, creative thinking on the part of pupils is often found to correlate with affiliative teachers. Thus, teachers who wish to evoke more creative thinking in pupils may try to emit more affiliative behavior themselves (Grimes & Allinsmith, 1961).

A sociological analysis of the classroom, however, does not pretend to give instant formulas for success. Instead, it provides teachers with tools for objectively viewing social variables and it enables teachers to predict the consequences of manipulating these variables. To help provide the framework for such an analysis, therefore, this chapter will examine education from a social perspective, beginning with the history of classroom research methodology. Thereafter, specific variables and their consequences will be discussed, and techniques for affecting change will be compared. And finally, applications, trends, and recommendations will be presented.

METHODOLOGY

As mentioned previously, one purpose of this chapter is to give teachers tools for observing their own classroom situation. Teachers need instruments for gathering and interpreting data about their classroom. Some of the commonly used techniques are teacher rating scales, sociograms, and classroom climate indices. A brief history of the development of classroom research is given here so that teachers will have a means of evaluating the instruments they choose. In addition to a description of certain instruments, some classical studies are included to indicate where classroom research has been and where it is going.

According to Withall and Lewis (1963), three major sources of influence have converged toward a social perspective on the classroom. One thrust has come from educational research. Input–output theory has attempted to relate input variables such as the demographic, personality, and training characteristics of the teacher to output, or pupil achievement. Another aspect of the thrust provided by educational research has been the planning of curricula to correspond to the psychological development of the child. The second influence on classroom research has come from the mental hygiene movement, which has emphasized the emotional side of the learning situation. This movement has proposed that the learning of ideas and skills depend on the pupil's emotional status. The third source of influence on social aspects of classroom research have derived from studies of group life and group dynamics.

Teacher rating scales were one of the first instruments used to gather data for an input–output analysis of the classroom. In early research, questionnaires filled out by administrators provided the information (James, 1930). Sometimes student opinions were also used. The criterion of teacher effectiveness was whether or not the teacher kept his or her job. Another rating approach was to have teachers place their own values on a rating scale (Wickman, 1928). These values were then correlated with pupil achievement to determine what input characteristics of the teacher produced what kinds and levels of achievement. The weakness of most of these rating scales was the lack of common criteria, reliance on subjective judgment, and inference of correlation of input and output beyond the validity of the data. However, teacher rating scales have been incorporated into present-day classroom research instruments. (Barr, 1952, gives a very complete description of teacher rating instruments.)

During the growth of the mental hygiene and group process movements, a variety of instruments was developed to measure social interaction. One of these instruments, the sociogram (Moreno, 1934), shows children's social position in the classroom in terms of the choices they receive and those they make. For example, children in a classroom may be asked to name the three other children they would most like to work with on a group project or would most like to sit with in school. The children's choices are then plotted in a diagram. The most chosen children are placed in the center of the sociogram and from the sociogram can also be seen when children are not chosen (isolates) and which children choose each other in mutual groupings (cliques). The sociogram is primarily a descriptive, not explanatory device—it does not tell why a situation exists. Details of administering a sociogram can be found in Gronlund (1959).

Categorization of teacher and pupil behavior has been another way of measuring social interactions. Anderson, Brewer, and Reed (1946) classified pupil and teacher verbal behavior as either "dominative" (telling the child to move, using warnings, punishing, calling to attention) or "integrative" (finding interests of the child, helping the child to define and resolve a problem, and commending spontaneous behavior). Anderson's studies showed that dominative teachers received aggressive, antagonistic behavior from their students, while integrative teachers received friendly, cooperative, self-directing behavior.

Thelen (1950) also worked with a categorization system, but classified behavior as either teacher supportive or pupil supportive. Using this index, Flanders (1959) found anxiety, apathy, hostility, and aggressiveness in the teacher-centered situation, while in the learner-centered condition he found less anxiety, more problem-solving behavior, and more emotional integration. Methods of observing for categorization were also investigated. Bales (1950), in his work on group observations, devised a 12-category system of work-group behavior, wherein the observer took the position of the recipient of the behavior being recorded.

Most of the studies discussed so far have focused on individual traits of the teacher or specific social interaction betwen the teacher and pupil. Many of these traits are more or less important. Therefore, even if the teacher knows about them, he may not be able to change them. During the late 1930s, research under the direction of Kurt Lewin attempted to characterize the overall classroom climate. These researchers wanted to see if leadership styles, rather than personality traits, affected group behavior. They also looked for what types of behavior occurred under each leadership style. The implications of the climate index approach to social research was that teachers who thought in terms of group process could modify and control the results of their group.

A summary of the classic study of Lewin, Lippitt, and White (1939) will make more explicit how climate research can help teachers modify their own classroom. Four clubs of five 11-year-old boys were formed. Each club met for 6 weeks under a specified style of leadership. Over an 18-week period, each club had three different adult leaders, who used democratic, autocratic, or laissez-faire styles. The styles rotated among the leaders. Two observers for each group kept a running account of the proceedings. Interviews with group members and parents were also obtained. The results showed that different leadership styles produced different social climates and different individual and group behavior. Groups with democratic leaders were more friendly, group minded, work minded, and had more initiative, high frustration tolerance, and greater pride in their finished products. Groups with authoritarian leaders achieved more in terms of work output while the authoritarian leader was present and in control but less when he was out of the room or not in control. Groups with laissez-faire leaders were frustrated by the lack of structure and, after attempting to impose structure from within, lapsed into unproductive, aimless behavior.

The significance of this study is that leadership styles had more effect than the individual leader's personality. It was one of the first attempts to observe and control the social climate variable. However, it was done under laboratory, not classroom conditions, and it has methodological flaws. Nonetheless, this study does show the importance of leadership behavior in establishing group climate, and it also shows that this climate, in turn, affects the performance feelings, and motivations of the group members.

After 1950, classroom research followed the approach exemplified by Lewin's work. The focus was on the classroom as a social milieu where learning and instruction occur. Research was aimed at understanding the individiual's frame of reference within the context of group values and pressures in a classroom situation. Several ways of observing and classifying social interactions are included here to give the reader a sense of the trend of classroom research. Wright, Barker, Nall, and Schoggen (1951) examined psychological ecology (the children's classroom interrelationships with the classroom environment) through anecdotal records. Withall (1956) worked from a sociometric angle, using time-lapse photography to measure teacher–pupil proximity. Wispé (1951) took a trait–treatment interaction approach to analyzing his data. In his controlled study of measuring student achievement under two teaching methods, permissive and directive, he classified what types of pupils did best under what teaching method. His study showed that teaching styles had no effect on brighter students, while the less able did better under the directive method. It should be pointed out again that the results of the studies mentioned should not be taken as formulas for teaching success. Often the studies were not conducted under reliable experimental conditions. However, they can given the teacher some idea of what variables exist, how they might be changed, and the possible results of making modifications. More detailed accounts of this kind of teaching research can be found in Gage (1963) and in Sears and Hilgard (1964).

Up to this point, our discussion has followed the development of classroom research, indicating methods of classification and observation of social behavior in the classroom and reviewing several important studies. Currently used instruments are directly derived from thos already mentioned. The sociogram is still in common use today. Category systems, like early rating and category systems, use ratings of teacher behavior, but the emphasis now is on observable social interactions with the pupils. Rosenshine (1971) discusses how to develop, use, and interpret observational instruments and he describes two basic kinds now used. One is the category method, in which each behavior of the teacher or students is counted whenever it occurs. The interaction analysis system of Flanders (1965) is the most frequently used category system. The other type of instrument is the rating system or questionnaire. Observers or students estimate the behavior of teachers on a 5- or 7-point scale. The Teacher Characteristics Schedule developed by Ryans (1960) is probably the most well-known. The improvement in the rating scales used today is that now they are descriptive rather than evaluative. That is, the rater does not use such terms as *poor* or *superior* when classifying behavior. For further information, the reader is referred to Gordon (1966), who gives detailed descriptions of a variety of methods and compared them on many points.

In retrospect, classroom research has moved from single-criterion research, such as teacher traits, to patterns, of social interactions. Presently, influences are coming from social psychology, psychotherapy, group dynamics, and information theory. And the emphasis now is on classroom management, communication patterns, and the achievement of specific socially mediated goals.

THEORY

A background in the methodology of classroom research gives us an idea of what kinds of data already exist and how to gather more. However, a major aim of this chapter is to provide tools for using social incentives in the classroom. Therefore, we need some basis for interpreting the data. A theoretical discussion of social variables can put the data into clearer perspective.

Learning and teaching occur in a social context, the classroom. Social theory as applied to the classroom can be used so that a better understanding can occur of how social incentives can be used to optimize classroom achievement. Of course, achievement in terms of cognitive skills is not the only aim of education. Self-esteem and social skills are also desirable, both for their own sake and as a prerequisite for acquiring cognitive skills. Social incentives can help in all these various areas of education.

The classroom is a place where information is transferred through channels of communication. Now, communication does not occur as an abstract event, but happens in a particular social context that has characteristics that affect the communication. Moreover, the people in the classroom are not any group, but rather a peer group, which has a structure and function of its own. Within the peer group, children take specific roles. Teachers themselves, though individuals, have certain powers because they play roles in relation to the pupil or peer group. Depending on teacher and pupil inputs, the classroom has its own climate. Yet school organization and features of the society at large put limits on the choice of classroom climate. A highly progressive classroom featuring a great deal of student control is unlikely to be tolerated in a traditional society; and a highly traditional classroom featuring a great deal of teacher control is unlikely to be tolerated in a progressive society.

Communication in the classroom, whether cognitive or affective, is information transferring from one individual to another, from one individual to a group, or from group to group. The individual's relation to the group will affect the impact of the communication. For instance, high school pupils may be members of a particular group, such as the freshman class, but they may use another group as a reference, such as the senior class. This reference group is one which individuals use as a frame of reference for self-evaluation, and attitude formation. They may not belong to this group, but they use it nevertheless. The reference group functions in setting the credibility of communication, selecting the exposure, and providing support for attitudes. The salience of the reference group depends on the topic of the particular communication. For instance, seniors' views on football may not influence the freshman who is not a football fan.

Person perception is a type of communication that is often influenced by a membership or a reference group. It is a process by which impressions, opinions, and feelings about others are formed. These perceptions may vary with the perceiver, his biases and personality, the amount of information available, and the extent of social interaction. We may ask, for instance, How do teachers come to form opinions of their pupils, or how do pupils perceive teachers? How do these perceptions affect subsequent classroom behaviors? Upon walking into a classroom the first day of class, students may perceive their teachers as "eggheads" because they belong to the teacher category (a part of this membership group), which has acquired, for some students' reference groups, the attributes of "eggheadedness." Thus, persons are often characterized according to certain characteristics of their group, such as race, profession, nationality, age, sex, or religious affiliation. Perceivers, often as a group, agree informally on the attributes that that particular category pos-

sesses. However, even though a discrepancy may often exist between attributed and actual traits, this rigid way of perceiving, known as *stereotyping*,
does not allow for individual differences.

The effects of changes of stereotyping in the classroom were demonstrated dramatically in Rosenthal and Jacobson's (1968) studies of teachers'
perceptions of pupils. Their data indicated that pupils tended to produce at
the level of the teacher's expectation. That is, when teachers were told that a
pupil was a low achiever, whether or not he in fact was, the pupil showed
little progress under their direction. Thus, once children are stereotyped as
stupid, they are treated as though they were. This stereotype causes the
teacher to behave differently toward them and negatively affect the student's
progress. Conversely, high expectations often elicit high achievement. The
point here is not that teachers should get rid of expectations, but that they
should guard against the harmful influence of stereotyping when forming
perceptions.

How pupils perceive their teachers also influences whether pupils
achieve the teacher's goals. For example, often pupil objectives are not
consonant with teacher objectives. Therefore, teachers must persuade or
induce pupils to do something contrary to their wishes. Of course, some
pupils are more prone to persuasibility than others and persuasibility in part
depends on whether the pupil perceives the teacher as relevant and salient.
Some personality attributes of the pupils, such as self-esteem and aggressiveness, have not been clearly linked to persuasibility. However, this lack of
information is not crucial here, for the major concern of this chapter is what
teachers can to to change the learning environment, rather than how pupils'
personalities can be changed. Since teachers have some control over the
circumstances of communication, several descriptive characteristics and techniques of effective persuasion will be presented here to facilitate this control.

It has been found that the degree of acceptance of a message depends
on the familiarity of the issue; the interest, involvement, and personality
dimensions of the respondent; the clarity of the issue; and the credibility and
personality characteristics of the communicator. For instance, if the teacher
is perceived as having low credibility, the teacher's message, to be accepted,
must not deviate far from the pupils' position on that issue. On the other
hand, it has been found that distance results in a high degree of change if
pupils are familiar with the subject, highly involved, and the issue is clear.
Thus, the teacher with low credibility can compensate by emphasizing these
other variables.

An example of personality interactions affecting persuasion efforts is
seen in experiments on reducing prejudice. These experiments have been
conducted to measure the effect of authoritarian or nonauthoritarian com-

munication on authoritarian or nonauthoritarian people. Nonauthoritarian communication slightly reduced prejudice among nonauthoritarian subjects, but increased prejudice slightly with authoritarian subjects. The authoritarian communication advocating the reduction of discrimination reduced prejudice in both authoritarian and nonauthoritarian subjects. The authoritarian booklet aimed at increasing prejudice produced an increase for extreme authoritarians, but reduced prejudice for extreme nonauthoritarians (Wagman, 1955).

Several phenomena of persuasion give clues to techniques that teachers might use when trying to create incentives for learning. Military research showed that soldiers who at first avoided listening to counterargument were most likely to be persuaded at some later point than those soldiers who were presented with counterarguments in small doses (Papageorgis & McGuire, 1961). This process of building up resistance of persuasion by hearing occasional counterarguments is known as *immunization.* Thus, once teachers have persuaded pupils to participate, they may wish to immunize pupils with counterarguments so that pupils will not be influenced by opposing factors such as peer group pressures.

Another phenomenon of persuasion is the "sleeper effect." It has been found that where the communicator has low credibility, the persuasive effect will increase over a period of time because the message is gradually dissociated from the communicator. For instance, rebellious pupils who perceive their teacher as being in the enemy camp and initially discredit anything the teacher says, may at some later point adopt the teacher's position if they have forgotten the source of the communication.

In the classroom, teachers usually have to persuade a whole group or individuals within a group. Groups may act as an agent of resistance or an agent of change. Teachers, therefore, need to understand group behavior in order to create a situation for persuasive communication. As agents of resistance, groups provide rewards for conformity: They filter information and they determine the level of credibility by such processes as stereotyping.

In the face of resistance, teachers may choose to use coercive persuasion, whereby they try to exert complete control with respect to the flow of communication and with respect to the administration of rewards and punishments. Under coercive persuasion, pupils *comply* with the teachers' wishes, but they do not adopt the teachers' rationale, as they do in gentle forms of persuasion.

If the group is operating in a democratic atmosphere, such as exists in a learner-centered classroom, change rather than resistance is more likely to be facilitated. Group discussion usually allows minority opinions to come out and be strengthened and, with less feelings of threat from authority, the group is better able to examine different viewpoints. The implication is that teachers should allow and even encourage dissenters to voice their opinions. If a large number of the members have committed themselves to change, they may subsequently carry along these dissenters through group discussion. Therefore, a democratic atmosphere is conductive to lasting persuasion.

In their effort to persuade, teachers often find student peer-group conformity to be a major obstacle. The crux of conformity is behavior based on norms. Therefore, teachers need to understand the operation of norms in order to change student behavior. A norm is defined as a standard or behavioral expectation shared by group members against which the validity of perceptions is judged and the appropriateness of feelings and behavior is evaluated. The concept of norm includes perceptual, cognitive, and affective responses as well as overt behavior. First-graders' positive attitudes toward learning to read are an example of conformity working to the teacher's advantage. Since most first-graders expect and are eager to learn to read, even those who have little aspiration to read may go through the reading process without the teachers' persuasion or coercion. In other words, the stragglers conform to the group norms. Thus, teachers can benefit by capitalizing on some existing norms and by converting other norms to suit their goals.

The degree of conformity in a particular classroom, as mediated by the peer group, of course, will vary. It varies with the focus of the group (task-oriented groups require less conformity than those that stress affiliative needs), and with the distribution of pressure to conform within the group (if pressed by group leaders, conformity becomes more crucial than if pressed by group members with low status). Note, too, that the peer group's pressure to conform in turn interacts with the individual student's status. Thus, a student with high peer-group status does not usually have to respond strongly to group pressure to conform, since he is already accepted. The lower-status student, however, will be fare more strongly affected by group pressures to conform because, if he is not responsive, he may be expelled from the group. If he wants to belong, he had better conform.

Conformity itself has been abstracted as a personality variable and has been studies under experimental conditions. Teachers who are interested in knowing the degrees of conformity in their own class may wish to measure it. Some of the frequently used paper-and-pencil instruments of conformity are the California F Scale (Adorno, 1950), the Edwards Personal Preference Schedule, and the Minnesota Multiphasic Personality Inventory.[1] The point is

---

[1] The Edwards and Minnesota tests are available from The Psychological Corporation, 304 East 45th Street, New York, New York 10017.

that, the stronger the need to conform generated in a classroom, the more the teacher will need to be aware of that need in teaching. By skillful use of persuasion, this pressure to conform can be harnessed to help the teacher achieve his goals for the class. Note that a more detailed discussion of theory and research on communication patterns can be found in Secord and Backman (1964).

Group behavior thus far has been discussed with reference to perception, persuasion, and conformity. The classroom, however, presents a special peer-group situation. Teachers, as teachers, play a special role in relation to the classroom peer group. If teachers can anticipate peer-group behavior and realize what their own powers are, they are more likely to affect peer-group norms and to be able to use social incentives to motivate classroom achievement.

The classroom peer group is not a formal institution like the family or school. In comparison to the adult peer group, the classroom peer group is usually less structured along socioeconomic lines. Since members are not concerned with each other in terms of production, as in a business situation, there is room for experimentation. Because relationships change frequently, especially with children in the first four years of school, the peer group has a transitory quality. It has a variety of functions, one of which is to transmit culture. It often reflects adult standards, teaches role behaviors, and provides a situation for the transfer of information.

The influence of the classroom peer group on the individual's behavior increases with the age of the child. Thus, a junior high school teacher (teaching children in the early adolescent years) has to be more concerned with peer-group pressures than does a first-grade teacher. However, as a corollary, the junior high school teacher can use these pressures for much greater potential impact. The present status of young adolescents as a functionless part of the greater society forces them to develop an even stronger peer group.

Coleman (1960) has studied extensively the influence of the school peer group on the individual. He took a sample of ten high schools in the midwestern area of the United States. Boys were asked if they most wanted to be remembered as:

1. A brilliant student
2. An athletic star
3. The most popular

Girls were given the following choice:

1. A brilliant student

2. An extracurricular leader
3. The most popular

When the results were plotted on a triangular graph, the responses of the boys centered near the athletic star vertex. The girls tended slightly less than the boys to want to be remembered as brilliant students. Coleman also asked students to name the classmates they considered to be in the leading crowd. He found that the leading crowd deviated from the student body position toward the athletic star vertex for the boys, and toward the activities leader or most popular for the girls.

Coleman then looked at the effect of social rewards, as defined by peer-group attitudes on academic achievement. For each high school, the average IQ of students who made A or A− (number of standard deviations above school mean) was correlated with percentage of other students mentioning "good grades" for the leading crowd. The relation was very strong. In schools where high achievement was valued, more bright students were high performers. Thus, if academic achievement is valued, bright students are more likely to put their energies into academic pursuits. Conversely, if athletics if valued, bright students are more likely to participate in athletic activities or areas other than academic pursuits. From these analyses, Coleman concluded that the adolescent subcultures in most schools in the United States are presently a deterrent to academic achievement, but that this same peer-group-derived energy could be diverted to academic achievement. How teachers might use peer-group subculture beneficially will be discussed in the next section.

Within a peer group, certain social roles arise, such as leaders and followers. However, in the classroom what may be more important is the teacher's social role as leader in relation to the peer group. Every role lends itself to certain images or stereotypes and certain expected functions. The stereotype of the teacher as "egghead" has already been mentioned. In addition, the teacher's personality may be stereotyped as idealistic, self-sacrificing, scholarly, virtuous, and humorless. The functions of the teacher in the classroom include mediator of learning, disciplinarian, parent substitute, judge, and surrogate of middle-class morality (Havighurst & Neugarten, 1962). (An old, but charming and insightful, treatment of the sociology of teaching including the roles of the teacher has been written by Waller, 1965 [1932].)

One of the most obvious and important roles of the teacher is that of leader, or wielder of power. Some of the types of power available to the teacher are expert, reward, referent, coercive, and legitimate. Power is a prerequisite of classroom control. How the teacher chooses to balance these powers greatly affects the overall classroom climate. For a moment, let us focus on the derivation and effects of the five types of powers mentioned.

1. Expert power arises because teachers have special skills in a subject matter. These cognitive or technical skills demand respect of the pupils. The teachers who emphasize their expert power tend to have a task- or achievement-oriented classroom. Pupils with high need for achievement tend to do well under this type of power (see Chapter 4).

2. Teachers' role as evaluator of pupils' work puts them in the position through their own social behavior to reward or punish. Teachers who use reward power are more likely to have classrooms that look to the teacher as arbiter or priorities and values. A system of positive reinforcement in which pupils agree with the teachers on what constitutes a positive reinforcer is most likely to be effective.

3. Since the teachers are the "older and wiser" members of the classroom, and hence represent the larger society, pupils regard them as a referent against whom they evaluate themselves. In this way, teachers serve as models to their pupils. The classroom atmosphere, in such cases, will be a personality cult centered around that teacher's particular personality.

4. Because the larger society assigns teachers to be in charge of the classroom, teachers have the coercive power to force pupils to do what they want, to a certain degree. Naturally, they cannot force pupils to want to learn, but, through the threat of punishment from outside the classroom, they can at least demand that pupils work while under the teachers' supervision. Teachers who wield coercive power set an autocratic atmosphere. Pupils who are willing to conform probably work best in this atmosphere.

5. Legitimate power represents those rights that the pupils feel teachers ought to have. Although this agreement varies greatly with the age of the peer group, most pupils grant that teachers may give assignments, judge the quality of work, and discipline the class as a whole. Most likely, a teacher stressing legitimate power will act as the resource person in a learner-centered climate. Pupils in this situation probably work best when teachers work with pupils to set most of the incentives.

While, theoretically, teachers are free to choose and balance these powers and roles and devise their own control patterns, in practice there are several limitations on choice. Pupils' expectations and the subject matter may modify the choice that is made. Furthermore, the balance depends on the teacher's personality, that is, what she is comfortable with. This personality factor is not to be ignored. Studies have shown that teacher success is often associated with warmth, and warmth implies spontaneity and acceptance of one's own feelings. A teacher forced out of her natural personality is unlikely to be spontaneous, accepting, or effective. Teaching style should be a matter of personal preference. Stephens (1967), for instance, promotes a whole theory of teaching around the idea of spontaneity. He feels that teachers should have a compulsion to talk about their subject matter. With regard to reinforcement, he advocates immediate and spontaneous correction through facial expression and verbal comment, rather than a deliberate resolve or sense of obligation, which may lead to postponement or neglect. This theory, however, is not meant to suggest that a teacher's personality cannot change or that teacher educators should not try to promote certain styles of teaching.

The discussion of the authority by which power is exerted by the teacher in the classroom inevitably leads to the question of classroom control. In research studies conducted on classroom control patterns, the kinds of control can usually be placed into one of three categories: undirected, teacher directed, or pupil directed. This classification system follows Lewin's three models of leadership, previously described (laissez-faire, authoritarian, and democratic). Cronbach (1963) summarizes the characteristics of each control pattern.

With the undirected pattern (from laissez-faire leadership), emotional security tends to be low because of low accomplishment. This situation produces high anxiety. Energy is wasted as pupils are disorderly and easily distracted. Learning skills are little better than those in spontaneous play. However, if the group, despite lack of structuring by the teacher, is able to impose structure on itself, then the pupils become very self-motivating. In the teacher-controlled group (authoritarian leadership), anxiety about what is to be done is generally low, since the teacher sets standards. Because the class is then quite task oriented, there is usually little social satisfaction. Efficiency is high, if pupils do not rebel against the teacher's directions. While content material is learned well, there is little opportunity to develop social skills or to learn to work independently of teacher supervision. Under group control (democratic leadership, where teacher and pupils plan together), frustration is common if the group feels that planning is a waste of time. However, enjoyment is high if the group feels that it is progressing and there are friendly interactions. In terms of efficiency, this group pattern leads to acceptance of goals and continued effort even when the teacher is absent. Cognitive gain is high, since free expression of ideas and feelings is allowed, but achievement is generally not as great as under authoritarian leadership. Group control provides an opportunity in social skills through teamwork, leadership, and self-control.

This classification system, of course, is only a set of generalizations convenient for making predictions. There is a lot of fluctuation, depending on the particular situation. The basic criticism of teacher and classroom research is that the variables are not well controlled and that they are complexly interpreted. Thus, the results of studies on teacher-centered or learner-centered classrooms are inconsistent, because climate depends on the nature of the task, personality and skills of group members, group structure, and especially the teacher's position in the group structure. These variables are so difficult to interpret and control that different results from seemingly similar experiments are to be expected.

The variables discussed thus far, types of communication, peer-group behavior, social role, and control patterns, have all centered on the classroom itself. The analysis of school organization, which has a wider scope, is one of the most recent approaches that permits classroom social variables to be seen in a different perspective. The institution of school can be regarded as a self-contained social system with unique organization and unique patterns of expectations binding on its members. Its function is education. The school is usually stratified by age at lower ages and by subject matter and level of difficulty at the upper levels. It has its own physical plant with rituals and ceremonies. Its values are usually middle class: It emphasizes punctuality, honesty, responsibility, and respect for property, along with a mixture of competitiveness and cooperation, and stresses mastery and achievement. Examples of its formal structure are age grading, time structure, physical space, subordination of staff, and the marking system.

Individual differences between schools are derived from the amount of influence from the various inputs. The current approach to schools is a "systems analysis of individuals, roles, subgroups within the entire construct of a school's way of carrying on the business of socialization" (White, 1969, p. 197). Eventually, this technique can be modified for use in the classroom itself. Studies to date have been on high school and college climates, using the College Characteristics Inventory, or CCI (Pace & Stern, 1958), which is a 300-item objective questionnaire for student description of environment, and the Organizational Climate Description Questionnaire (Halpin & Croft, 1963), which uses teachers' perceptions to judge climate on a continuum of "open" to "autonomous" to "controlled" to "familiar" to "paternal" to "closed." So far, results with these instruments have not provided a systematic understanding of the variables assessed. The difficulty of this kind of analysis is that the data are usually gathered at one point in time, rather than longitudinally. Furthermore, interaction effects have usually been ignored.

As an example of what kind of data and interpretation is involved in systems analysis, the results of some studies conducted on school organizational climate will be described here. Backman and Secord (1968) have singled out three areas of descriptive variables involved in school organizational climate. The first is the informal structure and culture of the student body. The second is the characteristics of the school: size, type of program, and faculty. The third is the background and personal characteristics of the students. Trow (1962), using the CCI, arrived at four types of college climates: collegiate, vocational, academic, and nonconformist. The source of differences between campus climate comes from fluctuations within the three variables mentioned above and from the interactions of those variables. Thus, the school climate sets another limit on teachers' choice of control patterns. For instance, academic teachers who are highly task-oriented may have to modify their techniques if they are teaching in a collegiate (high stress on social activities) atmosphere.

An institutional or formal structure is seen as a pattern of expectations and norms maintained by external rewards, such as social approval and money. This type of group, such as a business or a school, serves as a means to an end. When the end is reached, the group may dissolve or members change. The subinstitutional or informal structure involves maintenance by rewards that are intrinsic to the social interaction. Group membership is an end in itself. For instance, a work group may lower its output standard to alleviate the destructive costs of competition: hence, the disapproval of the high achiever so often exhibited, unfortunately, by high school student groups.

No matter what the type of purpose of the group, membership usually depends on the balance of rewards and costs (White, 1969). One of the teacher's duties is to make task activities related to high reward and low cost. Unfortunately, the student's peer group controls its own reward system, which may be in conflict with the one the teacher controls. This information should not be used to rationalize inactivity on the teacher's part. If the teacher is aware of the power of a reward structure, she can build and influence the peer group's reward structure and she can develop a social system in the classroom where her energies are spent less on behavior problems and more on teaching and guiding her students. (See, too, the introductory section of this chapter for a more detailed discussion of reinforcement and learning.)

Most tasks initially depend on external reward for maintenance. The eventual goal is to have intrinsic rewards maintain the activity. For example, to motivate or arouse the child's interest, the teacher may organize a class "treasure hunt," with a prize for the child or group that follows the map accurately. Initially, the child engages in the task because of the prize. Hopefully, in the course of time, map reading and hence following clues and directions will become fun and rewarding in themselves.

A discussion of the operation of reward structures in a group is incomplete without mentioning punishment. According to Thorndike (1932) and Skinner (1948), positive reinforcement should be used virtually at all times, because punishment basically is ineffective. Punishment suppresses, but does not eliminate, the undesirable behavior and does not replace unwanted behavior with wanted behavior. The study of Kounin and Gump (1968) gives a graphic example of the effects of a schedule of reinforcement versus a schedule of punishment. They took six classrooms containing 174 first-graders from a wide range of socioeconomic backgrounds. Of the six classroom teachers, three were judged punitive and three nonpunitive, according to the ratings of the principals and outsiders. All classes were judged to be well behaved and working at grade level. The children were interviewed on the following questions: "What is the worst thing a child can do in class?" and "Why is it so bad?" The results showed that children with punitive teachers showed more aggression in their misconducts, less concern with learning and school-unique values, some reduction in rationality pertaining to school conduct, and less trust of school.

Generally speaking, the major drawback of punishment is that it produces anxiety and fear, affects that are not usually conducive to learning. It has been found that behavior stopped by fear usually recurs spontaneously when the fear-inducing agent (the teacher) is not present. Furthermore, the use of punishment on the part of teachers often sets an example of what they are trying to prevent. However, punishment can have the advantage of stopping undesirable behavior immediately. For example, if several pupils are shouting or hurting their classmates, a teacher may use force to stop them from disrupting a classroom activity. Although the pupils' anxiety and hostility may thus increase, in the meantime the teacher has an opportunity to continue the classroom activity and otherwise deal with the problem that created the disruption in the first place. The ongoing classroom activity may eventually draw the disruptive pupils into its circle and give them an opportunity to exhibit positive behavior.

Before going into specific recommendations of social incentives in the classroom, several traditional incentives will be mentioned here to give an idea of how to examine the value of an incentive in light of reinforcement theory. Two of the most common incentives are marks or grades and winning in a competitive situation. Marks are a type of external reinforcement. While there is nothing inherently wrong with external reinforcement, it does not have the advantage of self-perpetuation that intrinsic reinforcement has. The task itself does not constitute the reward. Furthermore, marks generally lack immediacy or optimal timing, since they are given at the end of the task or term. They do not indicate progress through the task. An excellent discussion of marks and similar reinforcers is provided by Skinner (1968).

The incentive of winning through competition is a useful device in a classroom, but it may have several negative side effects. Like marks, it is an external reward. A pupil may have no interest in the math assignment, but may want to do well just to beat classmates. For the moment, this system works; the pupil does his or her math. However, what happens to math when the classmates are not there to compete against? Furthermore, competition may be costly, because pupils do not have the advantage of exchanging information and learning from each other. Later in life, they will need this skill of cooperation. Furthermore, the anxiety that competition arouses may interfere with the learning process. And if there are winners, there will also be losers. Competitiveness is better suited, then, to a society where an educated elite is desired. It is not as well suited to a society that wishes to educate the vast majority of its members.

APPLICATIONS

As mentioned earlier, it is assumed that the teacher's underlying goal is to create an environment conducive to learning, that is, an environment that will motivate the child and convert learning itself into a reinforcing experience, thereby motivating the child still further. The purpose of this section is to outline several methods that teachers might use to achieve their goals. These methods are applicable to cognitive and affective goals alike. There is no proposed right or wrong method for achieving these ends. However, the several approaches, offered here as options for the teacher's choice, are being worked with now.

1. Goal setting is a key aspect of motivation from the standpoint of reinforcement. DeCharms (1972) has experimented with goal setting in terms of a person's self-perception in the area of personal causation. He suggests that a person sees himself at some point along a continuum from "origin" to "pawn." By "origin," he is referring to the individual who intentionally initiates behavior to produce a change in the environment. The kind of change referred to here is usually small, tangible, and directly related to the initiator. The "pawn," on the other hand, feels that something external to himself compels him to certain behaviors. It is deCharms' hypothesis that an origin person is more likely to be motivated to achieve in the classroom than the pawn. For example, origin people feel that the work they produce is

directly related to the marks they receive. Pawns would see little relation between their input and consequent events. (See also Chapter 3, on locus of control.) DeCharms proposes specific steps to enhance "origin" behavior:

a. determine realistic goals
b. find out strengths and weaknesses of a person
c. determine concrete action
d. find ways to measuring progress

Generally speaking, these are steps of successful goal setting. However, deCharms applies them specifically to personal causation training. In one of his experiments, he first trained teachers in "origin–pawn" theory. He next measured the origin teaching approach in the classroom and the origin behavior on the part of the pupils. Finally, academic achievement was measured. The results showed that the training had effects on teachers and pupils both in terms of an increase in origin behavior and an increase in pupil achievement.

2. Goal setting is important not only from the standpoint of the individual alone but also from that of the individual in the group. First, as deCharms' work implies, the goals must satisfy the individual's interest in an obvious way. However, as the discussion of peer-group behavior indicates, the individual wants to hold the approval of the group as well. Many researchers are suggesting the use of group competition or games in academic as well as athletic pursuits. Group competition, unlike individual competition, promotes cooperation, at least within the group or team. Of course, there is still the possibility of hostility building up between groups. However, under a spirit of cooperation, ideas are freely exchanged and certain social needs are fulfilled.

3. The social aspects of peer-group acceptance can provide the social motivation and reinforcement that an academic task alone may not. In addition to being a source of reinforcement, the classroom is a place of norm setting. Coleman's study, for instance, described the importance of athletic ability in some adolescent subculture. However, since norms are situational and not inherent to the group, it is possible to change the conditions of the group in such a way that norms will be changed. That is, if pupils saw academic tasks and cooperation as beneficial, and athletic prowess and competition as costly, new norms might evolve. The now popular "sensitivity group" or "T-group" is an intensive method used for norm changing (Schein & Bennis, 1965). A group of people gather for the purpose of shedding their accustomed defenses built up through experiences in the larger society. Under the leadership of a trainer who creates a safe atmosphere, they work on

developing new attitudes and skills, such as openness, authenticity, and listening. Old norms, roles, and stereotypes disappear. It is hoped that the members will internalize the changes and carry them to a larger society.

Unlike the affect approach of the T-group, the Taba (Taba & Elkins, 1966) method tries to change norms cognitively. The teacher or leader provokes but does not openly evaluate pupils' thoughts. After the teacher throws out a question to stimulate divergent thinking, the peer group arrives at conclusions through discussion. The teacher never evaluates an answer as right or wrong. It has been found that goal setting is more successful when the peer group has power to raise and lower the teacher's goals. The Taba method represents one type of learner-centered climate where this is possible.

4. The teacher role itself can be used as a social incentive through the process of modeling. Again, there are no right or wrong kinds of models. For instance, identification can arise with democratic or authoritarian leaders. A pupil may identify with a democratic teacher because the teacher is concenred with emotional needs. Hence, the teacher becomes an object of liking. With the authoritarian leader, greater status and power may stimulate identification.

5. The systems analysis approach to classroom and school organization suggests a method of natural reinforcers that set an environment conducive to learning. The aim of this approach is to understand what variables and their interactions produce what results. After a certain degree of predictability is established, the next step is to regulate input variables to produce desired results. The name of this approach does not imply that the natural reinforcers are personal or put there by nature, but, rather, that they are part of the new ongoing system. The systems approach is, as the name suggests, systematic. Undesirable behaviors may be reinforced when personal and other environmental variables are unsystematically used. Skinner advocates instead the use of programed instruction, which sets goals and reinforces in small, specified, controlled steps. While some caution in the use of natural reinforcers is wise, environmental and personal reinforcers are unavoidable since they are a part of human society. Therefore, an awareness and understanding of social variables can help educators use readily available tools for achieving their goals. Some of these tools have been discussed in this chapter and they are summarized here to give educators specific ideas for a course in action.

a. *Assessment* of the present classroom situation is essential. Several possibilities are open, such as the sociogram for analysis of group dynamics. For themselves, teachers may wish to use formal teacher questionnaires or some evaluation of their own devising to examine their own attitudes and style.

b. *Resetting goals* in light of the current status comes next. Teachers need to look at how they perceive the class and how the class perceives them. Change may be warranted. For instance, they may wish to raise or lower their own and their students' expectations.

c. *Social means* or achieving goals can then be put into operation. Teachers must choose the kind and degree of method according to what they wish to accomplish.

   (1) *Persuasion:* To motivate pupils, teachers may need to increase their own credibility or raise the interest and clarity of the issue.

   (2) *Conformity:* Peer-group pressures and group competition can enhance learning once norms conducive to learning are established.

   (3) *Modeling:* Since the teacher role is one of setting an example to pupils, once teachers find a power system that fits themselves and the group, they can use their role as a framework to accomplish their goals.

   (4) *Personal causation:* Teachers can encourage pupils to see themselves as initiators of their own behavior.

   (5) *Reinforcement:* Teachers can coordinate the system of external and internal rewards in such a way that many social incentives eventually are internalized and become self-perpetuating.

RECOMMENDATIONS AND NEW DIRECTIONS

Before plunging into more classroom research and changes in teaching methods, one must reconsider these pursuits in light of the possible obsolescence of the traditional classroom. Innovative theoreticians like Ivan Illich (1970) are advocating the "deschooling" of society. Illich maintains that most learning, or at least the most valuable, meaningful learning occurs in the larger society, rather than in the schools. Jencks reinforces this idea with his hypothesis that the expenditure on schools and even academic achievement is not related to success in the larger society. Illich recommends replacing schools by a movement toward education in the community. Bremer and Moschziker (1971) of the Parkway Program have already put the community approach into practice. McClelland (1971), a classroom researcher himself, fully acknowledges the possible obsolescence of the classroom, but goes on to say that there are many characteristics of the classroom situation that are applicable to any learning situations. For instance, theories of reinforcement, peer-group behavior, and social role are still relevant. In place of classroom climate and school organization, one might substitute community climate and organization.

A dominant trend of education in this century has been a greater emphasis on the learner. Dewey's emphasis on the motivational and emotional aspect of the learner was the vanguard of this movement. Educators began to recognize that subject matter was not necessarily learned simply because it was taught. Postman and Weingartner (1969) are present proponents of this point of view. Much of the current research on the relation between teacher behavior and pupil achievement is analyzed in terms of the interactions between pupil traits, such as aptitudes and personality, and teacher personalities, such as cognitive styles and methods, or pupil traits and classroom climates (Berliner & Cahen, 1973). Wispé's study, mentioned earlier, was one of the early aptitude– or trait–treatment interaction studies.

In terms of future research, refinement of observational instruments is needed. The goals of classroom research should involve a two-pronged approach, general and specific, according to Travers (1971). He suggests that researchers should seek those conditions that tend to permeate the many learning situations, but also those conditions that state the specific relation between a given teaching procedure and the acquisition of specific skills.

With the many innovations in technology, more research in communication patterns is needed, with special reference to mass media. According to McLuhan (1964), not only is the information presented by media becoming a major source of learning material, but also the media themselves are teaching something to the recipient. Research to date indicates that mass communication serve to raise awareness, but does not necessarily change behavior. Mass communication is already coming into the schools through closed-circuit television and public educational television. Its effects on education need to be examined.

From the standpoint of teaching, a sociological perspective and an understanding of classroom or social incentives can help teachers become aware of what behaviors are associated with what circumstances. It is then possible for teachers to try to vary the circumstances to achieve their goals, whatever they may be. While specific teaching methods and goals are situational, there are certain pervasive goals of education. One of these goals is stated very well by Lee (1967), who speaks from an anthropological view of society and the individual. She proposes, "The individual experiences through himself, is motivated within himself, but needs society to enable him, to evoke him, to encourage, to guide him into strengthening himself into becoming a person who can be autonomous" (p. 62). At the same time, the classroom, as a microcosm of society, can provide many of the social incentives necessary to motivate and facilitate the child's contributions to the larger society.

ANNOTATED BIBLIOGRAPHY

Deutsch, M., & Hornstein, H. A. The social psychology of education. In J. R. Davitz & S. Ball (Eds.), *Psychology of the educational process*. New York: McGraw-Hill, 1970. Pp. 179–222.
The authors present schooling from a social psychological point of view, that is very close to that of Dewey. They give a comprehensive summary of theory and research to develop this perspective, and discuss current trends.

Gage, N. L. (Ed.). *Handbook of research on teaching*. Chicago: Rand McNally, 1963.
This book is a comprehensive collection of research on teaching up to 1960. It includes articles on theory, methodology, major variables, and specific grade levels and subject matters.

Krumboltz, J. D., & Krumboltz, H. B. *Changing children's behavior*. Englewood Cliffs, N.J.: Prentice-Hall, 1972.
A practical guide for teachers and parents who have specific goals they wish to achieve with their children. It discusses a variety of methods based on the theory of reinforcement, such as shaping, developing, and maintaining new behaviors.

Miles, M. B. *Learning to work in groups: A program guide for educational leaders*. New York: Teachers College Press, 1965.
The author starts from the assumption that most school activities function by group process. (In addition to the classroom, he mentions parent interviews, staff and committee meetings, and board hearings.) Therefore, he advocates a movement to increase skills in group functioning. He analyzes group behavior in practice terms, giving specific steps toward leadership and group training.

Rosenshine, B. *Teaching behaviors and student achievement*. London: National Foundation for Educational Research, 1971.
This book reviews about 50 correlational studies conducted in classrooms. The studies are selected with an emphasis of teacher characteristics and on pupil achievement. The reviews are organized around the following topics: teacher approval and disapproval, cognitive behaviors, variation in teacher behavior, enthusiasm, amount of student–teacher interaction, ratings, and demographic characteristics of teachers.

Sears, P. S., & Hilgard, E. R. The teacher's role in the motivation of the learner. In E. R. Hilgard (Ed.), *Theories of learning and instruction: The sixty-third yearbook of the National Society for the Study of Education* (Pt. 1). Chicago: University of Chicago Press, 1964.
These authors, like Rosenshine, review a number of teacher–pupil studies, but

they emphasize, instead, teacher behaviors. They categorize social interactions into affective, evaluative, and cognitive domains.

REFERENCES

Adorno, T. W., Frenkel-Brunswik, E., Levinson, D. J., & Sanford, R. N. *The authoritarian personality.* New York: Harper & Row, 1950.

Anderson, H. H., Brewer, J. E., & Reed, M. F. Studies of teacher's classroom personalities. III. Follow-up studies of the effects of dominative and integrative contacts on children's behavior. *Applied Psychology Monographs*, 1946, No. 11.

Backman, C. W., & Secord, P. F. *A social psychological view of education.* New York: Harcourt, Brace, and World, 1968.

Bales, R. F. *Interaction process analysis.* Cambridge, Mass.: Addison-Wesley, 1950.

Barr, A. S. The measurement of teacher characteristics and prediction of teaching efficiency. *Review of Educational Research*, 1952, *22*, 169–174.

Berliner, D. C., & Cahen, L. S. Trait–treatment interactions and learning. In F. N. Kerlinger (Ed.), *Review of research in education.* Itasca, Ill.: Peacock, 1973.

Bremer, J., & Moscheisker, M. *The school without walls: Philadelphia's Parkway Program.* New York: Holt, 1971.

Coleman, J. S. The adolescent subculture and academic achievement. *American Journal of Sociology*, 1960, *65*, 337–347.

Cronbach, L. J. *Educational psychology* (2nd ed.) New York: Harcourt, Brace, and World, 1963.

deCharms, R. Personal causation training in the schools. *Journal of Applied Social Psychology*, 1972, *2*, 95–113.

Dewey, J. *The school and society.* Chicago: University of Chicago Press, 1915.

Dewey, J. *Democracy and education.* New York: Macmillan, 1916.

Flanders, N. A. Teacher–pupil contacts and mental hygiene. *Journal of Social Issues*, 1959, *15*, 30–39.

Flanders, N. A. *Teacher influence, pupil attitudes, and achievement* (Cooperative Research Monograph, No. 12, OE-25040). Washington, D.C.: U.S. Office of Education, 1965.

Gage, N. L. (Ed.). *Handbook of research on teaching.* Chicago: Rand McNally, 1963.

Gordon, I. J. *Studying the child in the school.* New York: Wiley, 1966.

Grimes, J. W., & Allinsmith, W. Compulsivity, anxiety, and school achievement. *Merrill-Palmer Quarterly*, 1961, *7*, 247–272.

Gronlund, N. E. *Sociometry in the classroom.* New York: Harper, 1959.

Halpin, A. W., & Croft, D. B. *The organizational climate of schools.* Chicago: University of Chicago, Midwest Administration Center, 1963.

Havighurst, R. J., & Neugarten, B. L. *Society and education* (2nd ed.). Boston: Allyn & Bacon, 1962.

Illich, I. *Deschooling society.* New York: Harper & Row, 1970.

James, H. W. Cause of teacher failure in Alabama. *Peabody Journal of Education*, 1930, *7*, 269–271.

Kounin, J. S., & Gump, P. V. The comparative influence of punitive and nonpunitive teachers upon children's concepts of school management. In W. H. MacGinitie and

S. Ball (Eds.), *Readings in psychological foundations of education.* New York: McGraw-Hill, 1968. Pp. 232–240.

Lee, D. A socio-anthropological view of independent learning. In G. T. Gleason (Ed.), *The theory and nature of independent learning.* Scranton, Pa.: International Textbook, 1967, Pp. 51–63.

Lewin, K., Lippitt, R., & White, R. K. Patterns of aggressive behavior in experimentally created social climates. *Journal of Social Psychology,* 1939, *10,* 271–299.

McClelland, J. E. Classroom-teaching research: A philosophical critique. In I. Westbury and A. A. Bellack (Eds.), *Research into classroom process: Recent developments and next steps.* New York: Teachers College Press, 1971. Pp. 3–15.

McLuhan, H. M. *Understanding media: The extensions of man.* New York: McGraw-Hill, 1964.

Moreno, J. L. *Who shall survive?* Washington, D.C.: Nervous and Mental Disease Publishing, 1934.

Pace, C. R., & Stern, G. C. An approach to the measurement of psychological characteristics of college environments. *Journal of Educational Psychology,* 1958, *49,* 269–277.

Papageorgis, D:, & McGuire, W. J. The generality of immunity to persuasion produced by pre-exposure to weakened counterarguments. *Journal of Abnormal and Social Psychology,* 1961, *62,* 475–481.

Postman, N., & Weingartner, C. *Teaching as a subversive activity.* New York: Dell, 1969.

Rosenshine, B. *Teaching behaviors and student achievement.* London: National Foundation for Educational Research, 1971.

Rosenthal, R., & Jacobson, L. *Pygmalion in the classroom: Teacher expectation and pupils' intellectual development.* New York: Holt, 1968.

Ryans, D. G. *Characteristics of teachers.* Washington, D.C.: American Council on Education, 1960.

Schein, E. H., & Bennis, W. G. *Personal and organizational change through group methods: The laboratory approach.* New York: Wiley, 1965.

Sears, P. S., & Hilgard, E. R. The teacher's role in the motivation of the learner. In E. R. Hilgard (Ed.), *Theories of learning and instruction: The sixty-third yearbook of the National Society for the Study of Education* (Pt. 1). Chicago: University of Chicago Press, 1964.

Secord, P. F., & Backman, C. W. *Social psychology.* New York: McGraw-Hill, 1964.

Skinner, B. F. *Walden II.* New York: Macmillan, 1948.

Skinner, B. F. *The technology of teaching.* New York: Appleton, 1968.

Stephens, J. M. *The process of schooling: A psychological examination.* New York: Holt, 1967.

Taba, H., & Elkins, D. *Teaching strategies for the culturally disadvantaged.* Chicago: Rand McNally, 1966.

Thelen, H. A. Educational dynamics: Theory and research. *Journal of Social Issues,* 1950, *6,* 5–95.

Thorndike, E. L. *The fundamentals of learning.* New York: Columbia University, Teachers College, 1932.

Travers, R. M. W. Some further reflections on the nature of a theory of instruction. In I. Westbury and A. A. Bellack (Eds.), *Research into classroom processes: Recent developments and next steps.* New York: Teachers College Press, 1971. Pp. 23–40.

Trow, M. Student cultures and administrative action. In R. L. Sutherland, W. H. Holtzman, E. A. Koile, & B. K. Smith (Eds.), *Personality factors on the collect campus.* Austin: University of Texas Press, 1962. Pp. 203–206.

Wagman, M. Attitude change and the authoritarian personality. *Journal of Psychology,* 1955, *40,* 3–24.

Waller, W. *The sociology of teaching.* New York: Wiley, 1965. Originally published in 1932.

White, W. F. *Psychosocial principles applied to classroom teaching.* New York: McGraw-Hill, 1969.

Wickman, E. K. *Children's behavior and teacher's attitudes.* New York: Commonwealth Fund, 1928.

Wispé, L. G. Evaluating section teaching methods in the introductory course. *Journal of Educational Research,* 1951, *45,* 161–186.

Withall, J. An objective measurement of a teacher's classroom interactions. *Journal of Educational Psychology,* 1956, *47,* 203–212.

Withall, J., & Lewis, W. W. Social interaction in the classroom. In N. L. Gage (Ed.), *Handbook of research on teaching.* Chicago: Rand McNally, 1963. Pp. 683–714.

Wright, H. F., Barker, R. G., Nall, J., & Schoggen, P. Toward a psychological ecology of the classroom. *Journal of Educational Research,* 1951, *45,* 187–200.

9

Effects of Nutrition on
Educational Development

MARGARET NANCY WHITE

Northeastern University

The purpose of this chapter is to discuss the effects of physiological needs on the educational development of children. In more specific terms, the relation of nutrition, hunger, and disease to intellectual development and the motivation of learning behavior will be examined. Significant studies in the field will be reviewed, followed by recommendations for further research and for implementation of programs for change.

PHYSIOLOGICAL AND PSYCHOLOGICAL NEEDS

Before proceeding with problems of health status, it would be useful to discuss the relation between physiology and psychology. A physiological need is defined as a biological process involving a homeostatic imbalance (Murray, 1964). A dichotomy is sometimes made between physiological needs and psychological needs, with hunger, nutrition, thirst, and sleep in the first group, and needs such as security, intellectual stimulation, and self-actualization in the latter. Furthermore, physiological needs are considered innate (Fuller, 1962), while psychological needs are thought to be acquired or learned. However, a strict dichotomy between classifications is overly simplistic, since many needs have characteristics of both poles.

A. H. Maslow (1954) proposed a dominance hierarchy relation between physiological and psychological motives. At the bottom of the scale are physiological needs. These are followed by safety needs, belonging needs, love needs, esteem needs and at the top, self-actualizing needs. According to Maslow, the lower needs must be met before the child's behavior can be strongly influenced by needs higher on the scale. For example, a child who is chronically hungry can hardly be expected to be particularly concerned with matters of security, status, or performance in school. The hungry child's major concern is to get food and his psychic energies will be directed to that goal. One of the classical studies offering evidence for Maslow's theory was conducted among a group of conscientious objectors in Minnesota (Keys, Brozek, Henschel, Mickelson, & Taylor, 1950). During their schedule of semistarvation, they thought of little else but food and lost interest in all other activities.

Maslow's theory has implications for learning behavior and classroom achievement. If the child's survival needs are not met, he will not be activated by the motives necessary for learning. Therefore, though he may be in school, he is unlikely to be developing in his academic work. These losses in achievement will be difficult to make up. Furthermore, certain undesirable learnings may occur. For example, he may be learning that he is a failuure at school. Although Maslow's theory of dominance hierarchy has not been adequately tested within the upper-level motives, the basic premise of the relation of physiological and psychological motives is widely accepted (Cofer & Appley, 1964).

The relation between the two kinds of motives is further suggested by some neurophysiological findings. Hunger is apparently regulated by the hypothalamus, which reacts to the sugar level in the blood. This kind of regulatory process does not occur in isolation of other processes. There is evidence that the reticular activating system (RAS), which is a part of the central nervous system, is involved in sleeping, wakefulness, and fine gradations in attention. Sensory information such as that created by hunger pangs activates the RAS, which, in turn, prepares the cortex for related incoming information by creating a state of general and diffuse readiness. The cortex in return sends information that regulates the RAS by interpreting the importance of the incoming stimulus (Hilgard & Bower, 1966). For instance, hunger just before evening dinner is interpreted as usual and a person continues normal activities for that time period, but hunger while on a hiking trip through the mountains might create a considerable level of arousal. The interaction of the RAS and the cortex has implications for physiological needs and learning. That is, while a basic drive such as hunger is present and is activating the child, intellectual activities requiring a focus of energies in a different direction are ruled out. In short, the theory and research suggest that physiological motives affect the psychological motives needed for learning. This relationship will be discussed later.

HEALTH STATUS

The physiological factors treated in this paper—nutrition, hunger, and disease—are all part of the general topic of "health status." Malnutrition is defined as a nutrient imbalance resulting from the poor quality of the nutrient source, a deficit of one or more nutrients, or a reduction in diet below the minimum daily requirement (Coursin, 1972). The latter descriptor implies hunger. However, hunger usually bears the connotation of immediate physiological discomfort, while malnutrition implies effects on long-term physiological and psychological growth. The term *disease*, in this paper, will refer to all diseases, but particularly to those resulting from malnutrition. The two most common are kwashiorkor and marasmus. Kwashiorkor comes from a deficit of protein calories, compensated with calories from sugar and fat. Marasmus results from low intake of all calories.

In dealing with health problems, one must look at what and where they are, and to what extent they exist. Our intuitive judgments are sometimes quite misleading. For example, until the late 1960s, hunger and malnutrition as a problem in the United States of America went unrecognized. Later reports showed the gross inadequacies in the diets of many American children (Birch & Gussow, 1970; *Hunger, USA*, 1968; Myers, Mabel, & Stare, 1968; Myers, O'Brien, Mabel, & Stare, 1968; McGovern, 1971). The conclusion was clear. Hunger and malnutrition exist on a wide scale in the United States, a country whose population has, on the average, relatively high intakes of proteins and calories.

The problem of hunger in developing countries has long been known, and it still runs rampant. A recent statistic suggests that 30% of the world's children (some 300 million) are suffering from malnutrition (Winick, 1969). In terms of general health status, a 1960 estimate from UNICEF suggests that 750 million of the world's one billion children will live a shortened life because of hunger and sickness (Latham, 1969). The numbers have increased since then.

Within a particular region, the type of malnutrition must be carefully examined. For instance, in developing countries where babies are breast-fed, malnutrition in infants does not occur until after weaning, while in the

United States of America, where breast-feeding is less likely to occur, malnutrition often starts in the first months of life (Chase & Martin, 1970).
Ironically, even in well-developed countries, and even among the affluent,
there is a problem of malnutrition. With the development of processed foods
and increased choice of products, people tend to get their calories from fats
and sugars (Altschul, 1972). In addition, the affluent have the problem of
overnutrition. In short, there are few people whom malnutrition does not
touch in some way.

MEASUREMENT PROBLEMS

Quantifying nutrition and its effects on educational development is not
any easy task. Nutrition as a factor is difficult to single out from concomitant
variables. Furthermore, certain kinds of experimentation in areas of human
health are ruled out because they are unethical (for example, withholding
needed treatment to children in a control group). Measures of nutrition and
the experimental study of malnutrition are not well developed.

Animal models, though a source of well-controlled experimental data,
have limitations since human conditions are not necessarily analogous to
animal conditions. In clinical studies, anthropometric measures (height,
weight, skin fold) and biochemical analysis (urine content and hemoglobin
level) give an indication of nutritional status. Conditions at birth, especially
weight and prematurity, may reflect nutritional status. The nutritional habits
of pregnant and lactating mothers also give clues to the nutritional status of
the infant (Birch & Gussow, 1970; Jelliffe, 1968; Committee on Maternal
Nutrition, 1970). Yet even when clinical data from these measures are
available, the scope of problems of a given population is not necessarily clear.
Field studies of food assistance programs again provide much data, but an
adequate evaluation of these programs is lacking.

Assessments of the direct effects of malnutrition are often ambiguous.
Educational development cannot be used as a measure of the effect of
malnutrition because it usually depends on economic status and cultural
background as well as on nutrition. Thus, some indirect measures of the
effects of nutrition sometimes have to be used, such as measurement of the
brain itself, intelligence tests, and behavioral clues. Behavioral measures such
as tardiness and absences *may* reflect physiological conditions, and affective
reactions such as apathy, listlessness, and irritability *may* indicate a child's
need to conserve energy for basic functions. Such behaviors are not conducive
to classroom learning but neither are they necessarily indicative of poor
nutrition.

In summary, the methodology of measuring physiological factors and their psychological implications is far from perfect. Yet, as long as the problem exists, a solution must be sought. The clumsiness of the methodology must not become an excuse for inaction. In the next section, where specific studies will be discussed, it will be seen that there already exists sufficiently worthwhile evidence for action.

HEALTH STATUS AND ITS CORRELATES—A REVIEW OF THE LITERATURE

One of the major questions researchers have asked is, "How do specific nutrient deficiencies affect brain growth and learning behavior?" Findings indicate that malnutrition affects the physiological development of the nervous system and that learning behavior is indeed impaired. The degree of damage is still open to question.

The interaction of malnutrition and disease seems to have a synergistic effect in human beings. Vitamin deficiencies often set the stage for disease. Disease, on the other hand, can affect nutritional status. For example, Scrimshaw (1972) points out that a child who is frequently exposed to diarrhea and other infections suffers from protein loss in several ways. First, most solid food is withdrawn from the intestine, and often there is a decrease in protein absorption. Furthermore, there is an increased metabolic loss of protein. As a result, the infected child actually needs extra protein. Scrimshaw, Taylor, and Gordon (1968, p. 266) claim that, "in an estimated three-fourths of the world's population, an appreciable part of the excess morbidity and mortality in children is attributable to this synergism."

Animal researchers have found that protein-calorie malnutrition in monkeys results in delays in the development of neuromotor responses, a tendency toward hyperemotion, and negative reactions to novel stimuli (Levitsky, 1971). Coursin (1972) traced the effect of a vitamin B_6 deficiency. He found implications for epilepsy, mongolism, and phenylketonuria.

Winick and Rosso (1969) investigated the effects of general malnutrition by comparing brains of children who died of malnutrition to the brains of those who died of accidental causes. By determining diriboxynucleic acid (DNA) content, they estimated cell number in brains and found a significantly smaller number in malnourished children. Head size, lipid development, and dendrite arboreation were also reduced.

A longitudinal study using physical and mental growth measures was conducted in Cape Town, South Africa (Stoch & Smythe, 1963). The researchers followed two groups of children, one considered grossly malnourished, the other normal, over a period of 7 years from age 2. For intelligence measures, they used the Gesell Test, the Merrill–Palmer, and after age 6, a South African modification of the 1916 Stanford revision of the Binet–Simon. At the end of the study, there was a significant difference of 22.62 points in IQ between the two groups. The children of the malnourished group were also shorter, lighter, and had smaller head circumferences. However, the causal relationship was confounded by the fact that the normally nourished group also had a better home environment and had gone to nursery school.

The reversibility of damage caused by malnutrition is another basic question for research. It is generally hypothesized that damage is a function of time of onset and duration of malnutrition. It is thought that if periods normally characterized by rapid brain growth coincide with periods of malnutrition, the probability of irreversible brain damage is increased. Such a period is known as a *critical growth period.* In humans, for example, rapid myelinzation of the brain occurs during the last 6 to 8 months of pregnancy. This is followed by very rapid brain growth during the first 1½ or 2 years of extrauterine life (Canosa, 1970). Thus, malnutrition during these periods may have quite profound and irreversible effects on later learning and development.

Rapid growth periods are still the subject of much research effort. Several clinical studies give evidence for the critical growth hypothesis. Cravioto and Robles (1965) followed the development of 20 children in Children's Hospital, Mexico City, suffering from kwashiorkor, a problem caused by nutritional deficiency. Children under 6 months of age upon admittance did not regain mental age but, with older children, who were 15 to 41 months upon entry, recovery was more complete. The degree of recovery varied directly with age of admission.

In Yugoslavia, Cabak and Najdanvic (1965) studied 36 children who had been hospitalized for malnutrition between 4 and 24 months of age. When reexamined at ages 7 and 14, their physical development was normal, but mental development was significantly below that of normal Serbian children.

In a clinical study carried out in the United States (Chase & Martin, 1970), children who were hospitalized during their first year of life for undernutrition were compared to a control group 3 or 4 years later. The findings showed that the test group was lower in height, weight, head circumference, and developmental quotient (DQ). The degree of physical and mental development was correlated with duration of undernutrition. None of the children treated within the first 4 months of life had a DQ equivalent to the control group. However, it was noted social factors, such as paternal separation, the presence among parents of alcohol-related problems, and the number of siblings, were related to undernutrition.

The question of interactions between malnutrition and other variables, such as poverty, disease, and social class, is a pressing issue. Because malnutrition is often confounded by these other variables, they all should be studied in research on nutritional learning problems. Can learning problems be directly related to malnutrition, or to concomitant factors, or to an interaction of the two?

One animal study analyzing the effect of the interaction between environment deprivation and malnutrition indicates that stimulation can compensate for malnutrition (Levitsky, 1971). Cravioto's extensive work in a rural area in Guatemala results in the opposite conclusion. He compared children hospitalized for malnutrition to unhospitalized siblings. He found that a poverty environment in general has negative effects, but that severe malnutrition increases the chance of low test scores, intersensory integrative ability, in particular. (He used the Terman–Merrill, Gesell and Goodenough Draw-A-Man tests). Thus, personal hygiene, housing, and cash income were secondary to nutrition (Cravioto, De Licardie, & Birch, 1966).

The problems of malnutrition and disease are closely related to the problems of poverty. Although Cravioto found malnutrition to be a more significant variable than other environmental variables, the effect of the interactions of the variables is evidenced in the problems of infant mortality, low birth weight, prematurity, and infant malnutrition (Birch & Gussow, 1970; Gussow, 1970). In the United States, there is a great discrepancy in health care between those who are poor and those who are not. Low birth weight and prematurity are more prevalent among the poor. Mothers of short stature, more frequent among the poor and malnourished, are also higher risks for pregnancy complications. The poor and malnourished are also more likely to have children with low birth weight.

Low birth weight is a factor widely associated with problems of the nervous system. Studies show a relationship in which lower birth weight is moderately associated with lower IQ. Moreover, of children weighing less than 150 grams at birth, one-third have physical defects. Premature children are more frequently found to have personality problems in comparison with nonpremature children. They tend to work below their capacity and may have motor disorders of perception, cognition, impulsivity, and distractability (Birch & Gussow, 1970).

Frequently, ignorance of good nutritional habits is given as the cause of malnutrition among the poor. However, Birch and Gussow (1970) cite evidence that lack of economic resources, rather than ignorance, lies behind malnutrition of the poor. Once again, poverty and malnutrition interact.

The studies thus far discussed have been either clinical or experimental, in a laboratory sense. Although still on an exploratory level, a variety of

action programs aimed at nutrition improvement have already been implemented and evaluated. In physiological terms, effects of such food assistance
programs are inconclusive, but behavioral differences are more apparent. In
the area of nutrition education, researchers at Syracuse University (Lally,
1971) implemented an extensive program for pregnant mothers. Intervention,
both nutritional and cognitive, were continued for the young child. There was
evidence that mothers who joined the program at the beginning of pregnancy
put nutrition principles into effect better than those joining later. (It should
be noted, however, that the selection of mothers was not controlled.) Cognitive measures were also administered to the infants. Scores of 6-month-old
infants whose mothers had been in the prenatal program were compared to
scores of infants who entered the program at 6 months. There was a
significant difference between the mean IQ of infants in the program (117.3)
and the control group (91.3). The effects cannot be attributed to nutrition
habits alone, however, since the program included cognitive intervention.
Interactions were not analyzed.

Carter, Gilmer, Vander Zwaag, and Massey (1970) investigated the
relation of nutrition, health, and intelligence in urban and rural preschools
where lunch programs have been in operation. Though the results were
inconclusive, the methodology has merit for future research. Extensive health
measures were taken: medical history, visual acuity, audiometry, blood,
urine, and anthropometric measures (skeletal age, bone density, skin-fold
thickness, muscle circumference, and birth weight). A new measure, called
composite specimen analysis, was also used, which measures the child's food
intake, rather than what he is served. The Binet test was used as the
intelligence measure. No correlation was found between IQ and anthropometric measures, but there was a slight relationship between health measures
and IQ.

In the case of programs under the direction of the National School
Lunch Act (1946) and the Child Nutrition Act (1966), laws that provide
funds for free or reduced price lunch, breakfast, and milk, most studies have
looked for behavioral rather than cognitive effects. A 3-year study of Head
Start[1] children in the United States with a follow-up when the children were
5 to 7 years old, did look for physical and mental changes ("Hungry
Children," 1971). The children were given lunch or both breakfast and lunch.
Nutritional improvement was seen in those who were given both. The mea-

---

[1] Head Start is a program for poor children in the year preceding their entering
school. It is comprehensive in that it not only provides preschool education but also
nutritional, medical, and dental treatment.

sures included cranking, sorting, a cognitive task, and reaction time. It was found that, overall, well-nourished fast growers did the best; well-nourished slow growers did better than poorly nourished fast growers; and the doubly deficient did the worst.

Results of a recent pilot breakfast program in the United States have produced great enthusiasm for its continuance (Latham, Baldwin, Levitsky, Call, & Roe, 1971; Pollack, Irvings, & Vaupel, 1972). In physical terms, there has been less hunger-related illness, such as vomiting. Behaviorally speaking, work habits, alertness, and attention have improved. Falling asleep in class and hyperirritability have decreased. Corollary benefits have been improvement in attendance, lower tardiness, and less truancy.

Although there is a dearth of information on the effects of the federally funded National School Lunch Program, there is an abundance of information on the problems of running a food assistance project. There is strong criticism that, since food assistance programs are run by the U.S. Department of Agriculture, the programs serve as a marketplace for surplus crops, rather than as a boost to nutritional status (*Hunger, USA*, 1968; Hurley, 1969). In addition, school administrators frequently see the National School Lunch Program as a welfare burden, and principals view it as an administrative headache (Robin, 1971). Furthermore, the majority of the children who need a free or reduced-price lunch are not getting it. Each county can decide for itself if it will have a program. Since "reduced price" is yet undefined, cost can vary. Moreover, the atmosphere where the meals are served is far from ideal. School cafeterias are usually extremely regimented. Out of rebellion, food fights may occur. Teachers use deprivation of meal or snack time as a threat. Teachers and staff eat separately from the pupils. Thus, even though food is provided, the conditions hinder good digestion (Bettelheim, 1970; Ellenberg, 1970). The potential of school meal programs as aids in improving children's school learning and motivation are clear, but those in existence in the United States can scarcely be used as models.

IMPLICATIONS

Now that various studies on nutrition have been discussed, the question arises once again: What is the effect of malnutrition and its physiological consequences on motivation, intellectual growth, and learning behavior? The results of the research we have considered are often inconclusive. Malnutrition often exists in conjunction with other factors, such as disease, poverty, and poor parental education and, as Pollitt (1971) argues, these cannot be studied adequately except through sophisticated statistical methods. Yet implications for direct effects of malnutrition on the development of the brain and the rest of the nervous system are quite certain, as Winick's work indicates. Thus, despite the need for more sophisticated studies, we have one reasonable conclusion relating malnutrition directly to poor intellectual development by damage to the brain (Cravioto, 1971).

Cravioto's evidence of effects on intersensory integration have implications for lasting effects on intellectual development, especially if viewed in Piagetian terms. The President's Committee on Mental Retardation (1969) points out that intersensory integrative skills are necessary for growth of symbolic intelligence. These skills begin to develop at birth and involve the shifting of motor symbols to conceptual ones. Furthermore, intellectual development, which depends on interaction with the environment, has an invariable, sequential, and hierarchical order. For instance, during the first month the infant uses innate reflexes such as sucking. However, the reflexes of the malnourished infant are weakened. In social terms, weakened responses elicit reduced feedback from the mother. Thus, personality change may conceivably accompany malnutrition.

Hurley (1969) summarizes the effects of malnutrition by pointing out that it is among the most frequent causes of organic damage leading to mental retardation. Further, malnutrition leads to infections and disease, longer lengths of recuperation, and lessened capacity to benefit from intellectual stimulation. Psychologically, the malnourished child may become "insecure, suspicious and anxious. . . . The child is listless, dull and immobile. . ." (p. 182). In short, poor nutrition has potentially a long list of negative outcomes destructive of the developing child's school achievements and motivations.

In support of these arguments, Cravioto (1971) proposes a hypothesis on the indirect relation of nutrition and intellectual growth. First, the child suffers from loss of learning time. Second, there is interference of learning during critical growth periods, as the Piaget model suggests. And last, there are personality and motivation effects. The malnourished child is less responsive to stimulation. By seeing himself as a failure in school, he creates a negative self-image. His mode of adapting will not be conducive to further educational development. In short, the indirect effects of nutrition can be described as having a spiral effect on educational development.

Such indirect effects of malnutrition on educational development are apparent, though often difficult to prove scientifically. Subjective observations show that a well-fed child is much more inclined to learn than the hungry, malnourished, tired, or ill child (Shipman, 1969). Energy that would ordinarily be channeled into learning activities must be conserved to maintain basic existence. Most of the studies discussed examine only extreme cases of hunger and malnutrition. Effects of lesser forms may still be debilitating, but factual evidence is still lacking (Sandstead, Carter, House, McConnell, Horton, & Vander Zwaag, 1971).

RECOMMENDATIONS

The final question is: On the basis of current information, what action should be taken?

1. More data is needed from basic research using both animal and human subjects. Longitudinal studies should also be supported. Field studies are necessary to find out the status and nature of health problems. Much work needs to be done on the methodology of health surveys and physiological measures. Improved measures of intelligence are badly lacking. Latham and Cobos (1971) have already worked extensively on finding valid instruments for testing their sample in Bogata, Colombia. Too many of the aptitude and intelligence measures as well as behavioral expectations are set to American middle-class standards (Latham *et al.*, 1971; Vore, 1971). Once adequate instruments are established, they must be used to find out more precisely the impact on nutrition on motivation as it affects performance (Call, 1969).

2. As important as basic research is the need for action programs. Such programs must be comprehensive in order to treat the whole person (Pollitt, 1971). A nutritious meal here or there is grossly inadequate. As studies to date indicate, malnutrition coexists with the other variables of poverty and disease and usually interacts with them. Hence, well-run food assistance programs are a beginning, but comprehensive health care must accompany food.

3. Nutrition education is an important area in need of further development. Recent studies are showing increasing evidence that prenatal and postnatal health status of the mother affects the development of the child (Committee on Maternal Nutrition, 1970). Potential parents need to become aware of the relation of nutrition and other environmental factors on child growth (Hepner & Maiden, 1971). Availability of nutrition education, family planning centers, and health care for the mother would help ensure favorable child-rearing conditions.

4. Food assistance programs are another way of implementing change. These programs would provide meals at schools and food stamps or some equivalent to the families. Gussow (1970) recommends that responsibility of

health and nutrition should be taken on by the schools. This would mean the provision of medical care, breakfast and lunch, and even sleeping facilities. The argument further suggests that, although such services have not been proven conclusively to boost school learning, their mere existence teaches the child that somebody cares.

One of the major points that should be kept in mind is that, in instituting change, solutions must be adapted to the future. That is, not only should present needs be examined but also future needs. Resources and potential resources must be investigated. For instance, technology in food production and its consequences should be pursued. In administering the programs, people's needs, not the producers' and implementers' self-perpetuation, must be the guide. The target groups must be made aware of their problem, but moreover, must be involved in planning and implementing the solution (Birch, 1968).

ANNOTATED BIBLIOGRAPHY

Birch, H. G., & Gussow, J. D. *Disadvantaged children: Health, nutrition, and school failure.* New York: Harcourt, Brace, and World, 1970.
    The authors present a strong argument for the need of comprehensive health programs for improving education. The book seems to have the most complete literature review to date on the topic of health and nutrition as related to intellectual growth. The bibliography contains approximately 500 references.

Committee on Maternal Nutrition/Food and Nutrition Board, National Research Council. *Maternal nutrition and the course of pregnancy* (Summary report, U.S. Department of Health, Education, and Welfare). Rockville, Maryland, 1970.
    This report gives evidence and arguments for health care and nutrition education of pregnant and lactating mothers, plus many suggestions for further research and broad solutions to the problem.

Committee on Procedures for Appraisal of Protein-Calorie Malnutrition of the International Union of Nutritional Sciences. Assessment of protein nutritional status. *American Journal of Clinical Nutrition*, 1973, *23*, 807–819.
    This report advocates the need for a universal test of protein malnutrition and discusses and compares the value of current techniques; clinical, anthropometric, and biochemical.

Gunderson, G. W. The national school lunch program: Background and development (FNS-63-Food and Nutrition Service, U.S. Department of Agriculture). Washington, D.C.: U.S. Government Printing Office, 1971.
    This report presents the National School Lunch Program with a favorable,

uncritical bias. That is, it does not question the motives or political aspects of implementation. However, it gives a good summary of the history of food assistance in Europe and the United States as well as details of legislation.

Hunger, USA: A report by the Citizen's Board of Inquiry into hunger and malnutrition in the United States. Washington, D.C.: New Community Press, 1968.
Though far from being a comprehensive picture of hunger in the United States, this report gives an indication of problems in assessing hunger, the dearth of information, the inadequacy of assistance programs, and above all, the prevalence of hunger and malnutrition in the United States.

Hurley, B. L. *Poverty and mental retardation: A causal relationship.* New York: Random House, 1969.
This book is an indictment of present attitudes and policies in the United States concerning the poor. According to the author, retardation is caused by social factors. His evidence and conclusions are similar to Birch and Gussow; however, he arrives there by a more sociological and political path.

Jelliffe, D. B. The assessment of the nutritional status of the community. *World Health Organization Monograph Series,* No. 53, 1968. Geneva, Switzerland.
Jelliffe presents a detailed account of symptoms of malnutrition, methods of conducting surveys, and assessment measures, such as clinical, anthropometric, biochemical, and dietary.

Jelliffe, D. B. Infant nutrition in the subtropics and tropics. *World Health Organization Monograph Series,* No. 29, 1968. Geneva, Switzerland.
Here Jelliffe discusses practical aspects of setting up nutrition education programs. He discusses general principles regarding goals, consideration of the habits and values of the people being trained, and knowledge of local foods. He then takes up specific programs such as those for pregnant mothers and school-age children.

The school lunch bag: Community action to end hunger. Children's Foundation, 1970. (1028 Connecticut Ave. N.W., Washington, D.C.)
A loose-leaf notebook of step-by-step procedures for using existing funds to implement a school lunch program where there is none. It includes inventory sheets, cost estimates, history, legislation, and reference names. Even if the reader is not interested in starting a lunch program per se, the materials could serve as a model in communicating at a practical level.

REFERENCES

Altschul, A. Recent advances and problems in nutrition and food science and implications for child nutrition programs. For presentation at USDA–Rutgers University Conference on Improving Child Nutrition Programs through New Food and Nutrition Science, New Brunswick, N.J., June 27–29, 1972.

Bettelheim, B. *Food to nurture the mind.* Washington, D.C.: Children's Foundation, 1970.

Birch, H. G. Research issues in child health. IV. Some philosophic and methodologic issues. Presented in part to the Head Start Research Seminar, Washington, D.C., November 1, 1968.

Birch, H. G., & Gussow, J. D. *Disadvantaged children: Health, nutrition, and school failure.* New York: Harcourt, Brace, and World, 1970.

Cabak, V., & Najdanvic, R. Effect of undernutrition in early life on physical and mental development. *Archives of Diseases of Childhood,* 1965, *20,* 532–534.

Call, D. L. Research findings on the social consequences of malnutrition. Cornell Agricultural Economics Staff Paper, No. 8. Ithaca, N. Y., August 1969.

Canosa, C. A. Nutrition, physical growth and mental development. Paper presented at UNESCO Meeting on Deprivation and Disadvantage in Developing Countries: Effects of Malnutrition and Endemic Diseases on Education and Their Remedies, Hamburg, Germany, June 1970.

Carter, J., Gilmer, B., Vander Zwaag, R., & Massey, K. Health and nutrition in disadvantaged children and their relationship with intellectual development (Collaborative Research Report). Nashville, Tenn.: Vanderbilt University School of Medicine, 1970.

Chase, H. P., & Martin, H. P. Undernutrition and child development. *New England Journal of Medicine,* 1970, *282,* 933–939.

Cofer, C. N., & Appley, M. H. *Motivation: Theory and research.* New York: Wiley, 1964.

Committee on Maternal Nutrition/Food and Nutrition Board, National Research Council. *Maternal nutrition and the course of pregnancy: Summary report.* Rockville, Md.: U.S. Department of Health, Education, and Welfare, 1970.

Coursin, D. B. Nutrition and brain development in infants. *Merrill–Palmer Quarterly,* 1972, *18,* 177–202.

Cravioto, J. The effect of malnutrition on the individual. Paper presented at the International Conference on Nutrition, National Development and Planning, Massachusetts Institute of Technology, Cambridge, Mass., October 19–21, 1971.

Cravioto, J., & Robles, B. Evolution of adaptive and motor behavior during rehabilitation from kwashiorkor. *American Journal of Orthopsychiatry,* 1965, *35,* 449–464.

Cravioto, J., DeLicardie, E., & Birch, H. G. Nutrition, growth, and neurointegrative development: An experimental and etiologic study. *Pediatrics,* 1966, *38*(2) (Pt II, Suppl.), 319–372.

Ellenberg, N. J. Food in schools. *Phi Delta Kappan,* 1970, *11,* 316–317.

Fuller, J. L. *Motivation: A biological perspective.* New York: Random House, 1962.

Gussow, J. D. Bodies, brains and poverty: Poor children and the schools. *IRCD Bulletin,* 1970, *6,* 3–4, 9–13.

Hepner, R., & Maiden, N. Growth rate, nutrient intake and "mothering" as determinants of malnutrition in disadvantaged children. *Nutrition Reviews,* 1971, *29,* 219–223.

Hilgard, E. R., & Bower, G. H. *Theories of learning* (3rd ed.). New York: Appleton, 1966.

Hunger, USA: A report by the Citizen's Board of Inquiry into Hunger and Malnutrition in the United States. Washington, D.C.: New Community Press, 1968.

Hungry children lag in learning. *Opportunity,* 1971, *1*(3), 10–13.

Hurley, R. L. *Poverty and mental retardation: A causal relationship.* New York: Random House, 1969.

Jelliffe, D. B. Infant nutrition in the subtropics and tropics. *World Health Organization Monograph Series,* No. 29, 1968. Geneva, Switzerland.

Keys, A., Brozek, J., Henschel, A., Mickelson, O., & Taylor, H. *The biology of human starvation* (2 vols.). Minneapolis: University of Minnesota Press, 1950.

Lally, J. R. Development of a day care center for young children (Progress report, 1970–71. PR-156 [C6]) Syracuse University Children's Center, Office of Child Development.

Latham, M. C. International nutrition and later learning. In S. Sunderlin (Assoc. Ed.), *Nutrition and intellectual growth in children* (Bulletin 25-A). Washington, D.C.: Association for Childhood Education International, 1969.

Latham, M. C., & Cobos, F. The effects of malnutrition on intellectual development and learning. *American Journal of Public Health,* 1971, *61,* 1307–1324.

Latham, M. C., Baldwin, C., Levitsky, D. A., Call, D. L., & Roe, D. An investigation into the effects of hunger on classroom behavior and performance of young children (Proposal submitted in response to RFP-GD-71-5). Ithaca, N. Y.: Cornell University, 1971.

Levitsky, D. A. Nutrition, mental development and behavior. *Nutrition News,* 1971, *34,* 15, 18.

Maslow, A. H. *Motivation and personality.* New York: Harper, 1954.

McGovern, G. McGovern criticizes survey released by H.E.W.: Charges apparent manipulation of data. Release to the President, May 9, 1971. See also *New York Times,* March 6, May 2, & Aug. 30, 1971.

Murray, E. J. *Motivation and emotion.* Englewood Cliffs, N.J.: Prentice-Hall, 1964.

Myers, J. L., Mabel, J. A., & Stare, F. J. A nutrition study of school children in a depressed urban district. II. Physical and biochemical findings. *Journal of the American Dietetic Association,* 1968, *53,* 234–242.

Myers, M. L., O'Brien, S. C., Mabel, J. A., & Stare, F. J. A nutrition study of school children in a depressed urban district. I. Dietary findings. *Journal of the American Dietetic Association,* 1968, *53,* 226–233.

Pollack, B., Irvings, M., & Vaupel, S. *If we had ham, we could have ham and eggs . . . if we had eggs* (Food Research and Action Center). Yonkers, N.Y.: Gazette Press, 1972.

Pollitt, E. Poverty and malnutrition: Cumulative effect on intellectual development. *Les Carnets de l'enfance,* 1971, *14,* 40–52.

Robin, F. *Their daily bread* Atlanta, Ga.: McNelley-Rudd Printing Service, 1971. (Library of Congress No. 68-27171).

Sandstead, H. H., Carter, J. P., House, F. R., McConnell, F., Horton, K. B., & Vander Zwaag, R. Nutritional deficiencies in disadvantaged preschool children: Their relationship to mental development. *American Journal of Diseases of Children,* 1971, *121,* 455–463.

Scrimshaw, N. S. Statement to the UNICEF executive board. *PAG* [Protein Advisory Group] *Bulletin,* 1972, *2*(3), 1–9.

Scrimshaw, N. S., Taylor, C. E., & Gordon, J. E. Interactions of nutrition and infection. *World Health Organization Monograph Series,* No. 57, 1968. Geneva, Switzerland.

Shipman, V. Disadvantaged children and their first school experience: ETS–Head Start

Longitudinal Study. Vol. 1. Princeton, N.J.: ETS, August 1969. (Grant number CG-8256).

Stoch, M. B., & Smythe, P. M. Does undernutrition during infancy inhibit brain growth and subsequent intellectual development? *Archives of Diseases of Childhood,* 1963, *38,* 545–552.

Vore, D. A. Prenatal nutrition and postnatal intellectual development. Paper presented at Society for Research in Child Development, Minneapolis, Minn., April 1971.

Winick, M. Nutrition and intellectual development in children. In S. Sunderlin (Assoc. Ed.), *Nutrition and intellectual growth in children* (Bulletin 25-A). Washington, D.C.: Association for Childhood Education International, 1969.

Winick, M., & Rosso, P. The effect of severe early malnutrition on cellular growth of human brain. *Pediatric Research,* 1969, *3,* 181–184.

10

A Postscript: Thoughts toward an Integrated Approach to Motivation in Education*

SAMUEL BALL

Educational Testing Service

In the preceding chapters, we have dealt with a range of important constructs or concepts in motivation as they apply to education. How do they relate to each other? We have noted some relationships between anxiety and curiosity, between locus of control and need for achievement, between need for achievement and social pressures in the classroom. But a general theoretical integration is currently beyond the capabilities of the field.

Of course, the message to educators is quite clear that the teacher should "motivate the child." This idea comes up, in some fashion, in virtually every educational psychology textbook. Then the textbook presents its pet concepts. It may discuss level of aspiration, self-concept, interests, competition, reinforcement schedules, test anxiety—the list goes on and on. We can hardly fault providing a list for we have done that ourselves in this book. However, the fact is that, for any given child, there seems to be a preferred *motivational style*. We coin this term to indicate that each child has more or less of each of the long listings of motives. Assessing this internal integration

*Prepared for UNESCO under contract with IEA, ref. 206612, and published by its permission. © UNESCO 1977.

of motives, this motivational style, is perhaps a key to further understandings in this area.

In 1966, Lian-Hwang Chiu, in his doctoral dissertation, carried out a factor analysis on data from the eleventh-graders attending a comprehensive Connecticut high school. Using an item-sampling approach, he had the eleventh-graders respond to some 500 true–false items, some adapted from previously developed motivation scales (e.g., test anxiety, curiosity) and from others developed specifically for this study. Each item, however, was a member of 16 scales each developed to assess a specific motive.

A number of traditional psychometric operations were performed on the data to refine the 16 scales, and scores based on these scales along with achievement and aptitude scores were then subjected to factor analysis. On the basis of the analysis, five motivational factors emerged.[1] These factors were, at most, minimally related. That is, they were independent, motivational factors.

1. Positive orientation toward school learning (which involved persistence, high level of aspiration, positive academic self-concept, and positive feelings about past performance at school).
2. Need for social recognition (seeking positive reinforcement from the teacher, competing academically with classmates in order to be seen by them as doing well in school).
3. Motive to avoid failure (fearing failure, high test anxiety).
4. Curiosity (both epistemic and perceptual).
5. Conformity (working because it is "demanded" by the teacher or by parents, or, if relevant, by peer pressures).

As often happens, the development of a measuring instrument of 140 true–false items based on these five factors led to some useful conceptualizations that, in turn, led to some potential educational applications. We found that the best way of describing a student's motivation was through a graphic profile showing the student to be, for example, high on Factor 1, low in Factors 2 and 5, moderate in Factors 3 and 4. The students had motivational styles, which could readily and reliably be assessed and graphically presented for the students' own use and for the use of their teachers and counselors.

In general, we did not expect, at the high school level, that "adding" the motivational profile to aptitude scores would enable the prediction of achievement with much greater accuracy. Aptitude without much motivation is probably a better combination for a student than little ability and high

---

[1] The achievement and aptitude scores factored out as an independent cluster.

motivation, at least as far as school performance is concerned. Besides, aptitude scores probably include, to some degree, a motivational component. Moreover, prior evidence suggested a curvilinear relationship, rather than a linear one, existed between motivation and achievement. For example, we know that too much or too little anxiety affects performance negatively. Nonetheless, using a multiple regression model, the motivation scores, with anxiety added inversely, significantly added to the prediction of achievement based only on aptitude measures. In fact, in one small study based on 30 seventh-graders in a private school, the relationship between the weighted motivation scores and achievement was considerably higher than between their IQ scores and achievement.

We also noted striking differences between the motivation profiles of "overachievers" and "underachievers." The two groups were selected by school counsellors in a Yonkers, New York, high school. We then arranged matched pairings based on IQ scores within 5 points of each other. The overachievers all scored above the underachievers on Factor 1. The means of the two groups was similar on Factor 3—but the variances were markedly different. The overachievers clustered around the school mean for fear of failure; the underachievers either scored very high or very low on this factor. Underachievers presumably were either too anxious or too unconcerned to learn well.

Some early consideration was also given to teachers and their ideals of a "well-motivated student." We found great discrepancies among the profiles developed when teachers filled in the true—false measure as they would want their ideally motivated student to fill it in. Greatest contrasts occurred in terms of anxiety, curiosity, and conformity. Some teachers thought of their ideally motivated student as being very anxious and fearful at exam time. About an equal proportion of teachers thought their ideally motivated student would not be anxious and fearful at exam time. The majority of the items used in the student assessment differentiated the teachers when they considered their ideally motivated student. Perhaps it would be worth considering having students, teachers, and administrators look at student motivation profiles and teachers' ideal student motivation profiles for purposes of grouping, obtaining insights, and for guidance and counseling activities. Similarly, the motivation profile information generated from the students could serve as an excellent starting point for discussion with a student and with the student's parents about the ways the student is motivated (and not motivated) to perform in the classroom.

A great deal more work needs to be done before this integrated multivariate approach to motivation in the classroom can be recommended for practical general use. At least, however, it helps us to emphasize that the typical approach of earlier theorists deserves critical scrutiny. One motivational construct studied to the exclusion of others is not likely to provide educators with the information they need. Perhaps, in 10 years time, another book on motivation in education could be written in which *each* chapter were not about a single construct but about some aspect of an integrated approach. We'll work to that.

Author Index

Subject Index